Contents

Contents

Acknowledgments

This book is dedicated to Jodi—the most logical, helpful, and attractive sounding board on Earth.

To all the creative real estate professionals and industry idea people who constantly added their opinions about the needs and wants of second-home buyers. We would specifically like to thank Kevin Hawkins, Cookie Gaulding, Jim Hawkins, Rob Keasal, Vicki Fazzini, Richard Morse of Washington Exchange Services, Inc., and Venita Bishop of Section 1031 Services, Inc.—they all deserve a wonderful place on a quiet mountain lake.

—Tom Kelly

I'd like to thank the many friends and acquaintances who provided insights into the second home process. Specific inputs from John Carman, Jane Kirschner, Faith Holfelder, and Kathy Sanders were helpful in understanding the pitfalls of owning and managing second homes. Other, less specific, conversations with Anne Byrne, Jeff Dwyer, Judy McGuire, and Joe Tuccillo helped me understand the motivation behind the second home buyer. I hope I have disguised their stories enough to hide their identity but related them faithfully enough to do them justice. To all of them, my thanks.

—John Tuccillo

Introduction
It Makes Sen$e: Why Your Second Home Will Pay Off

If you opened this book, you are probably thinking of buying a second home as an investment, a vacation retreat, a retirement destination—or all three. Or you might already own a second home and you want some ideas on how to maximize its value as an investment. Well, relax. Everything you need to know is here. After you've read this book, you will be ready to do whatever you want in the housing market.

Just exactly who are we and how can we present ourselves as experts on real estate? We are a couple of incredibly knowledgeable sports buffs who can talk your ear off about baseball and basketball. In our spare time, we do real estate. Tom is a nationally syndicated radio host, freelance real estate columnist, and former real estate editor for *The Seattle Times*, whose syndicated column now appears in more than 40 papers. He also hosts a radio program, originating from the CBS affiliate in Seattle, that airs in more than 35 domestic markets plus 450 stations overseas via Armed Forces Radio. John is an economist (ugh!) and real estate consultant who spent 10 years as Chief Economist for the National Association of Realtors. He's written six books (on real estate) and is a regular columnist for *Real Estate Professional* magazine.

Introduction

We've talked with enough consumers out there—in person, on the phone, over the airwaves—and others who have offered feedback to our newspaper columns to know that there's a great deal of interest about second homes, especially in the real estate climate that's prevailed since 1995. We also know that there's a great deal of bad advice out these—most of it from self-help gurus whose "systems" are the magic carpet to real estate riches. Not! Think of it this way. If a guy had a way to make millions, why would he sell it for $39.95 at 2:00 a.m. on some cable channel? We can't think of a reason, either.

There's nothing being sold in this book except for the extraordinary value brought by a second home–this book explains how one additional property purchase can serve a variety of purposes over time while providing you with a significant financial asset. And that value is not just in the form of wealth accumulation. It also comes from the ability to enjoy your property—sunset over the lake, cocktails by the seventh fairway, a breathtaking mountain view just a short walk up the road. It's the total package. We want to present some common sense advice that will allow you to enjoy fully the pleasures of owning The New Second Home and to prolong that pleasure through most of your life.

Real Estate as an Investment

Before we begin, we need to be clear about our biases. Both of us believe deeply in the wealth-building powers of real estate. We think you can create significant wealth simply by exercising common sense. Look at it this way: If you think a house is good enough to live in, someone else will too, and they'll pay you for the privilege. The ownership of a real estate investment, particularly property you can personally enjoy—a vacation home, your retirement residence—is the most profitable investment within the reach of the average American.

This last point deserves some consideration because the conventional wisdom is still that common stocks offer the best returns over time. If you measure cash-on-cash return, this might be true, but when you look at total return, the picture changes. The ownership of real estate offers four distinct advantages over stocks. We expand on each of these later in the book.

- *Real estate prices are less volatile.* As we have seen in the opening years of this century, stocks can move a great deal in both directions. This makes ownership of stock a crapshoot, with profit solely dependent on timing. If you cashed out in December 1999, your returns were huge; if you waited a year, you probably lost a great deal. House prices fluctuate, but within a lesser range. If real estate prices don't shoot up the way stock prices do in a bull market, real estate markets don't crash the way stocks do when the bull runs out of steam. In short, it's a less risky investment. Because real estate makes up a large portion of the wealth of most American households, that's a good thing.

- *Real estate is a leveraged investment.* You can own property with an equity investment (down payment, but let's use stock market lingo here) of no more than 20 percent. In fact, there are many programs that let you buy with virtually nothing down. Most people can't do this with stock. You need to pay the entire price of the stock. So when the price of a stock rises 5 percent, you make 5 percent on your money. If your real estate rises by 5 percent in value, your return is upwards of 25 percent.

- *Real estate is tax advantaged.* Any interest incurred for the financing of real estate is deductible from ordinary income for tax purposes, and the 1997 tax law in effect eliminated any taxation of capital gains on one's primary residence for most Americans. Tax on investment property can be deferred and sometimes eliminated. We still pay capital gains tax on stock, and you can't deduct the interest on any debt incurred for the purchase of financial assets.

- *You can live in real estate.* Stock certificates are pretty, with great colors, cool writing, and embossed letters. Unfortunately, you can't go to sleep in them or stand on them to watch the sunset over the lake, or hold a party for your friends and family in them. They just (you hope) make you money. Real estate provides many different kinds of satisfaction that money can't buy.

The Perfect Place: The Multiple Uses of Real Estate

Let's consider a realistic example to illustrate the above. Joanne is a married 56-year-old whose last child is about to go off to college. When she was divorced 20 years ago, she got a real estate license as a way of supporting herself. While she hated listing and selling real estate, she loved investment and apprenticed herself to a small, private investment company as a property manager. Gradually, she learned the business and worked her way up to the creation of her own limited liability corporation. The partnership bought a small resort property ideal for small meetings and fam-

Introduction

ily reunions. She says, "My plan was to pay it off and it would be my own IRA. I could live off the rents or sell it and live off the proceeds." The rental income paid for the property and the cash flow enabled Joanne and her second husband to buy several other properties. Of these, most were completely profitable, and even when the cash flow was inadequate, the properties sold at a profit. Joanne sums up her investment experience this way: "…if we can't net 20 percent on our money, including the tax benefits, we won't even look twice. [Real estate investment] beats the market by a wide margin." [1]

But (as they say in the infomercial business) wait, there's more! This book is really about "the New Second Home" that Perfect Place that serves a variety of purposes over time. You can begin by using the equity you've built up in your primary residence to buy a second home, watch that investment appreciate, have renters pay for it, and then exchange that property (tax free) for another that will continue the wealth-building process. You will finally wind up with the home you want to live in for the rest of your life. You then sell your principal residence (again tax free) and live in your dream.

In short, buying the New Second Home is a tax-free process for which somebody else pays, and the magic of appreciation pays. It begins with the Investment Phase when you buy the property and have it appreciate, and have the mortgage paid down by rental income. After that you trade it (again tax free) for a property where you want to spend most of your time in your Cocooning Phase before deciding if that place will also host your Ultimate Phase.

The key to all this, the "secret sauce" of real estate investment if you will, is your ability to either evolve an owned property from a cash-generating investment to a retirement home, or use the property to trade for that retirement or vacation place you really want. You can do all this without sacrificing any of the appreciation that has benefited your investment. No expenses, no taxes.

The rest of this book will show you how to move through these stages. As you read this book, please understand that we support the purchase of real estate as an investment. It works—and it works for you!

In this book, we cover all the topics you need to know about buying an investment, vacation, or retirement property:

---

[1] We tell stories through the whole book. They're meant to illustrate what happens when real people buy the New Second Home. The names are changed, but the cases are real.

- How can real estate increase my wealth?
- How much can I afford?
- How do I choose where to invest?
- How do I manage my investment to best benefit from tax laws?
- How do I maximize the cash flow from my investment?
- How do I finance my investment?
- What renovations to an investment property really pay off?
- When should I sell?

At each step we offer practical advice about how to get started, where you can go for information, and how other people have managed to make, maintain, and profit from their investment in real estate. As we said above, none of this is magic. It is common sense applied to investing, coupled with some hard work.

Getting Started: The Investment Engine

OK, by now, you're saying, "Great idea guys, but I'm just now comfortable with paying for my first house. How can I buy an investment property?" Well, you don't know it, but you have under your control a marvelous engine to drive real estate investment. Probably the best way to buy a second house is to own a first one. That sounds ridiculously self-evident, but a lot of changes occurring in the real estate and housing finance markets make it so much simpler now to use a primary residence as the basis for building wealth in real estate and other areas.

Indulge us here in a little history. Way back in the Dark Ages (well, at least before 1980 or so), a house was a lumpy, fixed, static investment. It couldn't be bought or sold easily, like common stock. It couldn't be broken down into smaller pieces and used, like cash. It required a long-term debt for its holder to afford it, unlike bonds. It's a good thing you can live in it because it really wasn't good for much else! It was also a very risky asset to finance, because its value (and therefore the liability attached to it) was several times the annual income of its owner. In fact, the house was such a different breed of asset that it required a separate financial institution to provide credit to homeowners. We called these institutions savings and loans, and they disappeared in a spectacular wave of corruption and failure in the late 1980s.

Luckily, their demise coincided with the advent of information technology and the growth of mortgage market players like Fannie Mae and Freddie Mac, who began to develop the mortgage Veg-O-Matic. They sliced and diced mortgages so that the financial paper backed by real estate could in fact be bought and sold just like any other asset. The result has been a flowering of the mortgage market. It is now possible to custom tailor any mortgage for any property. You want a 5-year adjustable-rate mortgage (ARM) with a balloon payment that rolls over into a 25-year, fixed-rate mortgage, followed by a 1-year ARM indexed to the Yen-Dollar exchange rate? You got it. Want fries with that?

Now the house has become as much of a piggy bank as any other asset. If you want your asset portfolio to contain less real estate and more stock, you don't have to sell your house and move into a smaller place. All you need to do is refinance your mortgage, take cash out, and invest it in the stock market. If you want the reverse, prepay part of your mortgage with the proceeds form the sale of stock. In fact, if you have qualified for a line of credit secured by the equity in your house, you don't even have to call your friendly banker. All you need to do is write a check. By using the flexibility and the relative low cost of the mortgage market, you can move in and out of real estate and other assets at will, without even rearranging the living room furniture, much less moving out.

The market today makes it easier and cheaper than ever before to unlock the equity in your house and use it to diversify your asset portfolio. Joanne said it best when she called her investment property her own IRA. She used the equity in her primary residence to support the purchase of an investment property and, when the cash flow form that property and its appreciation allowed her to do so, she bought other real estate.

How much of a foundation do you have? The answer is readily available. You can ask a local real estate professional to give you an opinion as to the market value of your home. The real estate market has been roaring for the past six years, and the odds are that even if you bought as recently as five years ago, you're looking at an appreciation in value of 30 percent or more. On a house that cost $100,000 five years ago, that means your equity has risen by $30,000. That will serve comfortably as a down payment on an investment property selling for up to $150,000. And you're on your way.[2] This is a maximum, and you can clearly buy a lesser-valued property. But it shows how much investment power you have in today's market.

The first hurdle to overcome in real estate investment is to think of your primary residence as the foundation for your investment portfolio. It is the most valuable asset you own, and, because of the way in which

---

[2] Even if you're not buying investment real estate, it's always good to have a realistic idea of the value of your home at all times.

real estate is now financed, fits perfectly into a multi-asset portfolio strategy. It will be the financial engine for your next investment in real estate.

Getting Started: Basic Decisions

OK, let's get to the hard work. There are certain basics you need to know before you can invest in that second home. Let's rephrase that. There are certain basics you need to know if you are going to make the most of your second home investment. Anyone can lose money on a real estate investment—and many people do. This isn't the Ron Popeil "set it and forget it" oven. It's your money we're dealing with here!

Just as making money in the stock market requires that you pay attention to the basics of the market, so too does successful real estate investment require some study and knowledge. As much as the infomercials would like you to believe it, there is no "magic bullet," no set formula that will automatically guarantee that you will profit from real estate investment.

Later on in this book, we discuss the details of all of these basics. For now, we list them with a short description. Most of these refer directly to a property designed to generate cash flow through rental. The considerations are no less relevant in choosing a vacation home for your own use.

- *Choosing a property.* "Location, location, location" might be a real estate cliché, but there is a truth behind it. Successful real estate investment requires even more consideration of location than choosing a primary residence. Your profit will depend on the attraction of the investment to others, whether year-round or vacation renters. If you decide on a property based on your own desires, it's likely that your investment income, and thus your return, will be suboptimal. Why? Because you're not a renter and you will not evaluate a property with a renter's eye.
- *Choosing a community.* There's always a catch. Yes, you need to consider the needs ands wants of renters when you choose a property. But if you intend to use this property for yourself, you need to consider its location in a community. If the property will eventually serve as your retirement residence, you need to choose a place where you will be comfortable later in life. The house can be altered; its environment is set.
- *Financing the property.* One of the biggest changes that has occurred in the real estate market over the past 10 years has been the availability and cost of financing. Availability has expanded and cost has

fallen. We don't mean that interest rates are down. They are, but they will rise again. Rather, we mean that it's possible to acquire property with little or nothing down by using the equity in your primary residence or any of a number of mortgage programs that make it easy to buy real estate. The lower your cost of financing, the greater your cash flow will be and the higher your return on investment.

- *Understanding tax laws.* This is key to your investment success. The government has given you three major gifts through the tax laws. First, you can deduct the interest incurred on any debt used to acquire real estate. Second, the capital gains exclusion on real estate is very generous. Third, you can trade properties relatively freely without incurring any tax liability. Each of these will add to your return on investment. Understanding them will pay off handsomely.
- *Managing the property.* Having tenants, short- or long-term, will require that the property be managed effectively. This means maintenance and improvement, as well as simple rent collection. You will either do it yourself, or you will hire others to do it for you. Before you invest in real estate, you must decide how you will handle management. Management is a cost, and as such, it will diminish your cash flow. Either you will spend your time to do it, or you will pay someone else. Choosing the more cost-effective approach will affect the return on your investment.
- *Financial capacity.* You are responsible for paying for and maintaining your property regardless of whether the property is generating revenue. Real estate that will ultimately prove a good investment because of price appreciation and tax benefits might be a struggle to hold because of negative cash flow. So, before you invest, you need to create and hold a cash reserve to cover those periods when the house is not rented or when the rent is late or when the furnace gives up the ghost.

Evaluating Your Investment: The Math of Real Estate

Sometimes, talking about investments and rates of return and evaluating alternative opportunities sounds a lot like Abbott and Costello going through their "Who's on First?" routine. The language gets garbled, the concepts get fuzzy, and the misunderstandings abound.

> *Abbott: Okay, so we got this house we're gonna rent, y'see? And this guy who rents it pays us $100 a week.*

Costello: That's a good thing. So we make $100 a week. Boy oh boy, are we livin' now!

Abbott: Not so fast. Y'see, we need to pay part of this to the bank on account of they lent us the money to buy the house.

Costello: Let me get this straight; we have to pay the bank because we're usin' their money, right?

Abbott: Right.

Costello: But we're still gettin' a lotta dough!

Abbott: Not so fast. This guy we're rentin' the house to, he's not real reliable. He only pays every other month.

Costello: So let's throw da bum out and get somebody who will pay.

Abbott: We could do that, but it would take a couple of months and we get no rent, but we still have to pay the bank.

Costello: This sounds worse and worse with everything you say. How much money will I make from this here house?

Abbott: The way I figure it, you owe me another $25.

The root cause here is that it's all math. No one likes math, and no one likes to talk about money. If you're on a plane, within an hour you can find out anything you want about the person sitting next to you. As a matter of fact, they will volunteer information about their homes, families, jobs, politics, and opinions just about everything else in their lives—except their income and their net worth. For Americans, these are the unmentionables, never to be discussed unless absolutely necessary. Now it's necessary. We need to look at how to evaluate investments.

Any investment needs to be evaluated for its total rate of return over its holding period relative to alternative investments. The holding period is completely under your control. You might decide to buy a second home as a prelude to retirement—vacation in it now, live in it later. Or your second home can be the gateway to a third or fourth, and so on. The alternatives against which you compare a real estate investment are also subjective. Consider how you would use the money if you didn't buy that second home.

The total return to your investment in real estate, however, is not subjective. Rather, it has several very specific components. If you are evaluating the potential return from a second home, some of these must be estimated. It's usually wiser to be conservative in making these assumptions, because Murphy's Law will surface, but for each, there are guidelines available from experience.

Introduction

The components of total return that affect your profitability are:

- *Cash flow.* Rents provide a stream of income to sustain the expenses of the house and provide profit. In evaluating the investment, you need to adjust your projected rents in two directions. Each year, the rent should be adjusted upward for any increases due to inflation and improvement of market conditions. The entire rental income should be adjusted downward for any vacant periods because no income will be received for that time. Talking with property managers in your market will enable you to get a good feel for what rent levels are and what vacancy rates you can expect.
- *Appreciation.* Over the holding period, the house will change in value. For most holding periods and for most housing markets, the value will increase over time. This is particularly true given that you have control over when you will sell the property. It is very rare that investment property must be sold. Thus you can time the market to ensure a capital gain on the property. For information on appreciation rates, check out *www.realtors.org* and look at the research section for rates of price increase for real estate in most metropolitan areas throughout the United States.
- *Maintenance and renovation.* Any expenditure on a rental property to maintain or improve it is expense, and that will diminish your return. Similarly, any management expenses reduce cash flow to you. That doesn't mean you should let the property run down or quit your day job to manage it. It simply means that there are expenses attached to owning investment real estate. These need to be offset against cash flow and appreciation in calculating your return on investment. Two things need to be emphasized here.
  - First, major changes (repair or remodeling) in the property can be depreciated over an extended period of time. Thus the amount deducted each year is only a portion of the total expense.
  - Second, your estimate of repair and renovation expenses is sensitive to your chosen holding period. A roof replacement might be of concern if you are planning to own the home for 30 years, but not if your time horizon is 5 years.
- *Tax considerations.* The interest you pay to finance the purchase of the house is tax deductible. Because you benefit from this, it represents part of the positive return from your investment. Conversely, rental income is taxable to you and is thus reduced by whatever your marginal tax rate is. Finally, tax schedules will govern the allowable depreciation deductions for major home repairs

and renovations. IRS schedules will provide most of the information you need to factor in the tax considerations of real estate investments.

- *Discounting.* If I ask you to loan me $100 today to be repaid in a year, would you give me the money with no interest? Probably not. And if you put money down on a house, will that money earn interest in a bank account? No. You need to adjust your return for the time value of money. In other words, if your rental house yields a return of $10,000 in three years, you need to "discount" that return back to today to see how much it's really worth. Using the return on an alternative investment—perhaps a bank account—is usually a good assumption here.

All of these considerations can be plugged into a formula that will enable you to get a good estimate of what return you can reasonably expect on your real estate investment. That formula looks rather complicated but merely does what we described above. In fact, most advanced hand calculators have the formula already plugged in. All you need to do is put in your assumptions, and you can get an answer that will guide your decision. Check out some of the real estate calculators on the Web that are listed in the Appendix to help you along your way.

Let's Get Moving

All the preliminaries are done, the bands have left the field, and we've had the coin toss. You will receive and defend your own goals. Let's get the game underway! The book is divided into four sections. The first is the "what," and it details the potential for profiting from investment real estate. It presents general strategies that will allow you to get into the market efficiently. These include the very important tax strategies to get you to your Ultimate Phase. The second section helps you make the important location decisions about your investment: where to buy, what to buy, and how to improve the imperfect. The third and fourth sections describe how to maximize the return on your investment, both in terms of income and in terms of appreciation, including tips on when and how to get out. A final section describes the demographics of the housing market to give you some ideas on the nature of the rental and sales markets you will face.

So, here we go. Good luck!

PART 1

Our Secret Sauce
Keys to the New Second Home Kingdom

1

A Lifelong, Tax-Free, Second-Home Ownership Strategy

You hit home runs not by chance but by preparation.—Roger Maris

Millions of homeowners dream of owning a second home, for pleasure and profit, but they aren't sure they can afford it. Many who do own a second home are concerned that Uncle Sam will strangle them for selling it. Others are attempting to untangle the dilemma of being property rich and cash poor. Fortunately, there are now solutions to these two problems.

This chapter explains the simple strategy that will enable your next real estate purchase—whether for investment, vacation, or retirement—to serve all three of these purposes over time, tax free. We call this concept of tax-free lifetime homeownership "The New Second Home." In addition, if you already own a traditional second home or homes, or rental property, this chapter also charts your course to greater equity, tax savings, and additional leisure time in the place you really want to be. Subsequent chapters explore the many reasons a second home could be the best purchase you'll ever make. "Best purchase" no longer denotes only cherished family times—The New Second Home can become a huge, flexible, and versatile moneymaking, tax-saving asset.

The New Second Home Strategy is never limited by an owner's age or the location, or type, of property. Its goal is to provide you with a creative, new approach to obtaining the traditional second home. While we offer several different temporary and permanent twists, phases, combinations, and options (Interim, Cocoon, and Ultimate) here's the New Second Home Strategy in the simplest of forms:

1. Buy a rental property in the area you think you want to retire/get away. (Perhaps the down payment comes from a home equity loan on your primary residence).
2. For most of the year, rent it out—renters pay down your mortgage. Enjoy some personal-use days and get to know the area.
3. Sell your primary residence, collecting up to $500,000 tax free.
4. Move in to the getaway/retirement rental and deem it a personal primary residence. Make it cozy for your long-term comfort or wait two years and sell it to pocket another tax-free gain.

Building Ownership through a Series of Properties

The New Second Home can also be a long-term tax shelter for future retirement. For example, if you are 35 years old and plan to slow down at 50, you can buy a rental home disguised as vacation home, furnish it, enjoy some personal-use time and have renters pay for it (Interim Phase). When you have whittled every shred of tax depreciation advantage out of it, you can move in and convert it to a full-time private residence (Cocoon Phase) while still renting it out a couple of weeks a year. And because most mortgages "front-loan" interest, you will have used up most of your tax deductions from the mortgage in the 15 years you were working and renting the home. In the later years of the mortgage, when interest deductions are relatively low, you probably will be less concerned about your income falling off because you have promised yourself to slow down at age 50. While future tax proposals undoubtedly will change the current tax landscape, second homes still will be in direct sunshine when compared to other proposed restrictions on real-estate investments. You can sell your primary residence, pocket the gain, and retire in your second home (Ultimate Phase).

As mentioned in the Introduction, The New Second Home can be a one-step purchase or a process of stepping-stone moves designed to get you where you want to spend most of your battery-recharging time. Let's define the most important steps. You do not necessarily need all of them to accomplish your goal:

A Lifelong, Tax-Free, Second-Home Ownership Strategy

Interim Property—Often the only piece of real estate you can afford other than your primary residence. This can be a commercial property, rental house, vacant land, or apartment building you already own or plan to purchase.[1] This is usually an investment property that can be sold via 1031 Exchange (discussed in Chapter 2) to obtain a home that includes the amenities you'd like in a weekend getaway, or the last home you see yourself occupying. The replacement rental home could be converted to a principal residence after it has been "aged" to ensure the exchange. Then the former rental property could later be sold after the qualifying period of use as a principal residence (two years) and the exclusion claimed for the sale.

Cocoon Home—The home and area might be right, but you can't say you'll purchase and be there forever. This is sometimes a vacation property or second home that you already own. Perhaps it is mostly a rental now that you use for family vacations one or two weeks a year. It might have been the family cabin that you inherited from your parents. It could become your Ultimate home, but you are not sure at the moment if you would ever sell it.

Ultimate Home—You are never selling this place. It might eventually be your only personal residence or it might be your second personal residence. You want to spend every day you can here, and you probably will never rent it out. When you die, it goes to the kids. (If they don't behave themselves, it goes to charity.)

By buying one property—or series of properties—and having renters pay for it (Interim), then selling the property via the 1031 Exchange and buying one more to your liking (Cocoon or Ultimate) you defer (save) the gain on the rental property. Don't like your new neighborhood? Sell the home while it's still a rental property and find another via another 1031 Exchange. If you already have moved in and converted it to your personal residence, sell two years later and move to another place. Or borrow against the equity of your primary residence and use it as the down payment on a rental in The Ultimate Community. Rent the home in The Ultimate Community for two years, then move into it. Sell, or again rent, the previous home. When done correctly, all transactions would be tax free.

How is that possible? Not only is it possible, but it also is rather simple and actually OK with the Internal Revenue Service. Your intention at the time of the exchange is the only relevant fact. You can immediately there-

[1] The desire to own any sort of property in some areas is extremely strong. For example, in the exclusive Hamptons on Long Island, consumers are buying 10-x-20-foot garden plots as their "vacation getaway."

after change your mind and convert the usage of the property. However, because Uncle Sam cannot look inside your brain to see what your intention was, the IRS will examine the "objective manifestations of your intent" and attempt to determine what your intention truly was.

For example, let's say Fast Freddie, a longtime plumber known for his speedy house calls, owned one rental property—a cute duplex in the inner city he bought for $50,000 that was now worth $250,000. Freddie heard that the printing press around the corner—the employer of his tenants for more than a decade—was going to lay off most of its workforce. Freddie, an avid golfer, decided to exchange his $250,000 duplex for a golf course home in Florida worth $350,000 because he knew the house would bring premium rental income from Midwest Snowbirds, and those rents would more than cover the $100,000 mortgage payment, taxes, and insurance of the golf course home. After renting to an Ohio couple for a month, Freddie was named assistant pro at the course. The new job justifies the change in status of the golf course property (investment to private residence), so Freddie could move in, deem it his primary residence, and not have to worry about $200,000 gain resulting from the duplex. That's because the IRS probably would approve the conversion of golf course rental to residence because his personal circumstances changed (new job) and he wanted to move into the property.

Remember, your intention at the time of the transaction is the only relevant fact. You can immediately thereafter change your mind and convert the usage of the property. The IRS will examine the "objective manifestations of your intent" to determine what your intention truly was. (We will detail that process, plus examine other options, in Chapter 2.) However, if Fast Freddie had the mental intention from the start of converting the golf course property to a personal residence as soon as it was safe to do so, his entire transaction could be taxable. That was not the case—Fast Freddie's initial intention was to bank the big rental bucks brought by Midwest Snowbirds. Had he not accepted the new job, and the rental income was not as big as expected, he still could change his mind and convert the property into a personal residence. Fast Freddie should be prepared to prove that his intention had changed, perhaps by showing his rental income had not reached the volume anticipated.

Unknowingly, when members of Congress approved the Taxpayer Relief Act of 1997 (examined fully in Chapter 2), they completely overhauled and multiplied the possibilities for second-home purchase, use, and sale. Ironically, the reason why taxpayers are able to reap the advantages of having two homes in the first place can be directly traced to our members of the U.S. House of Representatives and Senate. Why are we able to deduct the mortgage interest on two homes rather than just one? It's because Congressional members "needed" two homes—one in their home state and another in the nation's capital. (Some accountants even refer to the curious guideline the "Congressmen's Rule.") When you couple the ability to own two (or more) personal residences simultaneously, then toss in the capacity to convert a rental property into a personal residence, you will be overwhelmed to discover the windfall profits brought by simple combinations of appreciation and tax savings. Let's examine several examples that are applicable to traditional age brackets and investment phases.

Before we do, take a moment to state aloud: "Moving into my rental is not a taxable event." And, "I can sell my primary residence every two years and pay no tax."[2]

The Couple That Already Has "Arrived"

As most taxpayers know by now, the 1997 tax legislation added a generous exclusion for sales of primary residences. If you own one or more residences, there are some tax-saving chess moves to be made—all aboveboard—but preparation and timing are always important. The basic gain exclusion qualification rule is simple: You must have owned and used the home as your main residence for at least two years out of the five-year period ending on the date of sale. If you are married, the full $500,000 capital gains break ($250,000 for singles) is available as long as one or both of you satisfy the residency and ownership guidelines (explored thoroughly in Chapter 2).

Let's say Hopalong Kennelly and his wife, Gertie, are married and own three homes. First there's their current main home, not far from the movie studio in Los Angeles where Hopalong works, which qualifies for the $500,000 capital gains exclusion. They paid $550,000 for the place, sell it for a net of $950,000, and put $400,000 of gain in their pocket because it is less than the $500,000 maximum exclusion. Hopalong and Gertie then move to their Scottsdale, Arizona, vacation home where Hopalong keeps his horses. After living in Scottsdale for two years, Hopalong and Gertie sell the home, pocket $475,000 (their net again was less than the maximum ($500,000) of tax-free gain and move to Vero Beach, Florida, where Hopalong can walk to the Los Angeles Dodgers' spring training baseball complex. After living in Vero for two years, Hopalong and Gertie can sell, pocket up to $500,000 in gain tax free, move again . . . the tax-free windmill continues and the gain goes in their pockets.

[2] Up to $250,000 for a single person; $500,000 for a married couple

You're right—few people want the hassle of moving to a new primary residence every two years. But you could, and the vacation home, or homes, you own now could be involved, tax free. If you permanently convert, or temporarily flip-flop, the status of rental properties to personal residences, more moneymaking possibilities quickly surface.

Single and Thinking about Selling

For example, Sally, 37, a single woman and schoolteacher, has a principal residence and a rental property. Both properties have significantly appreciated in value over the past decade. Sally sells her principal residence, takes her capital gain exclusion of up to $250,000 on that residence, and decides to move into the rental home. The rental unit now becomes her principal residence. Sally lives in the former rental house for two years and thereby satisfies the use and occupancy tests. Sally then sells the property and realizes another big-time gain, of which $250,000 can be excluded. It makes no difference that most of the appreciation on the second property was realized when it was a rental house. Sally has prepared, has met all of the tests to exclude the gain, and has done nothing illegal or immoral. In a world plagued by deliberate corporate and personal tax evasion, Sally hasn't even jaywalked. She's simply avoided significant capital gains tax while building a considerable nest egg by understanding the tax laws (discussed in Chapter 2) and carrying out a simple plan. And she'll do it again. She has used the cash to buy condominiums on both coasts. Sally will use one as a primary residence and the other as a second home, renting it periodically to friends until she eventually occupies it full time.

Depreciation Consideration

Depending on when Sally bought, converted, and sold, all of her gain might not be excluded. That's because depreciation taken on the rental property after May 6, 1997 will be subject to "recapture" and tax. Any depreciation taken before that date is "forgiven" and available for the gain exclusion. So if Sally had chosen not to depreciate the property at all, or had taken her depreciation before May 6, 1997 she could call the tune without having to pay the piper. If not, the amount she would have to pay would depend on the value of the property and the length of time she depreciated it.

For example, let's use some round numbers and say Sally's rental home was worth $100,000 when she bought it in 1997. The rental term ended five years later when she converted it to her personal residence. The county determined that 65 percent of value of the property was in the building (sometimes officially known as "improvements") while the land value was determined to be $35,000. Because residential property is depreciated over a 27.5-year schedule and only the improvements can be depreciated, Sally's taxable amount for depreciating her rental for five years would be $11,700. (5 years divided by 27.5 = 18 percent. $65,000 × 18 percent = $11,700). Depending on her other income, Sally's maximum capital gain bill would be $2925 ($11,700 × 25 percent = $2925) or less. That's not bad, considering the potential for gain she could pocket tax free.

Depending on your situation and what you might already own, there might be necessary side roads (Interim, Cocoon) to cruise before reaching your Ultimate decompression chamber. If you are starting from scratch, the fastest avenue is finding a rental in the eventual place you think you want to spend leisure time. Rent it out until you want to occupy it, and then move in. However, a gray area continues to loom around how long you must hold an investment property before deeming it a personal residence, especially if you acquired the property through a 1031 Exchange. This tax-deferred mechanism is for investment properties only—personal residences do not qualify. According to Carleen Snyder, real estate tax partner in the accounting office of Moss Adams, LLP, and other accountants, a home that has been a rental nest egg for decades usually is not an issue, but those that have been acquired in the past three years via a 1031 Exchange can be. That's because no specific "hold" times have ever been written or adopted. And, as mentioned earlier, intent at the time of the exchange should be toward another investment property. This is explained in the how-to section on 1031 Exchanges in Chapter 2.

"If taxpayers are going to convert the use of homes, I would like to see at least two tax years in the books," Snyder said. "If a person were to buy a rental in July 2003, I would prefer it remain as a rental property at least through 2004. That way, the conversion would not appear on a tax return until the 2005 return, and then actually be viewed sometime in 2006."

"The simple conversion of a rental home to a primary residence is not likely to show up on the IRS radar scope," Snyder said. "There are a lot of mom-and-pop rentals out there—couples with one rental home they have been nursing for years. Perhaps that property is the former family home they didn't want to sell— or couldn't sell—earlier in their lives."

While thousands of consumers own or have inherited mom-and-pop rentals, vacant land, or extremely valuable commercial property, most people do not understand the flexibility and versatility of their real property assets. One of the more underestimated financial bonuses available to the average consumer is the ability to convert an investment property into a primary residence. That tax-free fact, coupled with the $500,000 tax-free exclusion on gain from your primary residence is the easiest way to afford a recreational or retirement property without breaking the bank. In fact, it's an effective, realistic strategy in building equity and wealth.

Best Place to Start

If you own no other property, the best way to launch the tax-free vehicle that snowballs into The New Second Home kingdom is to purchase one rental. Get in the door to an investment property any way and in any place you can. If the property is in the area you want to spend your time, you can save some steps. If not, you are by no means out of luck. This property could be the overgrown eyesore in your neighborhood, a foreclosure you found on the Internet, a percentage of an apartment complex, a piece of raw ground you can buy for a bargain. Obtain the down payment via a home equity loan on your primary residence, a lump-sum bonus, or perhaps a small inheritance from Bachelor Uncle Bill with No Kids. Then have renters pay down your mortgage with their monthly rent while the home climbs in value, thanks to appreciation. You can then move into it or sell it—tax free, via a 1031 Exchange—and find a home that better suits your eventual recreation or retirement years. While we offer and discuss creative methods to help you finance your New Second Home in Chapter 5, one of the more logical ways to fund your purchase will be to take out a home-equity line of credit on your primary residence or refinance your residence and pull the cash out for the down payment. You could then get a conventional first mortgage or ask the seller to "play the bank" by arranging seller financing for you. Most home-equity lines of credit float a point or two higher than the prime rate. And, unlike mortgage interest, which is deductible on up to $1 million of debt on your first and second homes combined, the home-equity cap is $100,000 for a combined total of $1.1 million.

Throwing the Rental in Reverse

Converting a primary residence into a rental happens all the time—there is nothing underhanded about it. Some people flip-flop the use of their properties every few years depending on personal use, rental income, or other considerations discussed later in this chapter. In addition, with the uncertainty of the conventional financial markets, consumers are now, more than ever, attempting to hang on to as much real estate as they can afford. The subject of "keeping your home as a rental" often comes up when a new job opportunity surfaces. Typically, an employee is transferred to a new region, not knowing if the new professional environment will be to his or her liking. The reasons most often given for retaining your current home are (a) you might return soon, (b) the home will be in great demand as a corporate relocation or local rental, (c) houses in your area are rapidly appreciating. Now, add to that list, and certainly not at the bottom, the chance of selling it tax free and pocketing a significant gain. In the immortal words of Kenny Rogers, "you've got to know when to hold 'em . . ."

For example, Uncle Charley, a widower, bought his home in 2002 and relocates across the country in 2004 to take a new job as an assistant basketball coach at a community college. He's not sure if this new job will work out because he's heard the head coach is ornery and nasty to his players. So instead of selling his current residence, Uncle Charley decides to rent it out. If he can't get along with the head coach, Uncle Charley can return to his old house and lovely neighborhood.

Twelve months later, the head coach is fired and Uncle Charley is offered the position, complete with a pay raise and new car. He decides to accept the new post and wants to sell his old home that he rented out. Uncle Charley puts his old home on the market and is able to exclude up to $250,000 of the gain on the sale. He's able to do this because Uncle Charley used the home as a principal residence for at least two years during the five-year period ending on the date of the sale of the residence. Even though Uncle Charley hasn't lived in the home for more than a year, he did use it as a principal residence for two years during the five-year period ending on the date of the sale.

Personal Residence or Rental?

A home and a primary residence have different meanings, benefits, and drawbacks to tax persons. For example, do you want the depreciation and maintenance benefits of a rental home or the mortgage-interest deduction of a residence? A personal residence cannot be depreciated. An individual can have several homes yet only one primary residence. A home refers to where a person is physically living, as long as his or her stay is more than a temporary one. Primary residence involves both physical presence in a place and intention to make that place one's home. Residence without "the intention to remain indefinitely" generally will not constitute primary residence. An individual's motive for changing primary residences—even for tax reasons—does not raise red tax flags. However, consumers must show at least some sort of intent to establish a primary residence.

If you are considering making your vacation home your permanent residence, now or in the future, you should begin planning for a change in primary residence. If you have been using your vacation home as a rental, consider converting it to personal-use only for a period of at least two years. That way, if you have to sell unexpectedly, you can keep up to $500,000 in gains tax free. However, use caution and keep a paper trail. During the past two decades, more than two million individuals have migrated to the Sunbelt states of Georgia, Florida, Texas, and the Carolinas, plus the Southwest states of California, Arizona, and New Mexico. Some people who retain homes and remain active in business or community affairs in their original states are finding that state tax officials are challenging their change of personal residence. The states say that these folks are still residents for income or estate tax purposes because they have not abandoned their original personal residences.

This was not an issue in Uncle Charley's case just discussed. The home was his primary residence before he decided to rent it out. However, when intent conflicts with facts and circumstances, determining which residence is actually an individual's primary residence can be confusing. The determination is usually based on the individual's objective and facts such as:

- Registering to vote
- Having bank accounts and securities accounts
- Payment of local taxes
- Time spent in state of residency
- Continuous car registration and driver's license
- Furnishing, appointing primary residence more extensively
- Using state of residence address in registrations and applications

Not as important, yet certainly noteworthy, is the fact that some states impose a tax on the fair market value of intangible personal property owned or controlled by their residents. The intangible personal property that is subject to tax generally includes:

- Stock options
- Commodity futures and contracts
- Notes, bonds, and other obligations for payment of money
- Stocks and shares of incorporated or unincorporated companies, business trusts, and mutual funds.

States have numerous statutory exemptions from the intangible tax for particular assets such as money and cash equivalents, securities issue by the U.S. government, and interests in partnerships that are not publicly traded.

Tax planners say you can eliminate your intangible tax liability if you structure your planning strategies correctly and implement them on a timely basis. Consider timing your move to avoid the initial year's tax or by restructuring the ownership of tangible assets. You will also want to consider the state income tax consequences of a change of residence. If you have bonuses coming, stocks options, or other deferred compensation (as is the case for example, with many professional athletes), carefully plan how you receive these funds relative to your move to avoid excessive state income taxes. All of you art collectors will want to know that some states impose a sales tax or use tax on tangible personal property used, stored, or consumed in that state. Tangible personal property usually means personal property that can be seen, weighed, measured, or touched. The tax is imposed not only on retailers but also on consumers of tangible personal property.

According to Rob Keasal, residential tax specialist in the Pacific Northwest accounting firm of Anderson Zurmuehlen & Co., P.C., taxpayers often already own the property and would not have to pay a use tax for stepping across the border and changing residency. "In some states, when a rental is sold with tangible personal property, like a stove and refrigerator, it is considered incidental to the real property and no sales or use tax is paid when the property changes hands," Keasal said. "However, many states are getting tougher. I've seen at least one state that even has a use tax reminder on its income tax return."

Other accountants concur. States have become more aggressive in enforcing their sales and use tax laws. They have gone to great lengths—examining U.S. Customs reports, auditing tax gallery sales, personal checkbooks, and credit card statements and sharing that information with other states. Some states have enacted strict filing responsibilities and record retention statutes with respect to individuals who are subject to sales and use tax laws. Persons who relocate to states that have enacted sales and use tax laws might be liable for use tax on their purchases. For example, if you purchase goods from an out-of-state vendor that are shipped into your new home state, you might be responsible for paying use tax on those goods.

In addition, there can be other significant considerations, other than rental income generation and tax savings, for flip-flopping the status of a rental property to a personal residence, and vice versa. Many times, these reasons can be social or legislative. For example, property owners with cabins along the shore of a remote mountain lake held a community meeting to formulate a plan to halt, or drastically curtail, logging companies from taking acres of evergreen trees near their mountain paradise. Some of the folks attending the meeting said their questions and concerns would strike more of an impact on local legislators if they were registered voters of the local county. But most of the people in the room only visited the lake during the summer months, and transferring their voting privileges would mean transferring their principal residence. Clearly, many had come to depend on summer rental income to ease county tax and cabin repair costs. Making such a change could drastically alter how their cabins were currently used.

The personal residence or rental question also will surface when dealing with a lender. Chapter 5 offers some creative ways you might not have considered to help you get in the door of The New Second Home. However, the conventional method typically entails making a down payment (from savings, liquidating other assets) or taking out a home-equity loan on your primary residence for the "down" on an Interim, Cocoon, or Ultimate property. The remaining balance then can be financed over a term similar to the loan on your primary home—30 years, 15 years, or a variety of adjustable-rate mortgage periods. If the home is a second residence, the rates probably will be more favorable than if the home is rental unit, commonly referred to as a "nonowner occupied" dwelling. If you plan to rent out your home, the lender will want to see proof that you're actually going to generate a cash flow that will help pay the monthly mortgage plus taxes and insurance. In many cases, the lender will ask for a cash flow statement for a property showing its rental history. And don't count on your bank to take all of a home's estimated rental income into consideration. Even for a property with a long rental history, most lenders will only consider 75 percent to 80 percent of the total take. If possible, make purchase offers contingent on your loan being approved—some lenders will not extend funds in condominium developments where there are more renters than owner occupants. Also, make sure you know all insurance costs for your new property. The dizzy world of environmental claims has pushed some homeowner's insurance premiums out of sight.

We now have poured the basement foundation for The New Second Home. In Chapter 2, we explain the history and explore the possibilities of combining tax-free exclusions with tax-deferred exchanges, netting profits difficult to find in other investment opportunities. Think about it—what other financial instrument also gives you sand between your toes, snow under your boots, security, memorable family experiences, AND cash in your pocket?

The Problem with Timeshares

Consumers can sell their primary residence and move into their own rental property or second residence and then designate that property as their new primary residence. This move keeps the capital gains chain alive—as long as you live in your new residence two of the previous five years, you can sell the property and again be tax free. What often breaks the powerful capital gains chain powered by rising home values and appreciation is sinking all of your available cash—money that could go into an appreciating asset—in a timeshare instead of a second home or investment rental.

Timeshares work for a huge number of owners. But be careful. By the time you purchase (usually for cash), pay annual fees, exchange fees and sell, you'd be much better off financially by stashing the money in a small rental property, letting the tenants pay off your mortgage, and selling the asset a few years later and buying the getaway you always wanted to try.

The tragic events of September 11, 2001 definitely have consumers thinking closer to home. With that philosophy has come a renewed interest in driving the family car to vacation destinations that could be used a couple of weeks a year rather than hopping on a plane and crossing several time zones. However, timeshares—regardless of location—have never been an effective investment or tax move, and here's why:

Getting your initial outlay back is nearly impossible. You should view your cash outlay as a prepaid vacation, not a real estate investment. Online resellers obtain condo resales from developers, corporations, and consumers and sell them approximately for 20–30 cents on the dollar. Some companies no longer buy direct from consumers because it's more efficient to deal directly with developers. Potential tax advantages generally come only with interval ownership. The developer retains most tax breaks on right-to-use plans. If the interval owner uses the unit solely as a rental, the owner could deduct repairs, maintenance, depreciation, taxes, interest, and insurance. However, if you own 1/52nd of the unit (one week of the year) you can deduct only that percentage of repairs and maintenance. Really, is 10 bucks from a new, \$520 hot water heater really worth your time to claim? After a few seasons, you probably will be wondering: "Why didn't we just rent?" An annual fee of about

$500 for your timeshare, $100 a year to belong to the exchange company, plus $100 to exchange your week for another in the exchange bank—that's $700 a year before any travel costs. That sum will cover most of the cost of a nice three-bedroom condo in Palm Springs in the autumn. Plus, you can pick different dates and locations every year.

2

Linking the Key Ingredients:

Tax-Free Exchanges and Exemptions Can Save You Thousands

The avoidance of taxes is the only intellectual pursuit that still carries any reward.—John Maynard Keynes

Remember when people couldn't wait to be 65 years old? Ah, the retirement life . . . rowboats, goofy fishing hats with colorful, feathered lures, golf clubs, and recreational vehicles. The harsh reality is that the number of Americans 65 and older either working or looking for jobs has grown by 50 percent since 1980.[1] Sure, consumers are living longer, want to feel active and productive, but scores of others have been financially crippled by stock-market losses, health-care costs, and overwhelming fears about the solvency of Social Security.

In this chapter, we explain how, with one swoop of a pen, a once-in-a-lifetime tax exclusion became a potential bonanza every two years for homeowners and investors of all ages. We explore the curious history of the home-sale exemption and its less-celebrated cousin, the tax-deferred exchange on rental property. We will then detail how, when the two are strategically linked, the union compounds the potential for profitable,

[1] U.S. Census Bureau, The Older Population in the United States, March 2002.

tax-free returns for all consumers. The bottom line is that all owners of real property can now exercise options and combinations deemed taboo a few short years ago.

August 5, 1997: One Move Unlocks Countless Financial Options

When President Clinton signed into law the Taxpayer Relief Act of 1997 on August 5, 1997, he changed not only the $125,000, one-time home sale exclusion for persons over 55 years of age, but also the "rollover replacement rule." In essence, the home began to move from the "shelter" column into the "financial portfolio" column. Under the old law, a taxpayer could defer any gain on the sale of a principal residence by buying or building a home of equal or greater value within 24 months of the sale of the first home. Tax on the gain was not eliminated, but merely "rolled over" into the new residence, reducing the tax basis of the new home. If you sold a primary residence and failed to meet the requirements for deferral, the taxpayer faced a tax on current and previously deferred gain. The old law also contained a once-in-a-lifetime, $125,000 exclusion ($62,500 if single, or married and filing a separated return) of gain from the sale of the primary residence. The intent of the new tax code, which replaces the "rollover" provision and $125,000 over-55 exclusion, is to allow most homeowners to sell their primary residence without tax. It also dramatically simplifies record keeping for many people. Although it's still wise to retain proof of the original cost of the home and significant improvements, tedious collection and retention of invoices and other records to substantiate the cost of home improvements probably won't be necessary.

Accumulating Wealth through Residences

Many taxpayers, including seniors who have already used the one-time over-55 $125,000 exclusion, do not realize they are eligible to sell their primary home again—and do it every two years—under the Taxpayer Relief Act of 1997. The 1997 law repealed all former tax laws on primary residences and significantly changed the role of the home in regard to financial planning. Here are the keys to one of the best ways the average homeowner can now accumulate more wealth for retirement and an explanation of why the home has become the largest piece in the average taxpayer's financial puzzle:

In order to qualify for the $500,000 capital gains exclusion ($250,000 for single persons), you must have owned and used the property as your principal residence for two out of five years prior to the date of sale. Second, you must not have used this same exclusion in the two-year period prior to the sale. So the only limit on the number of times a tax-payer can claim this exclusion is once in any two-year period. (As outlined in Chapter 1, you can sell your primary home, then move into your rental or vacation home——stay two years—and sell it without paying tax on either sale.)

What is often misunderstood is that both the earlier one-time exclusion of up to $125,000 in gain for persons over 55 and the deferral of all or part of a gain by purchasing a qualifying replacement residence are gone. You no longer can utilize parts of either portion, and you absolutely do not have to buy a replacement home. Persons who used the $125,000 can make use of the new exclusion if they meet the two-year residency test. The law enables seniors to "buy down" to less expensive homes without tax penalties.

For gains greater than the exemption amounts, a 15-percent capital gains tax usually will apply.[2] Homeowners with potential gains larger than the excludable amounts should keep accurate records in an attempt to reduce their gains by the amount of all eligible improvements.

To qualify for the full exclusion, either married spouse can meet the ownership requirement, but both must meet the use requirement. Although exclusion can be used only once in each two-year period, a partial exclusion may be available if the sale results from a change in place of employment or health, or unforeseen circumstances. If you have owned the house fewer than two years, you would receive a proportional amount of the maximum exclusion under special situations. For example, if you owned a home for one year and made a $45,000 profit, the entire $45,000 would be tax free because your total exclusion was chopped in half to $125,000 from $250,000 because of the one-year time frame. Consumers can turn vacation homes (plus yachts and recreational vehicles) into principal residences simply by meeting the residency requirements. Divorced or separated spouses also are not out in the cold. If an "ex" lived in the home for two of the five years before the sale, that person is able to use the exclusion. However, nothing changes on the loss side of the primary home sale ledger—losses on the sale of the primary home still are not deductible. If a nondeductible loss seems unavoidable, it might be a good idea to convert the house to a rental property (where losses are deductible), but you would have to be able to prove the move was not just to avoid taxes. If depreciation were claimed on a property, the maximum

[2] Reduced from 20–25 percent in 2003.

capital gains tax liability would be 25 percent to the extent depreciation was claimed.

For married taxpayers who file a joint return, only one spouse need meet the two out of five-year ownership requirement, but both spouses must meet the two out of five-year use requirement. That is, if the husband has owned and used the house as his principal residence for two of the past five years, but his wife did not use the house as her principal residence for the required two years, then the capital gains exclusion is only $250,000.

For those who leave their home because of a disability, a special rule makes it easier to meet the two-year requirement—especially if you were hospitalized or had to spend a significant period in a similar facility. In such cases, if you owned and used the home as a principal residence for at least one of the five years preceding the sale, then you are treated as having used it as your principal residence while you are in a facility that is licensed to care for people in your condition. This rule enables the family to sell the home to raise cash for the expenses without incurring a large tax bite.

The Tax-Deferred "Swap" Is Really a Flat-out "Sale"

A tax-deferred exchange (commonly known as IRS Section 1031 Exchange) is really "legally sanctioned fiction," according to Richard Morse, a Bellevue, Washington-based attorney who specializes in the exchange process. The transaction will proceed just as a "sale" for you, your real estate agent, and parties associated with the deal. However, provided you closely follow the exchange rules, the IRS will "sanction" the transaction and allow you to characterize it as an exchange rather than as a sale. Thus you are permitted to defer paying the capital gain tax.

Section 1031 specifically requires that an exchange take place. That means that one property must be exchanged for another property, rather than sold for cash. The exchange is what distinguishes a Section 1031 tax-deferred transaction from a sale and purchase. The exchange is created by using an intermediary (or exchange facilitator) and the required exchange documentation. (See Figure 2-1.)

The "Like-Kind" Requirement

In an exchange, you must trade an interest in real estate, (sole ownership, joint tenancy, tenancy in common), that you have held for trade, business,

Linking the Key Ingredients

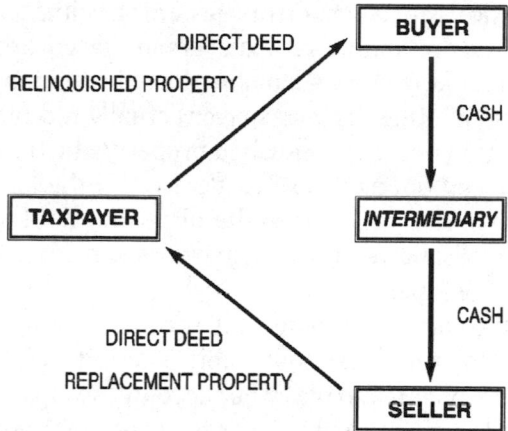

Figure 2-1

Capsule Exchange

First: You (Taxpayer) receive an acceptable offer for your property.

Second: You assign your seller's rights in the relinquished property purchase and sale contract to the buyer. The buyer gives "your" cash to the Intermediary. This is the first leg of the exchange.

Third: You make an acceptable offer to acquire the replacement property.

Fourth: You assign your purchaser's obligations in the contract to the Intermediary.

Fifth: The Intermediary acquires the relinquished property and instructs the Seller to deed it directly to you to complete the trade.

---

or investment purposes for another "like-kind" interest in real estate. The like-kind definition is very broad. You can dispose of and acquire any interest in real property other than a home or a second residence. For example, you can trade raw land for income property, a rental house for a multiplex, or a rental house for a retail property.

"The 1031 is absolutely my favorite part of the entire tax code—bar none," said Robert M. Levenson, vice president of LandAmerica 1031 Exchange Services, a member of the LandAmerica Financial Group. "It is flexible, it is versatile, and it offers both sophisticated investors and everyday consumers terrific financial opportunities. It is a valuable, underused instrument. While more and more taxpayers are discovering it everyday, most of them don't know how adaptable it can be to many situations."

The "No-Touch" Rule: If the taxpayer actually receives the proceeds from the disposition of the relinquished property, the transaction will be treated as a sale and not as an exchange. Even if the taxpayer does not *actually* receive the proceeds from the disposition of the property, the exchange will be disallowed if the taxpayer is considered to have "constructively" received them.

The code regulations provide that income, even though it is not actually reduced to a taxpayer's possession, is "constructively" received by the taxpayer if it is credited to his or her account, set apart for him or her, or otherwise made available so that he or she may draw upon it at any time. In a nutshell: "If you touch it (or even get too close), they will come."

Example: Willie, Whitey, Al, and Lou

In order for an exchange to be completely tax deferred, the replacement property must have a fair market value greater than the relinquished property, and all of the taxpayer's equity or more must be used in acquiring replacement property. This is known as trading up in value and up in equity, and it is essential for a totally tax-deferred exchange.

A true exchange—like a straight swap in baseball—rarely occurs. That's because two people rarely come together and look to deal properties of exactly equal value. Most of the time, the parties do not know each other, and their properties often are in different states. There are a number of different ways tax-deferred exchanges can be structured. They may involve two, three, or four parties and they may be quite simple or very complex. Typically, an exchange involves four parties—the exchanger (the taxpayer), a buyer for the relinquished property, a seller of the replacement property, and the intermediary who plays a key role, similar to the manager of a baseball team.

Here is an example of the parties and properties involved in a typical exchange:

Person	Role	Owns	Wants
Willie Mays	Taxpayer	Candlestick Condo	Bronx Bathhouse
Al Kaline	Buyer	Cash	Candlestick Condo
Whitey Ford	Seller	Bronx Bathhouse	Cash
Lou Pinella	Intermediary	nothing in deal	Exchange Fees

Relinquished Property: Candlestick Condo (Fair Market Value $500,000)

Replacement Property: Bronx Bathhouse (Fair Market Value $750,000)

Let's pretend that Willie Mays owns a condominium near Candlestick Point in San Francisco worth $500,000. The Giants have moved to their new stadium closer to downtown, and Willie believes the condo no longer is appreciating in value and thus wants to sell it. However, he doesn't want to pay tax on the sale and wouldn't mind having a piece of the Big Apple—like the Bronx Bathhouse. (See Figure 2-2.)

Whitey Ford, wanting to hold on to a piece of his famous past, has owned the Bronx Bathhouse near Yankee Stadium for decades. Whitey wants to do more traveling and feels his Bronx Bathhouse, worth $750,000, is no longer a good investment. He wouldn't mind being cashed out.

Al Kaline, who invested wisely after his retirement from the Detroit Tigers, has some cash and would not mind owning a piece of the City by the Bay. He'd like to buy Willie's Candlestick Point condo for cash.

Lou Pinella agreed to act as the intermediary for his friends so that each of the former baseball stars will end up with what he wants in the deal. When the exchange is complete, Willie will own the Bronx Bathhouse, Al will own the Candlestick Condo, and Whitey will have his cash to travel.

Different Types of Exchanges

Simultaneous Exchange: Title to the relinquished property is transferred directly to the buyer. The buyer pays cash to the intermediary. The intermediary pays cash to the seller, who transfers title to the replacement property directly to the taxpayer. The taxpayer thus avoids receiving any cash during the transaction, which would be immediately taxable.

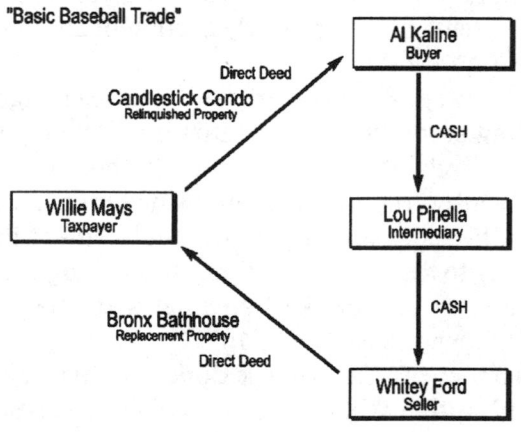

Figure 2-2

In our example, Willie transfers title to the Candlestick Condo to Al. Al pays cash to Lou. Lou pays cash to Whitey, and Whitey then transfers title to the Bronx Bathhouse to Willie. The exchange must be properly documented in accordance with IRS regulations.

Delayed Exchange: An exchange in which the relinquished and replacement properties close on different dates but not more than 180 days apart. The majority of exchanges are delayed exchanges.

Often, the taxpayer does not yet know what replacement property he or she wants to acquire but is required to close the sale on the relinquished property. When that is the case, a deferred exchange is necessary. The structure of the deferred exchange with intermediary is essentially the same as the simultaneous exchange with intermediary, except that, because the replacement property is not known at the time the relinquished property is transferred to the buyer, the two legs of the exchange take place at different times.

The exchanger (Willie) has 45 days to identify the property he wants as the replacement property. The transfer of the replacement property must still close within 180 days of the transfer of the relinquished property.

First Leg: The title to the Candlestick Condo is transferred to Al; Al pays cash to Lou. Lou holds money in Qualified Trust Account. The delay after closing on relinquished property can be no more than 180 days.

Second Leg: Willie does not want to sell the Candlestick Condo directly to Al in a taxable sale and then buy another property at a later time. He wants to do an exchange. However, Willie has not found the property he wants in exchange for the Candlestick Condo.

Within 45 days, Willie identifies the Bronx Bathhouse as the property he wants. Within 180 days of the transfer of the Candlestick Condo, Lou uses the funds from the first leg of the transaction to pay cash to Whitey, who then transfers title to the Bronx Bathhouse to Willie. Lou, and the ballplayers, must remember to properly document all time frames in this exchange. (See Figure 2-3.)

The **Straight Swap:** The two-party swap, or exchange, is the purest form of switching properties. As the name implies, only two parties are involved, and they exchange their properties. Both steps of the transaction occur simultaneously. Title to the relinquished property is conveyed by the taxpayer to the seller, and title to the replacement property is conveyed by the seller to the taxpayer. But rarely do straight swaps come out equal in real estate—not unlike Ken Phelps to the Yankees for the Mariners' Jay Buhner. (See Figure 2-4.)

Willie exchanges his Candlestick Condo for Whitey's Bronx Bathhouse. The result is that Willie has title to the Bronx Bathhouse (with a higher market value than the Candlestick Condo), and Whitey now has

Linking the Key Ingredients

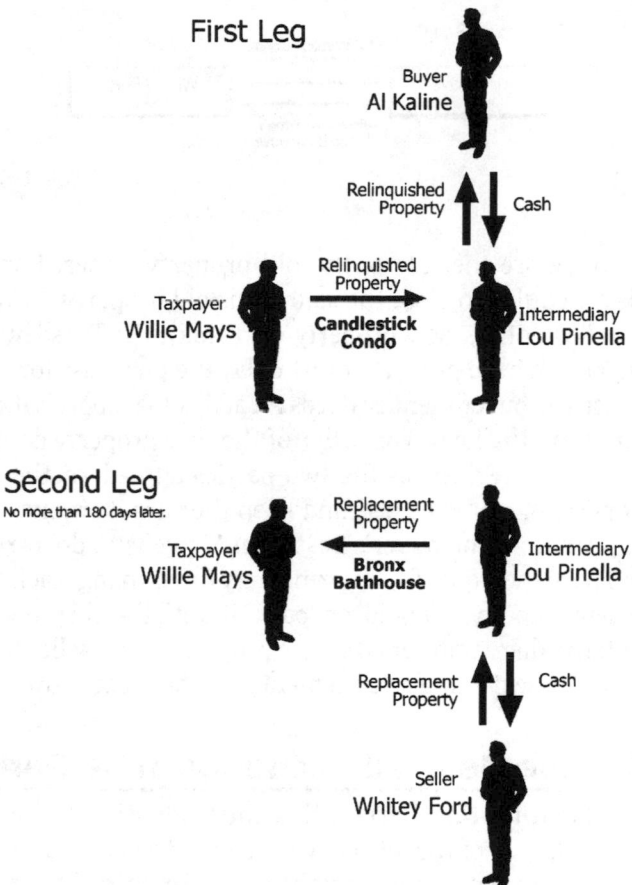

Figure 2-3

title to the Candlestick Condo. So the two have to work out the balance. Perhaps Whitey gets Willie to sign a few of his old jerseys and gloves to sell on eBay for astonishing prices.

Reverse Exchange: Sometimes a more costly and difficult method. If you follow all of its requirements, you should be in the clear. If you fail to meet all of the procedures, your exchange might still be successful, but will be subject to second-guessing by the IRS in the event of an audit. The ruling (Revenue Procedure 2000-37) came late to the party. The basic Code Section 1031 will not let a taxpayer buy the replacement property, or new property, until after he or she has sold the old, or relinquished property. Nonetheless, taxpayers have fallen into situations beyond their control where they needed to take title to the

Figure 2-4

new property before the sale of the old property closes. For example, someone is scheduled to close the sale of his old property on Wednesday and the purchase of his new property on Friday. On Tuesday, he learns that the buyer of his old property must delay the purchase for a couple of weeks because the buyer's lender needs an additional appraisal completed before it will fund the loan. The seller of the new property demands that the buyers close on Friday, as the two parties agreed, or the seller will sell the property to someone else and keep the earnest money.

In this situation, the buyer's best alternative is to do a "reverse exchange" and have their qualified intermediary (or exchange facilitator) take title to the new property and hold, or "park" it until the old property closes. Then the intermediary transfers the new property to the seller to complete the exchange. These parking arrangements are the meat of the new ruling.

What Are the Delayed Exchange Time Periods?

The 45-Day Identification Period: You must identify the replacement property by midnight of the 45th day following the close of the first leg. You won't lose your leg, but you might lose your shirt. That's because if you complete the deal without playing within the IRS' field of play, you could open yourself to tax liability. Your offer to buy the replacement property does not have to be accepted during this time period, and it is easy to identify a property. You are not required to wait until your first leg closes to identify a property. You should contact your Intermediary if you want to identify more than three properties.

The 180-Day Replacement Period: By midnight of the 180th day following the close of the first leg, you must complete your exchange by taking title to the replacement property you identified or your carriage to tax-free land turns into a pumpkin on the side of the road. These two time clocks—180 days and 45 days—begin to tick when the first leg closes.

Playing the Dealer: If you wheel and deal properties quickly and often, the IRS might think you are in the business of simply playing for a living. You are not supposed to exchange for the sole intention of reselling the property. This type of activity does not qualify for an exchange. So how long do you have to hold it before you can dish it? Lots of gray matter has been massaged over this gray issue. Attorneys grab their thumbs and invoke the infamous Rule of Thumb before all sides of the deal to "please wait at least one year."

What Is "Boot?"

"Boot" is an informal term that refers to Italy AND non-like-kind property. You will pay capital gain tax if you receive any net boot. Two common forms of boot are debt boot and cash boot. Debt boot refers to loans against the first-leg property that are paid off at closing. Cash boot refers to your net equity in the first leg property.

Taking Off Your Boots: To avoid paying taxes on the boot you received as part of the first leg, you must give boot as part of the second leg. *First*, you must acquire a property that costs as much as your net sales price. *Second*, you must reinvest the net equity—that is, give cash boot. *Third*, incur new debt that is equal to or greater than the debt you paid off.

Assume, for example, that the outstanding debt on the Candlestick Condo is $250,000. That gives Willie $250,000 down on the Bronx Bathhouse, and he assumes the remaining debt of $500,000. Thus, Willie received mortgage boot in the amount of $250,000 (the amount of debt on the Candlestick Condo, which he was relieved of in the transaction). Because a debt of $500,000 was placed on the Bronx Bathhouse, Willie is considered to have paid or given mortgage boot in this exchange. The amount of mortgage boot received ($250,000) is more than offset by the amount of mortgage boot given ($500,000).

Cost Basis: The purchase price plus some expenses associated with the purchase. Willie purchased his property, the Candlestick Condo, for $225,000. So Willie's basis in the Candlestick Condo is $225,000.

Adjusted Basis: The cost basis decreased by depreciation and increased by capital improvements. Willie's basis in the Candlestick Condo is $225,000. During the time he owned the property, he made $25,000 worth of capital improvements to the property, and took $50,000 worth of depreciation. Therefore, Willie's adjusted basis in the property is $200,000. Even if a taxpayer's adjusted basis in a property is greater than his or her basis, no tax is owed until there is a gain, and there is no gain until the property is transferred.

Realized Gain: The difference between the net sale price and the adjusted basis.

Recognized Gain: That portion, if any, of the realized gain that is subject to tax. If you sell, the realized and recognized gain will be the same. If you exchange, the recognized gain will be zero. For a transaction to result in total nonrecognition of gain, the taxpayer must receive property with an equal or greater market value and equity investment than the property exchanged, and receive no boot. Looking at our example, Willie was able to conduct an exchange that resulted in total tax deferral. He acquired the Bronx Bathhouse, a property that was greater in value than the Candlestick Condo. He placed $500,000 of debt on the Bronx Bathhouse, which was greater that the debt he was relieved of on the Candlestick Condo ($250,000). The $250,000 netted from the Candlestick Condo was used as a down payment on the Bronx Bathhouse. Willie's adjusted basis in the Candlestick Condo was $200,000. The gain on the Candlestick Condo was $300,000 (the difference between the consideration received for the property and the adjusted basis). By exchanging the Candlestick Condo, Willie deferred the total tax that otherwise would be due on the gain.

Replacement Property Basis: The exchange allows the tax to be deferred by carrying over the taxpayer's adjusted basis in the relinquished property to the replacement property. So Willie's adjusted basis in the Candlestick Condo is carried over to the Bronx Bathhouse. The basis is increased from $200,000 to $450,000 because of the additional debt on the replacement property.

Capital Gain Tax Rates: Long-term capital gain appreciation is taxed at 20 percent. Depreciation of real property is recaptured at a 25-percent rate. The total tax will be a combination of these two components.

How Is Money Held and Protected? The intermediary does not take any of your interest. The funds are protected from theft by using a Qualified Trust Account. The bank is cotrustee, and your signature and approval is required before any funds can be withdrawn. The funds can only be used as you direct.

How Should You Select an Intermediary?

1. Recognize that you are selecting a service provider, NOT a product.
2. Determine what benefits/value you desire from that service provider.
3. Your Intermediary should be knowledgeable about exchanges, escrow, and real estate law.
4. Your Intermediary must be accessible. What good is an intermediary if you can't get your questions answered?

If you pay for service, expect a service. Really, who needs to reach a voice machine five times in a row?

Once you have completed your tax-deferred exchange, you can always trade again when another property or area piques your interest. For example, Al Kaline might want to swap the Candlestick Condo for a house on a golf course in Scottsdale, Arizona. Kaline then completes the swap via a Tax-Deferred Exchange and then rents the golf course home to former major league baseball players. After about two years, as long as Kaline can show the original exchange was for investment (rental) purposes, Kaline could choose to move into the Scottsdale golf course house and designate it his primary residence, tax free.

Linking Rentals in the Real World

So much for our baseball legends . . . In the real world, Brian and Kathleen Richards could not wait to be 55 years old. Now, the couple, and a growing number of adults like them, is looking at renewing their financial life every two years—or preparing a place to land before they jump. That's because the Taxpayer Relief Act of 1997, allowed the Sarasota, Florida couple to keep up to $500,000 on the sale of a primary residence every two years. (As mentioned, that amount slides to $250,000 for single persons.) The secret sauce in the Richards's recipe contains the following ingredients: three rental homes, the ability to "move in" to each one of them every two years, and the option of selling each property via a 1031 Exchange.

The Richards took their "one-time exclusion" of $125,000 in 1995 when they both turned 55. They sold their large family home overlooking the water near Sarasota and bought a small home in a golf course community not far from the sand of St. Pete Beach. They had charted their financial course well and put down $50,000 of the gain on a condominium near Winter Park, Colorado. They discovered the area seven years before when visiting one of their children in graduate school at the University of Colorado in Boulder. They love not only the slopes but also the summer hiking and mountain biking. They now rent the condo for a majority of the snow skiing months, yet retain at least a week for themselves for a family reunion during an extended President's Day Weekend. The rental income covers the mortgage and maintenance, the renters are helping to pay off the debt, and the unit is appreciating every year. They could easily sell the St. Pete Beach house (pocket up to $500,000 in gain tax free) and move into the condo—now worth far more than the debt owed. If they tire of the snow, they can sell the condo in two years (pocket up to $500,000 in gain again), and head to another property.

What's extremely enticing is the fact that the average homeowner does not have to own three rentals to attain a similar goal. While you could conceivably live off appreciation if you were smart enough to predict rising home values in specific markets by moving there and then selling, tremendous flexibility comes from owning one tiny, seemingly worthless, rundown rental now and using it to achieve that sunny recreational place or retirement oasis. In fact, in Chapter 4 we'll show you how to find a good deal, and then give you some creative ways to finance in Chapter 5.

3

Balancing Dreams, Affordability, and Investment Potential

I always try to balance the light with the heavy—a few tears of human spirit in with the sequins and the fringes.—Bette Midler

There's a magazine called *Unique Homes* that displays the most fabulous properties imaginable, the stuff dreams are made of. These estates range in price from the high six figures into the millions of dollars and are located in all parts of the United States and many foreign locations. It's a dream book and it serves a useful purpose. We all dream, and real estate seems to be the stuff of dreams for most Americans. Those dreams are useful because they often drive us forward to do things that are meant to reach those dreams. Most often we don't reach those dreams, but the effort is beneficial because it gets us to do things that are good for us.

That movement toward the dream is the focus of this chapter. In it, we discuss how you formulate the long-term goal of your real estate investment activities and how you judge which options will best move you toward the dream. It's about starting with an Investment Property and trading up to a Cocooning Property or an Ultimate home. So this is all about planning. It's about setting out at the beginning of the process and determining its end. And then it's about starting small and growing.

Let's start with a basic premise: your reach exceeds your grasp. In other words, when you think about the house you want to live in late in your life, it's likely to be grander and better located than the house you now inhabit, or can even now afford. That's OK. It's the end of the process you care about. You intend to eventually live in that house and enjoy all the things you envision it affords. In this chapter, we look at how you can visualize the house you eventually want to live in, and how you plan to get there from where you are now.

Envisioning Your Dream Home

For example, consider John Lombardo, an accomplished professional . . . After years as a highly regarded trade association executive, he branched off to form his own consulting company. But when he did this, John also created in his own mind a vision of where he would like to be in 10 years. Always having been interested in his Italian ancestry, John decided that he would live most of the year in Tuscany and conduct his business from there, using the Internet and visiting clients during a three-month annual residence in the United States. In his many trips to Italy, he had explored the various towns that would be candidates for residence and had found the perfect location. This allowed him to flesh out his future life in Italy. He knew the sights and sounds of the town, how the breezes felt on his face, the smell of the flowers and herbs, and had even laid out his daily routine, including faithful dog. Back in the United States, he took language classes so that he could better speak Italian. This attention to detail kept his vision alive, and in the process stimulated his energy in, and desire for, his business. Sure enough, after 10 years, he had arranged his affairs in such a way that his trans-Atlantic lifestyle became a reality. The dream became the reality.

When we talk about a dream home, we're not talking about the here and now. Clearly, there are neighborhoods you would like to live in and houses you would like to inhabit as your household grows and develops. Perhaps the house is in the ideal school district, or perhaps it has the perfect flow for entertaining, or perhaps it's within walking distance of the wonderful downtown attractions you love so much. All that is fine, but it's only the beginning of the process we describe here. When we talk about a dream house, we mean the place to wind up after you have used The New Second Home to gradually increase your wealth and then sell your principal residence, combine the proceeds with the profits you have made on The New Second Home and get the home you have always dreamed about for your later years.

Envisioning your dream house is both difficult and important. It is difficult because right now you don't know what will excite and interest you when you are ready for it. Tastes change and so do household circumstances. That golf course community that excites your fancy now may, because of arthritis, give way to a more urban environment, perhaps one in a university town setting where life is quieter and safer and yet it's easy to access a multitude of cultural activities. Home styles and technology will surely change so that what you will want then cannot even be imagined now. It's a really tough process!

Despite this, it is very important that you carry a vision out in front of you. Without that vision, it will be impossible to make the right decisions in the interim. When to buy and when to sell, whether (or how often) to rent or to use, owning in vacation communities or urban areas—all of these choices can be best made by reference to the vision you have developed. Without an end point, no direction can be labeled "good" or "bad," "right" or "wrong." With one, your decisions are almost automatic.

The paradox here—that it is necessary to create a vision and that it is difficult to do so—needs to be resolved. The solution comes from revisiting your vision every five years or so. Formulating a vision now starts you on the road; revisiting it periodically allows you the flexibility to stay on the road and wind up where you really want to be. The traditional path of the traditional second home is to buy a vacation home, use it for years, and then retire to it. If you change over those years (and you probably will), the house and the location might not really suit you when you retire, and you might feel trapped. Creating and then revising your vision allows you to use the investment and tax program outlined in this book and still wind up in a dream location.

Creating that dream, like everything else in this book, is a straightforward process that requires some work and some thought. It should be done jointly—by everyone who will participate in the dream house. If you want to include children, close friends, and other family members, that's fine. But it's only fine if they will have some responsibility—either physical or fiscal—for the property. Planning with people who will eventually lose interest in the property or give up their stake in it will likely leave you stuck with their tastes and thus dissatisfied with what you have at the end of the process.

Whoever participates in the decision making, the best process of envisioning your dream house involves creating the most detailed picture you can. If at the end of the process, you can engage all your senses—

touch, sight, smell, taste, hearing—in envisioning your dream house, it will seem more real to you and it will motivate you to move through our wealth-building process. Additionally, the dream house could—and should—be very much outside your grasp. Dreams are unconstrained, and your conception of the dream house should be as well. As you develop the vision, remember that the controlling factor is not whether it exists, but rather whether you can fully envision it. Creating that kind of vision involves the following steps.

- Begin by setting a time frame. When will you want to reach the goal of your dream house? Do you want to wait until retirement to take up residence, or will you want to use it, at least part time, well in advance of that? How long do you intend to live there? Answering these questions will not only help you envision the dream location, but also set the timetable for the wealth-creation process that will enable you to reach the dream.

- Move a little deeper into the process by looking at the things you enjoy now in your leisure time. These will make up the bulk of your activity in the dream location, so the location ought to accommodate them. If you enjoy reading, plays, movies, and lectures, then an urban location will be best. Access to golf, fishing, or hiking will dictate a vacation community. Don't worry about whether your tastes will change; remember you are revisiting the vision every five years or so. You might want to "edit" these activities to account for whatever limitations you might foresee on your ability to enjoy these activities. For example, if you feel that as you age you will eventually give up playing golf, you might want to plan on a place that enables you some options rather than a location that is purely a golf community. Going through this step will enable you to define the type of location that will best suit your needs.

- Next focus in on the type of house you want. How much room do you think you need? If you are planning on sharing the home with family and friends, more bedrooms and more living space are needed than if you plan to be there with only your immediate household. How much time do you want to spend dealing with care and maintenance of the property? You might envision a great deal of land, perhaps a farm, where you can walk the fields with your faithful dog on spring mornings. If you do this, you also need to envision taking care of those fields, as well as the rest of the grounds involved. Even if you choose a more developed area, would you rather garden or have the time to play golf? Focusing on these decisions will help you choose the type of house as well as the type of ownership that best suits your vision.

- Get more detailed. Think of the configuration of the dream house and the amenities you want in it. Should it be single level or multi-level? Will you want it "wired" so that you have access to the Internet? (This is important in the interim as well if you are looking to rent out your investment property.) What type of appliances do you want in the kitchen? How about a security system? Do you want the potential for wheelchair accessibility? In other words, design in your mind the perfect house and then visit it—again in your mind—often. The more familiar you become with the house, the more you will want to be in it.
- Revisit the vision. Every five years or so, haul the vision out and review it. In the interim, your tastes might have changed, and your family situation might be pointing you in a different direction, both in the near term and in the long term. As you change, revision the dream location as necessary. In other words, go through the process again with your current status. You're doing this to remake the vision, but you're also doing it to assess your progress along the road to your dream. As you look at your vision again in light of the changes that have happened to you, also look at you real estate portfolio and determine whether your current holdings are on the right track. Do you need to use the tax-free exchange program to dispose of something you intended to hold? Is investment in a vacation community a better proposition now than it was at your last review? Do you need to be in a different location to take advantage of population shifts and appreciation differences? Answering these questions will provide a valuable "midcourse" correction to your progress.

These are the steps in the visioning process. It is sufficiently detailed so that it has the feel of reality, yet is beyond your grasp far enough to motivate your activity. The key to remember in any visioning process is that end results do not link directly into current reality. The link is indirect. The first investment house you buy is only a step on a path that might have many way stations. It leads to the dream, but is not itself the attainment of the dream. The mistake that many investors make is that that they see every investment as a final step. In this book, what we stress over and over again is that real estate investment is part of a process that enables you to build wealth over time by leveraging the tax system. Creating a vision enables you to have a specific orientation, and having that orientation forms your decision making in the interim. Getting to that vision is a long-term process that might lead you into ownership of properties you don't necessarily like, but will move you along the route to your vision.

Understanding What You Can Afford

Now that we've discussed how to determine the end point of your journey, let's look at square one. Where do you start along the path to your dream house? Learning where to start depends on knowing what you can commit to your investment. There are two methods for determining how much you can afford to buy in the way of investment real estate.

The first is the asset method. Begin with your current wealth position. Draw up a balance sheet of your assets and liabilities. If we were writing this 10 years ago, we might have advised you to exclude the equity in your primary residence because homes and mortgages were illiquid instruments and you couldn't reasonably tap home equity to finance other investments. Now that the mortgage market has become more integrated with the other financial markets, moving in and out of home equity and debt is very easy.

If you own a home, or if you have teenagers preparing for college, you've wrestled with the forms provided by your friendly Realtor or your neighborhood student loan provider. So you are doubtless familiar with creating your own balance sheet.

Begin by listing all your debts, including mortgages, student loans, car loans, other loans, and credit card debt. Offset against these all of your assets, including the market value of your house, retirement savings, and all other financial and real assets. The net of these two numbers will give you your net worth, or the amount you have available to transfer into an investment home. Of course, this should be a positive number, or else declaring bankruptcy might be a viable option.

Writing down this balance sounds simple and should give you a good guideline number, but the reality is more complicated. Some of your assets might be unavailable for reinvestment. For example, if your retirement program does not have a loan program attached, those assets are tied up until you reach age 59-1/2. Withdrawing retirement savings prematurely subjects the taxpayer to a 10-percent penalty as well as includes the withdrawal amount in ordinary income for tax purposes. It would take a rather large rate of return to make the alternative investment worth the withdrawal. So to determine exactly what you have available for investment purposes, subtract those restricted retirement savings out. What's left is your capacity for acquiring investment real estate.

The resulting numbers here don't have to be great for you to get into the investment real estate game. With as little as $10,000, you can control a modest yet lucrative investment or vacation property. As we shall see, the asset side is the real limiting factor. Once you acquire the property, the actual cash flow cost to you should be relatively low. Rental income will offset the monthly outlay (including mortgage payment). But getting into the property will require having sufficient other assets to reallocate to providing the down payment on an investment property.

The second method to determine your capacity to buy investment real estate is the income method. This uses cash flow, rather than net worth, as the deciding variable. Once again, it requires offsetting positives and negatives. Calculate all your monthly obligations—mortgage and other loan payments, credit card debt, tuition payments, etc.—and subtract them from your monthly income. There should be something left (if not, go to the next step, getting a second job!). We'll call this discretionary net income, and it is the amount that is available to pay for the net carrying cost of an investment property.

As we have mentioned often, this is a net cost because rental income will cover a good part (hopefully all) of this negative cash flow. The ability of your discretionary net income to support an investment property is substantial because of your ability to rent the property for some or all of the time. To prove this to yourself, try a little exercise. Look in the real estate section of your local newspaper for a likely investment property. Now calculate the gross cost of owning that property. This will include the mortgage (pick your own down payment), a property management fee (again, 10 percent is likely), and some provision for replacing house components like plumbing, electricity, roofing, siding, and other depreciable items.

When you've calculated this figure, determine what the house would rent for. If it's purely investment, this should be full time; for vacation properties, determine how often and for how long you intend to rent it. Decrease this number by 10 percent to account for likely vacancies. Compare the estimated rental income with the gross cost of owning, and the balance will either be the net cash flow to you or the amount you need to supply to carry the property. Please note that this is a cash flow number and ignores the tax benefits of owning investment real estate.

Financing Your First Investment Property I: The Down Payment

After you have done the financial calculations, you can look for your first investment property. In Chapters 6 and 11, we describe how to determine the right community for your acquisition and how to choose the right house to maximize your chance for gain. Following those rules will help you get a running start toward your dream house. Using the tax rules laid out in Chapter 2 will enable you to move to progressively more valuable properties in a profitable way until you make your last move—into the dream house.

There are three major sources of financing for your first investment property.

- *Reallocate current nonhousing assets*. You might want to liquidate other assets in order to acquire real estate. In fact, the transfer of assets out of stocks and bonds and into real estate during the first years of the twenty-first century has been the major reason that the housing market has boomed all over the country. Most people made this move because of the long slump that affected stocks after April 2000, and this provides a keen insight into how you should think about using other assets to finance the investment real estate purpose. When you reallocate current assets, you sacrifice the rate of return generated by those assets. In order for the transfer to be worthwhile (remember the comments above about premature withdrawal of retirement savings), the rate of return offered on the new asset over the entire holding period must at least equal the rate of return on the old asset plus any costs of making the transfer. Before you reallocate assets, do the math and make sure that the net to you is positive.

- *Borrow against home equity by refinancing*. This has been an attractive strategy for many American homeowners in the low interest rate environment of the early twenty-first century. As house prices have run up, there has been a marked increase in the wealth of many American households, and they have taken advantage of this by refinancing their homes. In some cases, the refinancing is for the purpose of reducing the monthly payment on the home. In other cases, it has been used to sustain the spending patterns of the household in the face of a sluggish economy. In yet others (and here we get to the important point), the proceeds from refinancing have been used as the down payment on another piece of property. The advantage of using refinancing to support a real estate investment is that rates on mortgages are lower than on any other form of borrowing, often lower than the rate of return that would be given up if other, nonhousing, assets were to be liquidated. The downside of this is that you have reduced your "equity shield" in the house. This is the protection you have if house prices slump or if you wind up unemployed and forced to sell your principal residence. Of course, having two homes to sell (counting the investment property) in a reduced price environment doubles your exposure. Additionally, refinancing the house restarts the clock on the payment of housing debt. If you had plans to retire debt free, this might force you to reconsider those plans. But, hey, this is about revisiting the dream every five years, isn't it?

- *Take out a line of credit*. You can avoid some of the risk of refinancing the house by taking out a line of credit secured by the value of your principal residence. Usually, the rate of interest charged on the credit line is about the same as mortgage rates, so it is still relatively low-cost borrowing. But because it is an additional loan, it doesn't increase the term of your current mortgage. You still can pay off that debt as planned. More importantly, the line of credit can serve as a working capital reserve to help you take care of all the ordinary expenses of owning an investment property and covering those periods when the house is not rented. Finally, you use only as much of the credit line as you need, so you don't automatically incur a large additional debt.

Financing Your First Investment Property II: The Mortgage Loan

To illustrate a postmarriage situation, let's look at the case of Joan Sherwood . . . As a result of a divorce, Joan owned her home without any mortgage debt. She decided to make an investment in a second home, in this case a rental property located near her principal residence. To do so, she took out a mortgage loan. Over time, she refinanced that mortgage as rates declined and turned a negative cash flow into a positive. She was the anomaly: someone with a mortgage, but only on her second property, not her principal residence.

The odds are that you will be using a mortgage loan to finance your first investment property. If you don't pay cash for the house, and if you are not buying in a vacation development where financing automatically attaches to the property, you will need to seek out your own financing. What should you do?

Your choice of mortgage will depend on three factors:

1. *Potential rental income*. Matching the monthly mortgage payment to the potential monthly rental income is a good strategy. You will be working backwards here. First you look at the income that the property will (ideally) generate, and then you will determine what mortgage instrument requires a payment close to that. It's really simultaneous: House price and interest rate determine monthly payment, and monthly rent is matched to house price. This is a safe way to proceed. Matching rental income and mortgage payment increases the proba-

bility that your actual out-of-pocket outlay to carry the property will be minimized.

2. *Money available at closing.* There are a variety of mortgage instruments that allow for different rates of interest depending on down payment and fees paid at closing. Generally, the less you put down, the higher the monthly cost. This occurs because lenders require either a 20-percent equity shield, mortgage insurance, or some other form of credit enhancement. All of these add to the monthly mortgage payment. In addition, lenders allow you to buy down the rate of interest on your mortgage by paying fees at closing. These fees, called points, will increase the money you need to bring to the closing table, but will decrease your monthly mortgage payment. The bottom line here is that you have a choice: you can trade off money down at closing for monthly payments. The exact combination you want will depend on your capital resources and your net discretionary income.

3. *Holding period.* If you have created your vision of the future, you should have an idea of how long you intend to hold an investment property before you trade it up for a better house. This holding period will help you determine the kind of financing you want to use. If your holding period is short—say three to five years—you might want to finance the property with a variable-rate mortgage. Although these can increase in rate over time, you can usually get one with a rate fixed for your holding period, and that rate will often be less than that on a long-term mortgage. Conversely, if you have a longer time horizon—say 10–20 years—a more conventional fixed-rate mortgage might be the best choice.

Once you have considered these three factors, you can identify the type of mortgage you want on your home. You should then investigate what might be available. In the last 10 years, there has been a proliferation of financing instruments offering low-down-payment requirements at relatively low interest rates. Most of these are unavailable to investors, but they are worth looking at. Fannie Mae is the leading provider of these instruments, and you should consult with a real estate professional to get information about their availability.

There is one final program that could help you own that first investment property. The federal government provides a tax credit for investors in rental properties designed to house lower-income households. The Low Income Housing Tax Credit reduces the cost of your investment by refunding to you a portion of your outlays. The rules are very well defined and there are income limits on tenants and price limits on properties, so you need to school yourself in the intricacies of the law. But if you do so, it could open an avenue for investment that will prove a terrific starting point.

Planning the Investment Potential of Your Second Home

Once you can envision your Ultimate dream home, and you have an idea what you can afford, the final step is to find the property you can afford that has the best investment potential to take you in the direction of your Ultimate home. Key questions include:

- How long will you hold onto this particular property? The time horizon you have will determine the quality of the property you buy and how much money you want to put into the property both at the time of purchase and subsequently. Painting, structural alteration or improvement, landscaping, and furnishing will all depend on how long you intend to keep the property. As a rule, the later in life you choose to invest in real estate, the shorter should be your holding period for the house as an investment.
- How often do you plan to use the property? The manner in which you choose and decorate a vacation retreat as opposed to a rental property—vacation or otherwise—is extremely sensitive to your use. If the property will be predominately for your own use, with occasional rentals or loans to friends and family, you will locate in a place that pleases your family and choose amenities that reflect their tastes. If this will be predominately rented, then you need to please some idealized but unspecific rental population. So your own planned use will determine the location of the property (see below) as well as the expenditures you will make on upkeep.
- Will you sell it eventually, or do you want to move in yourself? This will determine your need for durability in the house. If you intend to eventually live in the house, you'll take better care of the property and be more selective with your tenants. As a general rule, the closer you are to retirement, the more likely it is that you will buy a house that you can live in for a long time. If you are far from retirement, it's a better strategy to choose a purely rental property, and then later use the 1031 exchange rule (see Chapter 2) to acquire a place that really suits you. Areas change—as do your tastes—too much over 20 or 30 years for you to set your plan that far in advance.
- How does the purchase of investment real estate fit into my entire portfolio? Presumably, real estate will take its place among your other

assets, both financial and real. The scope of your real estate investment, and thus the house you buy, will be affected by the proportion of your portfolio that you have targeted for real estate and the amount of that allocation already taken up by your principal residence. *As a general rule, the older you are, the more liquid your assets should be.* As your approach retirement, one house might be more than enough, with the bulk of your assets in forms that can easily be turned into cash.

The success of your investment is sensitive to your answers to these questions. No investment exists in a vacuum; it is an action on your part designed to increase your wealth and make your capital grow. It is also a channel to increase your well-being and is dependent on your stage in life and what other assets you hold. The best route to success in investing is to have a plan. If you don't have a plan before you buy, then your buying decision will be difficult at best and wrong at worst.

Location, Location, Location

Your investment property likely will be used mostly by other people. Whether you're purchasing a vacation home that you will use a few weeks per year, or whether you're buying a property that you will lease throughout the year, it will be used by others more than by you. The return on your investment will be determined in large part by the revenue derived from the property. That will be driven by its appeal to potential renters. You need to choose a location for its attractiveness to potential renters rather than its attractiveness to you.[1]

For example, let's look at Cliff . . . Cliff was a writer who needed a great deal of time to create the great American novel. He wasn't always a writer. He'd just left a career as a highly paid executive of a communications company. His wife, Nancy, had also just retired from teaching. Both knew that they needed to plan for a long retirement, but neither wanted to work at all, even part-time. Cliff wanted to devote himself full time to his writing. His wife wanted time to indulge in her hobby, painting. She also managed their retirement income, a combination of their two pensions and the proceeds from the sale of their principal residence. Cliff and Nancy still owned two homes, one in Nantucket they had inherited from family and one they had used for vacations in Naples, Florida. They hit upon the solution to their need for both time and income, and in doing so, invented

---

[1] Even if you intend to live in the property eventually, its viability until then will still depend on rental income. If you really don't like the property, you can always swap it out for another. See our discussion of tax-free exchanges in Chapter 2.

the investment real estate version of the reverse commute. They rented one of their homes in the high season (Nantucket in the summer, Naples in the winter) and lived in the other. They didn't enjoy the best of climates, but the income from the rentals was enough (along with the income from their pensions and other investments) for them to live comfortably, to write, to paint, and to travel when the Nantucket winter or Florida summer became too much. Sometimes, appealing to renters rather than yourself pays off handsomely.

Renters tend to value convenience to transportation, employment, and entertainment more than space and landscaping. Choose a property that will appeal to the renter, not to you. And decorate the property to accommodate renters. Furniture will rub against walls, so use sturdy paint. Appliances will get more than usual wear, so buy cheap and buy sturdy. The renters are paying for your asset, but remember, nobody ever washed a rented car. Even if you are thinking of eventually living in the house, consider both your and the renter's preferences. For more on this, see Chapter 3.

Choose the Right Property

If you choose a location, you have also probably envisioned your target renter. The next question is what type of property you will look for. This is a decision similar to location but focuses more on the configuration of the actual dwelling rather than the neighborhood in which it is located. The number and types of bedrooms, the size of the lot, and other amenities, will all factor into your decision as to the specific property to buy.

Besides looking at the location of the property relative to schools, transportation, shopping, and entertainment, your target renter will be more attracted to a home that suits his or her needs. If you seek families, then a quieter, more spacious property convenient to schools will be best. Yards where children can play safely will be a big plus. Where you are renting to groups of unrelated adults (think about the cast of *Friends*), multiple bathrooms and larger bedrooms are a must.

Doing your homework here will pay off.

- Ask other investors and real estate professionals about the demographics of the rental market
- Check the 2000 Census for the population structures of renters in the areas where you are looking at investment property
- Talk to resort and vacation community managers about the types of renters who enjoy that community

With this background, you will be able to choose a property that will be in high demand by potential tenants.

Do the Math

It's easy to profit from investment real estate. It's also possible to lose your shirt. The incredible stories that populate the world of infomercials are just that: They lack credibility. This business is not even close to being automatic. Unless you bring a good business sense and a sharp pencil to your investment, you'll spend many sleepless hours wondering why you ever did this, and feeling worse because the only thing on TV as you pace the carpet are those very same pie-in-the-sky, easy-money infomercials.

Before you make your investment in real estate, you need to do the math. You need to discover whether this potential financial move will end up benefiting your wealth or whether you would be better off holding the cash in your checking account. Follow these steps:

- Calculate the total cost of the investment. This cost consists of the down payment on the property, the settlement costs of the transaction, and the interest foregone because you chose to buy this property rather than invest in something else. The two most common omissions here are to forget the settlement costs and to ignore the opportunities that might have been seized if you had not chosen to invest in real estate. Settlement costs can run up to 3 percent of the price of the property. The proper measure of the opportunity cost is the rate of return on some low-risk security like a Treasury bond.
- Figure an estimate of the monthly cost of owning and maintaining the property. This includes the monthly mortgage payment—including the payment on your home equity line of credit if this is how you are financing the down payment—and monthly maintenance, like utilities and repairs. If you make any major alterations or repairs on the property, you can spread the costs over a number of years, but you should include some monthly charge to your costs of ownership.
- Determine the rent that you can reasonably expect to charge in your market. This can be determined by reference to other properties being rented in the area. The help of a real estate professional will be valuable here. The rent you charge should at least cover the cost of owning and maintaining the house. But you're not going to get this rent every single month. There will be gaps between tenants, and some tenants will miss a month or pay late. Because the house will go through periods of vacancy, you need to adjust your rental income estimates to reflect

these gaps. Doing so allows you to more accurately project your cash flow. After all, you are not buying the house to lose money.

- Estimate the price at which you will sell the property. This is tricky because real estate markets boom and slump with regularity. You have no way of knowing what will be the condition of the market when you plan to sell. Flexibility here, of course, is a great asset, because you can choose to sell when the market is up. As a general rule, if the property is a pure investment, you will always sell for more than you bought, because you can time the sale.[2]

- Factor in the tax consequences of your investment. The tax laws favor investment in real estate. Interest paid to finance the purchase of real estate is deductible against income, and major repairs or renovations that enhance the attractiveness of the property to potential renters can be amortized over a number of years—the Feds will tell you how many for each type of change—and deducted from income as an expense.

All of these positives and negatives will net out to the expected return on your investment in real estate. But, as we discussed in the introductory chapter, all this needs to be adjusted for the time value of money. Simply put, a dollar given away today is worth less than a dollar returned tomorrow. This is because you forego the use of that money and the satisfaction it can bring you, and because inflation reduces the buying power of money. If you don't adjust for the time value of money, your estimates of the return from your investment will be biased upward. Check with an accounting professional to find the right way to factor in the time value of money.

Conclusion

Balancing what you want with what you can afford can be tricky. It's natural for our reach to exceed our grasp, so you will probably never get all you want. The key to reconciling needs and wants is to operate simultaneously in two time frames. The first time frame, that of the future, involves envisioning in great detail that place where you will eventually live, usually at the end of your life. The more detail you can summon about this place, the greater will be the possibility that you will reach it or something close.

---

[2] If you intend to live in the house later, or swap it out for another vacation or retirement house, you will be trading into the same kind of market (up or down) in which you are selling. So the transaction will be a wash.

The second time frame is the present. If you are not now a real estate investor, that present is the starting point. In it, you ask yourself: what can I do now to begin to move toward that dream house? If you are currently an investor, the question becomes: How can I use this property to move closer to my vision of the future? The answers in both cases will be in terms of a particular property, a plan for the property, and a strategy to acquire and hold it. It will allow you to use the tax strategies we describe in this book to move ever closer to your end point. You should keep asking yourself that question on a regular basis, every time you need to make a decision to buy or sell a property. Asking will keep you on the path toward your goal.

4

Proven How-To Avenues for Finding a Good Deal on Your New Second Home

Creativity consists of merely turning up what is already there.—Bernice Fitz-Gibbon

There are always avenues through the back door. In this chapter, we offer some casual, yet high-percentage methods of accessing that alternative entry. Interim, Cocoon, or Ultimate property bargains often are bypassed by many of today's high-cash, no-time-to-spend-looking buyer. And you'd be surprised what you might be able to find in second-home property options with decent terms and conditions. It might not put you on the 50-yard line of the Gold Coast, but it WILL be yours. Who knows what more you'll be able to find once you have your foot in the door and your toes in the sand conversing with neighbors at the community beach?

A terrific local sales person in the right place, and/or a few hours of legwork at the courthouse (or "eyework" on the Internet) could have you relaxing before you know it.

When Realtors gather for marketing seminars hosted by high-profile sales wizards, they are usually encouraged to "farm" specific neighborhoods where they live and work. That means getting their message out in every conceivable way—friendly conversation, newspaper ads, church and school bulletins, terrific testimonials—that they want to be, and have been, the agent of choice in a particular region.

Having an agent working for you in the area you want to buy is key, but there is no substitute for driving and walking individual blocks, meeting people, and viewing properties. It's the best method of ascertaining noise, traffic, wind, number and type of neighbors, and where the sun hits the house (dock, deck, yard) at different hours and seasons. Owners also like to know, and see, who might be purchasing their cherished property down the road—even if the owner chooses to hire a real estate professional to handle the transaction. Obviously, if your target area is miles from home, personal visits become few, and professional sales people and the Internet become crucial. Here are three experiences, and how-to charts, to help you on your way.

Direct Leap to the Ultimate Getaway

Michael McDonald discovered the spot two decades earlier while attending the wedding of a college classmate. He was looking for a safe place for his wife and sons while he worked the Alaska salmon season, and he'd always loved the region northwest of Boise, Idaho While driving a lake road near McCall, a "for sale" sign tacked to a large hemlock caught his eye. He scribbled down the telephone number of the vacant land, the first step toward the best times of his life.

However, first came a summer of county property searches, percolation tests, wildlife clearances, easement restrictions, power line extensions, shoreline permits—and incredibly generous neighbors . . .

McDonald contacted owners of the cheapest cabins and vacant lots to see if they would consider selling. He tracked down the lake plats at the county courthouse, copied the lot numbers, and found the listed owners through tax records. He then wrote letters and got several "maybe" responses. Many of the interested parties were adult children whose parents had passed away in the past few years. The young couples loved the lakefront property but found a difficult time making ends meet. They now had young children of their own, very little time to maintain the cabins from the bitter snows of January and February while having to scrape to pay the property taxes and insurance on a place that now had become a burden. In fact, they could use the cash from a sale. They had inherited the cabins at the time of their parents' death, so the value of

The Gateway to that Getaway

If you are out driving to that must-have area for the perfect second home, it might not take long to realize that virtually everything you see resembles a lazy summer fastball—high and way outside of your price range.

Here is our list of Top 10 Tips to get squared away before buying in the middle of nowhere:

1. Set your budget. Don't take on anything—debt or building—that will max your limits.
2. Don't buy on impulse—it is better to come back at a different time of day and take another long look.
3. Take notes and photographs as a reminder. Swift photo processing exists even in remote spots.
4. Ask to see the electrical supply. Is it adequate?
5. Check the condition, if any, of the septic tank and drain field. If it fails, is there room for a substitute system?
6. Ensure that there is a water supply. If pumped from a lake or stream, look for filters.
7. Obtain a copy of the title report.
8. Ask the owner why he or she decided to sell.
9. Talk to the neighbors. Ask about the history of the lot, cabin, area, roads, weather.
10. Make any purchase subject to an approved building permit.

the cabins had been "stepped up" to the fair market value the year their parents died. The children would owe little tax, if any, on the sale of the cabin.

One Boise man, a widower in his 80s who had not spent much time at the lake since his wife had died 17 years earlier, responded to McDonald's inquiry. He asked that McDonald contact his attorney about a vacant lot on the east side of the small lake community. It turned out the man, a Mr. Allen Rock, had been involved in the original platting of the community and at one time had owned quite a bit of property in the region. He said he thought all his lake lots had been sold long ago. Rock was quite impressed with Michael McDonald's letter. Not only was it short and to the point, but it also conveyed the genuine idea of "family time" that originally lured Rock to the valley over half a century ago.

Rock's attorney researched his holdings and concluded that Rock did, indeed, own the vacant lot and would part with it for $20,000. McDonald told the attorney he would buy the 50-by-250-foot property contingent on the approval of all services. It wasn't waterfront, but it was $20,000, across the only street in the community, and with a terrific view of the lake. It was almost better than waterfront because the lot in front was too wet for a building permit and McDonald also would be dodging the higher waterfront taxes—as good as waterfront, yet just across the street. There were no problems with power or water. All the cabins were served with electricity from the local public utility district, and the power poles were clearly seen standing tall and true 100 feet from the lake road behind the cabins. Most residents had pumped drinking water out of the lake for years, but now they also were served by two community wells that were dug and linked eight years earlier.

The only thing that stood between McDonald and a buildable dream lot was an approved septic-system design and percolation test. The lot had the required square footage, but water from the side of the hill periodically made the ground soggy. While doing property research at the courthouse, McDonald had met Dave Fannuchi, a registered sewage disposal designer ("Designs by Dave") who said the drain field design, percolation testing, and required county paperwork would cost $295. McDonald considered doing the job himself (a designer or engineer was not required at the time) but felt his chances for approval would be better if a professional did the work.

After two pile-driving-like thrusts of the post-hole digger, Dave Fannuchi knew the first of three percolation test holes was going to be marginal. In order to gain an approved septic permit for a conventional onsite sewage treatment system, the county required 4 feet of good soil without any sign of significant water in three widely spaced areas on the lot. There was some water three feet down, and the two other test hole areas did not look as promising as the first. Fannuchi was correct in his prediction—he hit water fewer than 22 inches into the second hole, and the third hole had even more water at the 14-inch mark. There was one other large, dry spot, but the requirement for a 100-percent reserve drainfield on or near the property also had to be addressed.

"This is going to be a marginal lot, Michael, even if we applied for waiver," Fannuchi said. "The alternative system—even if the county approves it—is going to cost you big bucks, probably more than the lot itself."

Fannuchi cornered the deputy health inspector after church services two days later and drove the official out to the lot McDonald was trying to "perc." The deputy decided the dry area of the lot was too small to adequately accommodate the septic system and basically said not to spend any more money—the lot would definitely be denied a sewage-disposal permit. He guaranteed his opinion would be upheld by the district supervisor. McDonald was more than disappointed when he got the news. Without a septic permit, he could not build a cabin. He also found out from a neighbor over the weekend that the tiny community association did not allow alternative systems. A few potential buyers in the past decade had tried to push an alternative system for the waterfront lot across the street, but both the county and the association denied the attempt. Adding to the McDonald's sting was the fact that most of the cabins were on lots smaller than the minimum size required for septic approval. They were built when the laws were less stringent, and "grandfathered" into the new guidelines. Should McDonald try to buy one of the few available lots nearby, then have Fannuchi design a pump system to reach the new lot? Maybe with the additional area, he could pass the septic inspection. All it took was a cursory look: Fannuchi said the adjacent lot had problems, too.

McDonald decided to walk away from the lot with the dynamite, unobstructed view of the lake. However, the experience was not worthless. He had found a lot, its owner, history, taxes, neighbors, market value, and requirements for building. It did not work out, but at least he knew why it didn't. More importantly, he had met Dave Fannuchi. Two weeks later, after church services, Fannuchi drove McDonald to a small cabin on the east side of the lake. The hills to the west dipped in this area, providing long afternoons of hot summer sun and postcard sunsets. The setting was golden—battered but usable dock, a sturdy, treated-wood deck on the waterside of the house that met an attractive lawn. The lawn rolled down to a pea-gravel beach.

"Great spot," McDonald said. "If it's for sale, I probably cannot afford it. I pretty certain I am looking for more of a fixer, or even a vacant lot."

Fannuchi mentioned to McDonald that the property had been the lake getaway for a prominent Boise family that had roots in the area for four generations. The cabin, with one bathroom and several bunkbeds, had mostly been used for church socials and weekend retreats. Fannuchi and his brothers had cared for the cozy spot for decades, applying linseed oil to its exterior while adding a new set of cedar shakes to its roof. A few moments later, a green Jeep scattered the gravel on the road near the front of the cabin.

"Michael McDonald? I am Allen Rock. Dave tells me you are still looking for a place."

Rock sold the cabin to McDonald. McDonald contends he will never sell it—an Ultimate place.

Need an Interim Step? Give It the Old College Try

One of the more consistent and stable real estate markets for traditional second homes and rental properties are the residential neighborhoods surrounding established colleges and universities. Why? The school isn't going anywhere, and visiting faculty, staff, and students always are going to need a roof over their heads. Not only are recent retirees "buying down" to smaller college towns with their educational amenities and vibrant social and athletic environment, but more and more small business owners with relatively small groups of employees also are moving to smaller college towns for the convenience of research and a larger entry-level employee base. Buying a home in a college town, letting visiting faculty members rent it out and thereby reducing your mortgage, is a great way to build an asset. For parents with college-age children, researching a rental in a college town makes a lot of sense and provides an attractive alternative to dormitory living. When the child graduates and you are finally free of tuition bills, expensive textbooks and outrageous cross-country airline tickets, sell the college rental via 1031 Exchange and buy a rental condo in Maui. After a couple of years of not enough sunshine, your doctor suggests that you relocate to a warmer climate where it does not take a hairdryer to warm your limbs in February. . .

Your Continuing Education Course to College Rentals

One of the safest real estate moves is investing in a single-family residence, or duplex, in close proximity to a college or university. You will have a constant pool of renters, even if you eliminate the uncertain category known as "undergraduate males." If you are considering purchasing in a college town, it's always a good idea to know an adult who lives within a 30-minute drive of your rental property. That way, if the entire Greek Row camps in the backyard for the weekend, you can at least send someone to count the tents.

Here's some quick suggestions you will not find in the campus bookstore:

1. Ask the Housing Office what percentage of undergraduates live on campus. Are freshmen and sophomores required to do so?
2. What is the cost of dormitory living? What amount does the school earmark for food?

3. Does the school offer off-campus units? If so, how many and what is the monthly cost? Gauge your rent from this information.
4. Does the school accept private homes as rentals to its faculty? If so, what is the referral fee?
5. Initially, advertise your home for rent in faculty and administration circles only. Ask that your attractive flier be posted in the faculty lounge.
6. Remember, not all faculty members are married with children. Two professors, or more, can share your place.
7. Married graduate students often are ideal renters. One spouse is the breadwinner, the other a dedicated student. They pay the rent on time, are quiet, and watch movies at home on the weekends
8. While there are a lot of tobacco users on any campus, don't allow them to live in your home.
9. If you begin to get desperate for occupants, remember that female undergraduates are usually gentler on a dwelling than young men. When in doubt, allow an extra girl (the added income will pay off).
10. If you are facing foreclosure and thus must rent to undergraduate males, send a cleaning service once a week and build the charge into the monthly rental amount. Not only will the service curtail damage, but also you can ask about extraordinary findings. When in doubt, do not allow an extra boy (the added income will not cover the extra wear and tear).

Not all college towns have big-time prices that only can be handled by the wealthy—or math majors. Let's say you found a home in a college town that costs $127,000. You would make a down payment of at least $12,700. If you finance the remaining $114,300 at an interest rate of 6.5 percent over 30 years, your principal and interest payment will be about $725 a month. Toss in taxes, fire insurance, and a few light bulbs, and you will be looking at $900 a month. That's not too bad, especially if you can get four mature students to pay $250 a month rent, not including food and other essentials. Students could probably eat and live in a dorm for less (young women rarely eat dormitory food anyway), but this way they have an alternative to noisy halls, and the parents have a fairly secure, four-to six-year venture. If you are a parent with college-bound kids, take a look down the road before you start visiting homes for sale on quaint university streets. How many years do you expect your child to live there and, if she transferred, would you want to rent to students who are not family members? Many accountants advise parents with college kids to estimate what home prices will be when the child's course work is done. Will that market appreciate 5–7 percent a year, or perhaps 30 percent in five years? If your child is headed to a major college or university, the chances are very good your investment will show at least modest appreciation. Some college towns once thought unrealistic because of sluggish sales prices are experiencing a comeback. But just how much appreciation is necessary to make the numbers work? One rule of thumb is if the house appreciates as much as the parent's annual tax bracket, the deal might definitely be worth doing. For example, if you are being taxed at 28 percent and feel the investment will appreciate 28 percent in the time you hold it, it could be a nice option for everybody involved.

"I usually recommend the parent think condo rather than single-family dwelling," said Ned Porges an agent with Century 21 Real Estate. "This is to minimize maintenance and upkeep issues while the student is in school—grass cutting, gutter cleaning. "What student would prioritize these issues to the top of the list to protect the investment?"

A big decision, mentioned in Chapter 1, is how to treat the home as far as Uncle Sam is concerned. The college dorm alternative could either be a second home or an investment property. Typically, the student manages this rental investment while mom and dad reap the tax benefits and appreciation that come from owning a rental home. Often the venture won't work because some buildings near schools are too expensive for the numbers to make it worthwhile. Also, there is the initial problem of handling the down payment and monthly expenses in addition to skyrocketing tuition fees. There are areas that continue to zoom, bringing more interest from parent-investors. With the stock market now more of an "iffy" option for many folks, a rental in a college town has become more appealing. If the property definitely is going to be a rental, you can't rent to your children and their friends for a song. The IRS will not allow you to show a taxable loss on the property if you personally use it for more than 14 days or 10 percent of the total rental period. "Personal use" includes renting to any relative unless you charge a "fair market rent."

If the student-partner does not pay rent, depreciation cannot result in a taxable loss. Expenses may be deducted, but not to the point where an actual loss is shown.

Proven How-To Avenues for Finding a Good Deal

In order for the parent-student partnership to work, students must be responsible landlords. One mom, Vicki Lloyd, a Realtor with Prudential California Realty in Mission Viejo, Calif., said she had used the student-as-landlord idea as a solution to expensive, off-campus rental rates near San Diego State University. On-campus housing is scarce on many college campuses, forcing kids to look elsewhere. What makes Vicki's story more compelling and attractive to parents considering the possibility of a college rental is the FHA loan wrinkle. Loans insured by the Federal Housing Administration (sponsored by the U.S. Department of Housing and Urban Development) permit expanded guidelines, such as loan-to-value ratios. More importantly, FHA allows for children to remain on the title as owner occupants, even though the parents supply the down payment and are the actual purchasers.

Here is Vicki's story:

"Another way to consider this is to compare the cost of buying with local rental rates, like we did in San Diego. My daughter and her four friends wanted to rent a three-bedroom house. The going rate for single-family three bedroom homes within walking distance to SDSU was about $1900 a month for a 1950s vintage house with nasty old carpet, original kitchen, and ugly bathrooms. At the time, you could buy a home of similar size and condition for about $190,000.

"My daughter, one of her roommates, and both sets of parents decided to try to buy a house instead of renting. We found a very clean house with three bedrooms in the front and a one-bedroom 'granny unit' in the rear for $226,000. We put only 10 percent down, and included the students on the FHA loan, as only FHA will give owner-occupied rates with nonoccupant coborrowers.

"We had immediate cash flow of $2400 a month that covered the mortgage, taxes, insurance, gardener, and even a 'carpet replacement allowance'! My daughter and her friend took care of writing the leases, depositing the rent in the bank account, and keeping an eye on anything that might go wrong.

"Those girls have now all graduated and moved on, but the house is now rented to the younger sister and her roommates for the next two years. And the property value has appreciated almost $150,000!"

If you do not have children, or feel they are not mature enough to head up a dorm-alternative household, there are still attractive rental possibilities for your potential property that do not include underclassmen seeking the next "Animal House." The number of visiting professors to college campuses always is underestimated, as are the number of staffers (secretaries, security, catering, librarians) who often are terrific rental-lease prospects. Notes to human resource representatives have worked wonders in landing mature renters, as have inquiries posted in faculty lounges and on-campus faculty living areas. Graduate students (some married) also form a significant, yet not-targeted, renter pool. Sometimes, professors seek alternative housing for highly coveted students.

For example, several years ago, Leo Stanford, then dean of the Institute for Theological Studies at Seattle University, was trying to locate a group home for a number of his graduate students. Several of his applicants were former nuns relocating from other states. Needless to say, the women were not eager to occupy rooms of an undergraduate high-rise dorm dominated by college freshmen. Stanford contacted an investor friend whose wife was an associate on the Seattle University faculty. The investor did not own property in the area but told Stanford he would see what might be for sale. A quick drive through the area revealed no "for sale" signs, so the investor copied down the addresses of several large houses within a four-block walk from campus. Today, the investor would have been able to enter the addresses into the county's real property database to determine the owner and tax assessment. Then, however, he had to make a trip to the county treasurer's office to determine the owners' names and mailing addresses. The investor found a willing seller who not only would make the home available so that the former nuns could occupy the house in time for the fall term, but the owner also agreed to provide seller financing. The arrangement worked for all parties involved—Stanford used the example as a recruiting tool, the former nuns (none of whom owned a car) found affordable housing walking distance from campus, the investor secured an appreciating asset while the nuns covered his monthly housing costs, and the seller got a quick, clean sale. What made the deal run smoothly was the investor's ability to meet and communicate with the eventual seller the intent of the rental. People will often listen when they hear that former nuns need a place to live.

Foreclosure Bargains by E-Mail—Without the Snidely Attitude

Remember Snidely Whiplash? He was the animated cartoon character who would twirl his long black mustache, tip his black top hat to the lovely farmer's daughter, and then unroll a long sheet of paper that read "Deed." The honky-tonk piano would reach a crescendo—bad news was just around the corner. Snidely was preparing to foreclose on the family homestead, and all in the community desperately tried to keep that fateful day from occurring.

While the image Snidely Whiplash has been associated with some of today's predatory lenders, most banks genuinely do not want to foreclose on real estate. Why? All of them will tell you it costs them money to maintain and resell the homes they are forced to take back. In a capsule, they are in the lending business and not the real estate business. The fastest way of getting banks out of the property business is to expose their real estate-owned property, or REO, to the greatest number of potential buyers as soon as possible. Hence, the Internet has been a godsend not only for lenders trying to clean their books of unwanted real estate, but also for second-home shoppers seeking an Interim, Cocoon, or Ultimate property. And, there's no Snidely-like attitude.

In fact, some of the largest online marketplaces for foreclosures will be very pleased to e-mail you, free of charge, a summary of the type of properties you are seeking as soon as they are added to the company's database. Looking for a condo near the town of Kihei on the Hawaiian island of Maui? As soon as a unit hits the eBay Real Estate folder (*www.ebayrealestate.com*) you will receive the property's address, square footage, listing price, number of bedrooms and baths, the type of loan (government or conventional lender), and the deadline for bids. Lender properties are sold through an online offer negotiation process using eBay's Offer Management System (OMS). You submit an offer, and the seller will then accept, counter, or decline. All further negotiations flow through the OMS. Government properties (HUD, VA) are sold by online auction (and also can be found at *www.hud.gov*). You may submit a bid online, and the highest bid wins the property. To submit a bid for government auctions, you must register with the agency offering the property. The key to getting what you want is being able to pull the trigger when the right property surfaces. So it's not a bad idea to tell Uncle Joe on vacation in Maui (or a local Realtor) to pull on his Aloha shirt and check out the address you just received via e-mail.

Another key company for second-home bargain seekers is Fidelity National Asset Management Solutions Inc. (*www.fnams.com*), which also offers an automatic e-mail feature for registered users. FNAMS has become a sort of foreclosure clearinghouse for conventional lenders, managing and liquidating REOs properties for 18 of the nation's top mortgage makers, including Washington Mutual, JP Morgan Chase & Company, Key Bank, ABN AMRO, Citi Corp, PNC Bank, and Cendant. FNAMS also gives its lender-clients the option of eviction services including relocation allowances ("give me the keys NOW, and we'll give you some moving money") for occupants reluctant to move on with their lives.

Tom DiMercurio, president and Chief Operating Officer of Fidelity National Asset Management Solutions, said his company would try to liquidate at least 6500 foreclosures a year for the foreseeable future. "Once we get a property, everybody's got a shot at buying it. The Internet's been a gold mine, especially for the little guy who knows what he wants in a specific area." The average listing price is about $125,000. But don't expect all of them to be run-down properties recently trashed by college kids on Spring Break. Here is a recent "Foreclosure of the Week" on the FNAMS Web site that would reach the upper limit of the Ultimate category:

> *"Stamford, Fairfield County, Connecticut. The Ultimate lifestyle awaits within this stately, uniquely gracious, stone and brick villa. Masterfully blending classic European design and modern grandeur, the supremely spacious residence encompasses 10,600 square feet of opulence on main and second levels, with an additional self-sufficient 3,000 square feet of luxury on the walkout lower level. A show-stopping entry, grand public rooms, superb master suite, perfect artist's studio and spectacular pool only begin its architectural achievement . . . residential excellence, top-notch shopping, first-class business and cultural opportunities with marinas, beaches and woods . . . "*

The Internet also has saved time, money, and miles for second-home buyers trying to locate bargains before foreclosures become official. To find out what information your county of interest makes available online, check out *www.netronline.com* and Simply click on "Property Data Online." Then select the state you want and then the county. And before you resort to the old-fashioned way of looking through the legal notices of your newspaper for public auctions, sheriff's sales, and trustee sales, check the newspaper's Web site. Many newspapers encourage readers to peruse their online Classifieds, and it's often easier—and cleaner—for the user. In addition, related services often are found on the site, including attorneys, property managers, inspectors, and surveyors. Some financial services—some you've never considered that could help you over the threshold of your New Second Home—are the focus of Chapter 5 .

RVs Can Be a Second Home, but . . .

Yes, Virginia, your second home can be an RV . . . but don't plan on it appreciating like a lakefront cabin.

While an RV (recreational vehicle) can qualify for the mortgage interest deduction as a second home—it is personal property and not real property. This means interest rates on loans probably will be higher than a home mortgage. According to the Internal Revenue Service, all "second homes" must be used as security of the loan[1] and must have basic sleeping, cooking, and toilet accommodations.

Virtually all RV types—motor homes, van campers, travel trailers, truck campers, and even some folding camping trailers—are equipped with these facilities.

Loan terms for new, large RVs typically range from 10–12 years, with some lenders willing to extend to 20 years. While many dealers offer their own in-house financing, RV loans can be obtained from credit unions, banks, savings and loans, and finance companies. And there can be an investment side to an RV purchase, but only through renting it out—rarely by making money on resale. Depending on time of year and area, dealers and rental outlets generally charge between $70–$170 a day for motor homes and from $50–$120 a day for truck campers and travel trailers. Individuals who rent their units personally typically charge less.

According to Richard Morse, attorney and tax-deferred exchange specialist, RVs can be exchanged much like rental homes in a Section 1031 exchange. However, rental homes are real property and recreational vehicles are personal property.

"You certainly can do personal property exchanges," Morse said. "The timelines are the same, but personal property exchanges are much more stringent. You must trade an RV for an RV, a truck for a truck."

Looking for out-of-the-way spots and curious folks, much like the late Charles Kuralt? RVs are terrific for travel, but unlike a conventional second home, they usually will decline in value the longer you own them.

---

[1] The IRS publishes two booklets that contain helpful information regarding the tax deductibility of loan interest. Copies of "Publication 936—Home Interest Deduction" and "Publication 523—Selling Your Home" are available by calling the IRS at 1-800-829-3676 or by visiting *www.irs.gov*.

5

Can't Afford That Getaway?
Eleven Overlooked Financing Options

You cannot afford to wait for perfect conditions. Goal setting is often a matter of balancing timing against available resources. Opportunities are easily lost while waiting for perfect conditions.—Gary Ryan Blair

You hear it all the time:

"No way I could consider a second home. I've still got kids in school. I put all my extra money into my IRA."

In this chapter, we explore how Individual Retirement Accounts—plus some other unfamiliar alternatives—can help you on your way to your goal of a second home. These roads could take some extra labor to pave (like finding a bank that will establish a real estate IRA), but the effort could provide you with the seed money for a weekend getaway and other financial rewards. Self-directed real estate IRAs are not only relatively easy, they are also not subject to some of the guidelines that apply to employee-sponsored qualified plans enforced by the Department of Labor. The bank, as directed by the individual, has complete and total control over the investment. In addition, the bank, as account holder, has an obligation of investigating each investment to be considered. This personal due diligence is a substitute for the rules that govern some employee-sponsored qualified plans. You can invest self-directed IRA money in a wide range of investments, including stocks, bonds, mutual funds, money market funds, saving certificates, U.S. Treasury securities, promissory notes secured by mortgages or deeds of trust, limited partnerships and . . . real estate. This includes single-family homes, timber parcels, gorgeous getaway condos, and office properties.

To prepare for your real estate IRA, designate the amount of your retirement funds that you wish to use in the property deal and open a new IRA account with an independent administrator. The best place to start is an independent community bank— then get set for the possibility of a long afternoon of shopping. Many banks will not service real estate IRAs (some will say "never heard of it") because it must act as owner—pay the taxes, collect servicing fees—paperwork that many lenders don't want or need. Community banks, however, will offer this trust account service for existing customers, especially if the bank can easily see that there's plenty of value in the purchase and a great potential for appreciation. And remember, because there are no limits on the number of IRA accounts a taxpayer may have, you will not be restricted to just one purchase.

The guidelines covering real estate IRAs are stringent. If you break one of these rules, you could jeopardize your tax-free status on your account.

- The land or house must be treated like any other investment.
- All rental profits must be returned to the trustee.
- You cannot manage the property. But your trustee can hire a third party—a real estate broker, or local manager—to collect rents and maintain or improve the property.
- The house or property (or proceeds from its sale) must remain in the trust until distribution at retirement. If a trustee is instructed to sell the property, funds can be transferred to another account for reinvestment.

You cannot use IRA money to buy your own residence, or any other property in which you live. It has to be investment property. But when you retire, you can direct your IRA to turn it over to you as a distribution at the current market value.

The problem with real estate IRAs is lack of funds to make a meaningful purchase. That's because until the rules are changed or modified,

---

Real Estate IRA Sources

Mid Ohio Securities—*http://www.midoh.com/*
Oarlock Investment Services—*http://www.oarlock.com/*
Entrust Administration—*http://www.entrustadmin.com/*
Creative Real Estate Online—*http://www.creonline.com*

---

your IRA cannot take out a mortgage or really be leveraged in any way. All properties purchased using a real estate IRA must be purchased with cash, and the trust then holds the property free and clear. One way to crack a huge nut is to get another—or several—investors to buy shares in one property.

For example, Terry and Molly Rausch, high-school sweethearts who grew up on a Wisconsin lake and later got married during a huge gathering on its western shore, used real estate IRAs to acquire a large waterfront parcel that they knew would appreciate tremendously in the next two decades. Here's a quick look at their story and the steps they took to get it done:

The couple found an isolated parcel through an auction catalog for $79,500. The property, with 188 feet of waterfront and a skeleton dock, sat on the market for months, then years. The spread had six, separately deeded lots—three on the waterfront side below the lake road and three larger lots comprising the uphill portion. The listing price came spiraling down from $170,000 to $149,000 to $129,500, and finally to $99,500. The property had "flipped" because of poor drainage, yet the Rauschs were more than well acquainted with the property. They were certain that a long-time friend could design and install a septic system and drain field on the small, southwest corner of the uphill property. The problem was funds—they didn't even have enough for a down payment. And if they borrowed the down payment from another family member, how could they afford the monthly payments on the note, given the financial demands of their young family?

What they both had were IRAs. Molly had a mutual fund that was not performing in an all-star fashion, while Terry had some high-tech stocks that were high flyers at the time. The couple had started their IRA contributions at the same time. The approximate value of Terry's was $37,000, while Molly's was about $35,500. They had heard about a real estate IRA from a college classmate, and then telephoned a branch of a national lender to inquire about the possibilities. The bank's trust department did not handle such affairs, yet had "heard" that a smaller, in-state lender had considered real estate IRAs in the past. The couple contacted the trust officer at the bank. In order to fulfill a "due diligence" requirement, she requested a market analysis from the Realtor who originally listed the property for sale. That analysis showed a $129,000 value.

The trust officer suggested the couple purchase the property by contributing a total of $70,000 from their IRA accounts. Terry would pitch in $37,000 and take three lots, while Molly would contribute $33,000 and govern the other three. That way, the property was purchased for all cash, and the taxman would raise no red flags.

The couple had their assets sold and transferred to the community bank. The trust officer provided the couple with compliance documents required by the U.S. Treasury and FDIC for self-directed IRAs. However, the service was not inexpensive—the bank would charge a 1-percent of market value annual fee with a $500 minimum fee on any balance. Because the market analysis had shown the market value to be $129,000—the couple had to pay $1290 per year for the service—or $645 per account. In addition, there would be the usual property taxes and association fees.

The offer—$70,000 all cash in 30 days—was quickly accepted by the seller. The auction company already had most of the paperwork in order, so the deal moved quickly to escrow. The couple soon owned 188 feet of waterfront on a lake they had enjoyed all of their lives. Their friend was successful in designing a septic system and drain field on the top portion of the land. In a few months, they conducted a successful lot-line adjustment that gave them two, 94-foot-wide buildable waterfront lots (the county minimum was 90 feet) that would share the same drain field.

What if some summer visitor happens to make the Rauschs an offer they can't refuse? If the price is right, they can always get out of the investment. All they need to do is instruct the trust officer to sell the property and have the funds reinvested elsewhere. In fact, if the Rauschs had purchased the property with Roth IRA funds or converted their conventional IRAs to Roth IRAs for the purchase, the appreciation of the property would come to them tax free after they reach age 60. That's because once a taxpayer reaches 59½, you may withdraw any portion of the proceeds of sale after they are deposited in the IRA.

Seller Financing

Unlike previous generations, today's second-home buyer often knows what he wants and where—and the possible alternative solutions on how to finance it. Cash talks, and some of these guys can roar. However, others don't always bring all their cash to the table, preferring to quickly slash through a list of the real estate possibilities—"carrying the paper," "lease-option," "pick a partner"—before choosing the final avenue (your friendly banker).

An extremely common down-payment method has been a sizable draw from a home-equity line of credit secured by a principal residence. In some cases, a rustic cabin does not qualify for bank financing due to inadequate water supply, septic, or electrical service. The seller must agree to "play the bank" and work out private financing with the buyer known as seller financing. The parties are free to negotiate terms, including down payment amount and the interest rate on the loan. Often, if the down payment is minimal, the rate on the loan could be higher than the conventional market, and vice versa. Any type of equally agreeable arrangement is permitted. Later, when the property is brought up to local codes, the buyer-owner can often refinance to a conventional mortgage product.

Lease Option

It is difficult to find the right cabin in a short period of time—especially for an out-of-state buyer. Although you hear about people buying "the first house we saw," potential buyers also spend months researching house size and style, neighborhoods, schools, churches, and commute times before doing any deal. For those who do not want to be forced into a tight time frame, renting or leasing with an option to buy can be a sensible alternative. Renting for a year to 18 months is quite common among newcomers. Many real estate agents know of available houses. Sometimes, this rental or leased home can turn into the permanent home for the renters, which is why a lease with option to buy is sometimes preferable. A lease option can buy time to research the area while getting a portion of the monthly rent credited toward the down payment.

Many owners make a commitment to purchase another house before selling their old one. If the first house does not sell, they are faced with making payments on both houses. To avoid this debt load, the owner agrees to lease out the first house for 12 or 18 months.

The lease agreement includes an option allowing the tenant to buy the property within the lease period. Here's how a typical lease-option works:

- The owner and tenant agree on a purchase price, often a figure based on today's market value plus an estimate of the average rate of inflation (let's guess 3 percent) in the next 12 months. Let's say the agreed-upon amount is $165,000 and represents the home's value 12 months down the road.

- The owner charges the tenant a nonrefundable fee for the option. The amount can vary, depending on how eager the seller is to move, the size and quality of the home, etc. Typically, the higher the fee, the better the tenant maintains the property. The fee—let's say it is $1500—is in addition to the monthly payments, and it gives the tenant the right to purchase the property for $165,000 at any time within the 12-month lease period.
- The monthly rent is typically greater than market rates because no down payment has been made, but a portion of it applies toward the down payment. The owner and tenant decide what portion will be credited. For example, if the monthly rent is $1000, $500 could be credited to the down payment.

Owners should read their mortgage agreements carefully before considering a lease-option. Some lenders may activate a due-on-sale clause if the borrower enters into a lease option with another party. Many times, lenders will permit a specific lease option period if notified in advance. And lenders are usually more willing to participate when they are assured of future business—like the seller's or buyer's new purchase loan. The owner and tenant must be sure to specify both lease and sale terms in the agreement. For example, it's a good idea to set an interest-rate ceiling in the agreement, or agree that the owner will finance the sale if conventional interest rates are at a certain level. This guards against the tenant being unable to qualify for a loan because interest rates are too high when it's time to exercise the option to buy.

Lease-option forms are available at some stationery stores that carry professional forms. If you are concerned about the language of the agreement, consult an attorney or escrow officer.

Pick a Partner

Another popular option is having two families, or couples, or individuals combine their assets and purchase the property as partners. It often makes sense, especially for couples that enjoy being together yet know they will never be able to afford a getaway of their own.

However, the secret, underestimated ingredient is time. People who buy a second home and retain a primary residence often do not spend as much time in the second home as they had planned. And, when a block of time surprisingly surfaces, they often find themselves traveling to a place they never have been or using the period for a family reunion. (That's why timeshares make sense for a lot of people—who don't have the time or money to blow on the whole enchilada. But they're not a good investment.)

Here's a pick-a-partner example. Let's say the Johnstons and the Schaefers are golfing buddies. Nancy Johnston would love a place in Palm Springs—an escape from Midwest winters, but she and her husband, Steve, do not have the cash to buy a condo outright and can't handle the monthly drag of an extra mortgage payment. Nancy does have some cash she inherited from her grandmother. One day, while playing golf with David and Pat Schaefer, Pat discloses that her uncle is closing out a new subdivision on a golf course in Palm Springs. The couple could get a bargain price from the uncle, but do not have the cash for a down payment. David's new job, however, gives them a comfortable monthly cash flow. A deal is made where the Johnstons would make the down payment and the Schaefers would make the monthly payments plus pay for all greens fees for three years. After three years, they refinance or sell the home and the Johnstons get their down payment back with a minimal interest allowance. The two couples split any appreciation upon sale.

Equity Sharing

The partner process also works in investment property and sometimes is known as "equity sharing." In investment property, a cash-poor buyer who knows of a good investment often seeks a partner to "front" the down payment. The two form a partnership to share the profits of the sale. Generally, there are three principals involved in an equity-sharing agreement in an "owner occupied" situation—a lender, investor, and purchaser. The investor negotiates and secures a loan from the lender and buys the property. The purchaser (with little up-front cash) then buys the property from the investor. Those two parties then share in the profits from the increase in equity over a predetermined period of time, normally five to seven years. The investor puts up the money for the down payment while the purchaser lives on the property, maintains it, and makes the monthly payments. Both investor and purchaser share major repair bills, depending on the agreement and who is occupying (purchaser or renter) the home.

The investor often makes about 50 percent on his initial investment, plus tax deductions on interest taxes and depreciation. The buyer gets

---

Alternative Financing Sources, Tips, Terms

The Mortgage Professor—*http://www.mtgprofessor.com/*

GMAC Real Estate—*http://www.gmac-real-estate.com/Buying/AltFin.htm*

Peterson's Alternative Financing Options—*http://iiswin-prd03.petersons.com/finaid/fa-private.asp*

Mortgage 101 Glossary of terms—*http://nt.mortgage101.com/*

---

into a home for little up-front cash, while enjoying part of those tax benefits and the chance to establish credit. The part of the deal that's probably the most misunderstood is the ownership split. The purchaser does not automatically get a 50-percent stake in the property. Typically, the purchaser gets 50 percent of the increase in equity over a specified period of time.

Equity sharing differs from a lease option in two key ways. First, if the prospective lease-option buyer does not exercise the option to buy, all of the payments made have secured no equity—similar to renting. Second, all payments made in a lease option are not necessarily subtracted from the purchase price. In an equity share, the investor usually requires the buyer to pay the equivalent of three monthly payments in advance. These three payments are subtracted from the last three months of the 30-year term schedule. The payments provide the investor with a little operating cash and are credited to the buyer at the time of sale.

If you are considering equity sharing, ask a lot of questions and have an attorney review all documents. The concept is a legitimate way of buying and selling real estate, but be sure all terms are explained. Investors can be found in the "Money to Lend" and "Real Estate Loans" section of the newspaper. Check into any investor's background and don't be pressured into signing an agreement until you clearly understand the process.

Finding a Way with VA

There's another possible avenue available for second-home purchase, one that is often overlooked by veterans of military service. While federal regulations require that all loans insured by the Department of Veterans' Affairs be used only to acquire a "primary residence," it is possible to purchase a second home using your VA loan guaranty. As in many cases involving the use of real estate, the definition of primary residence is the place you live "most of the year." So if you use the home more than six months of the year, it can be defined as your primary residence. For example, let's say you are getting ready to retire and want to buy a home in Arizona. You want to avoid the sizzling desert summers, so the plan to is to use the home October through April. That seven-month period would constitute the largest block of time you lived in any one place. Therefore, your new home in Arizona would qualify as your primary residence.

"The VA requires that you move into the home in a reasonable amount of time and that you keep it as your primary residence," said Paul Johnson, VA loan specialist for Washington Mutual Bank. "If those are your intentions at the time you apply for the loan, then there is nothing to keep you from using your VA guaranty to purchase the Arizona property."

"Once used, then gone" is not necessarily the case with VA loans, even though it's a common belief. While loan ceilings and guidelines are subject to change, those eligible have been able to borrow up to $240,000 with no down payment, or the conventional ceiling of $322,700[1] with a 25-percent down payment. The crucial requirements for eligibility are an honorable discharge, an eligibility certificate, and the ability to make the loan payments. All VA loans have a funding fee; for a borrower's first VA loan the fee is 2 percent of the loan. That 2 percent is reduced to 1.2 if the borrower puts more than 10 percent down. The VA will guarantee a maximum of 25 percent of a home loan amount. So if a veteran wants to borrow the maximum no-down-payment amount of $240,000, the VA will guarantee $60,000, which can be viewed as a substitute for the cash down payment. Veterans who want to purchase in a high-cost area or refinance a home loan with a price in excess of $240,000 can either do a 25-percent down payment on any amount over $240,000 or have sufficient equity in their property for that amount.

For example, let's say the new Arizona home will cost $265,000. The maximum VA loan amount would be $240,000 with no down payment, and the veteran would need to come up with a cash down payment of 25 percent of the amount greater than $240,000. Because the difference is $25,000, the cash down payment would be $6250, and the mortgage amount would be $258,750. In addition, the funding fee must be paid in cash for loans greater than $240,000. If you purchased a previous home with a VA loan and the buyer assumed your loan, your eligibility can be restored only when the assumer has paid off the loan. The only other

[1] Maximum amounts constantly change. Loan ceilings can be adjusted annually.

alternative would be if the assumer were an eligible veteran who is willing to swap his or her available eligibility for yours. And some borrowers still haven't gotten the word that reservists are eligible for VA programs. After 50 years of offering loans only to vets who served active duty, the VA changed its ways in 1992. Men and women who have completed six years in the Army, Navy, Air Force, Marine Corps or Coast Guard Reserves, or the Army National Guard or Air National Guard are eligible for VA home loans, including no-down-payment programs. If your next move is to a recreation or retirement home that will soon become your primary residence, the VA can be a great way to go.

Four Inexpensive Strategies That Put You in the Driver's Seat

In the section above, we've discussed some alternative methods of funding a potential property purchase. In addition, there are preliminary approaches that can put you in prime position before any real cash is exchanged.

1. Option—The clearest and strongest right that can be granted to give a potential buyer flexibility in the future. Under this plan, the buyer, or option grantee, is given the right to rent or buy a specified property during a specific period of time. However, the buyer, usually having paid a fee to obtain the option, is under no obligation to perform. To be enforceable, the option should set forth the price, dates, and terms on which the option is exercisable.

2. Right of First Refusal—An alternative to an option. Unlike an option, a right of first refusal does not entitle the holder of the right to force the other party to sell or lease the property. Instead, if and when the seller decides to sell the property, the holder of the right of first refusal can require the property for the same price and terms that the owner is willing to accept from the third party. A right of first refusal is not as strong for the potential buyer than the option. That's because it does not set the price for the property in advance, and it allows the owner to decide whether and when to sell or lease. A property owner generally will resist granting a right of first refusal because it can negatively impact the marketing of the home. (What buyer is going to get excited when another holds the first right of refusal?)

3. Right of First Negotiation—In order to counter the negatives of a right of first refusal, the seller and buyer can agree to a right of first negotiation. This provision says the seller must notify the holder of such a

right (potential buyer) that the seller intends to sell the property. The parties then have a specified period of time in which to negotiate a mutually acceptable deal. The obvious advantage of right of first negotiation over a first-refusal for the seller is that the right of first negotiation period ends *before* the owner or any third party or broker invests time and money in negotiating a deal. Hence, there's no confusion on the marketing side. A right of first negotiation does not give the holder of the right any assurance that the parties will reach final agreement on the price and terms for the transaction. If the exclusive negotiation period lapses without an agreement on price and terms, the owner generally is free to sell the property to a third party.

4. **Right of First Offer**— This is similar to the right of first negotiation. In some property deals, the parties will provide for a right of first offer ("RFO") in favor of the buyer. The holder of an RFO has the first right to make an offer for the purchase of the property before the owner can sell the property to a third party. The seller is given a specific period to accept or reject the offer, and if the seller rejects the offer, he or she is free to sell the asset to one or more third parties, with the only restriction being that he or she cannot accept a price that is less (or in some cases less than a percentage of) the price offered by the holder of the RFO. The RFO is used, for example, where a purchaser of a parcel wants a right to buy the adjacent parcels when they become available for sale yet the owner is unwilling to give an option or right of first refusal. The RFO holder (buyer) can be afforded additional protection by requiring the owner to make an offer to the buyer containing the terms (including price) that the owner will accept, before the owner can offer the property to a third party. This often produces the price that the owner will accept. However, the owner still controls the timing of any potential sale and is not obligated to reduce the price asked for the property even if it is off the charts. Eventually, the owner may be obligated to sell the property at the "off the charts" price to a third party if the RFO holder elects not to accept the owner's off-the-charts offer.

Flexible, Versatile Reverse Mortgages Can Help Seniors Buy, or Stay Put

In 1989, HUD tried to help "home-rich, cash-poor" seniors with a program that would enable them to take cash payments out of the home's equity. These reverse mortgages carry a variety of payment options. And repayment of the loan is not required during the homeowner's lifetime unless the property is no longer occupied as a primary residence.

National Reverse Mortgage Sources

U.S. Department of Housing and Urban Development—
http://www.hud.gov/

National Reverse Mortgage Lenders Association—
http://www.reversemortgage.org/

Financial Freedom Senior Funding—*http://www.finan-cialfreedom.com/*

Seattle Financial—
http://seattlemortgage.com/revmort.html

Wells Fargo Home Mortgage

"A lot of people think these mortgages are so final," said Dr. Elizabeth Irwin, 82, who used a reverse mortgage to buy a new home in Seattle-area retirement community. "But they aren't final. You can end it when you feel like ending it. You still own your home, and you can still do what you want."

The homeowner cannot be displaced and forced to sell the home to pay off the mortgage, even if the principal balance grows to exceed the value of the property. If the value of your house exceeds what is owed at the time of your death, the rest goes to your estate.

The loan is aimed at individuals 62 years or older who own their homes—either debt-free or close to it—and who have a need for additional cash. According to HUD, approximately 70 percent of America's elderly own their own homes and 80 percent owe nothing. The potential reverse mortgage market continues to be absolutely huge. Reverse mortgage payments to homeowners are based on age, interest rate, type of plan selected, and value of the property.

The flexibility of the reverse mortgages has come a long way since the instrument was first established in 1989. Once perceived only as a last-ditch effort to keep the family home, they are now used to buy homes, purchase cars, make needed repairs and improvements, finance education, pay for in-home care, or provide supplemental income. The loans are still expensive, with fees near four percent of the loan amount.

HUD's Home Equity Conversion Mortgage (HECM) is one of the more popular reverse options available today. The HECM loan limit, which often follows the increases in the Fannie Mae/Freddie Mac loan limit, varies by geographic area. All HECM loans have been guaranteed by the Federal Housing Administration, the agency established by the National Housing Act of 1934 to stabilize a depressed housing market and provide insurance on loans to homebuyers who otherwise could not find loans. In 1983, the government ceased to control the interest rates on mortgages insured by the FHA and started allowing the rates to "float" with the rest of the market.

The reverse mortgage, which must be on a primary residence, can also be used to acquire a second home. Let's say Betty and Joe Zito of St. Louis have a home valued at $235,000. Joe is 72 years old and Betty is 68. They execute a reverse mortgage on their residence based on her age and an expected interest rate of 7 percent. They could net a lump sum of approximately $106,000 on closing of the reverse mortgage. Shortly thereafter, they purchase a vacation condo in New Mexico. They put the $106,000 into the New Mexico condo and add $19,000 from Joe's retirement funds. They now own the New Mexico condo free and clear.

After a decade of no loan payments, they chose to downsize. They sell their primary residence, pay off the underlying debt, and move to the New Mexico condo. Using an average appreciation rate of 4 percent on the primary residence and a 7-percent interest rate on the loan, the balance on the loan would have increased to $253,198 and the value of the home increased to $347,857. If the home netted that amount upon sale, Betty and Joe Zito would put $95,659 in their pocket. Also, remember that they have made no mortgage payments for the past 10 years.

What other interesting wrinkles can you generate to help you get in the door of The New Second Home? Given the property and location, there might be a special loan program or individual that could provide more help than you ever dreamed. Research is key—in fact, it could provide the keys to your next property.

While the strategies we just discussed can help you get in the door of a property, getting the second home that you long for, where you want, can be accomplished—tax free. Remember, acquiring The New Second Home can be one purchase—and it can also be a stepping-stone process. In the next chapter, we'll detail those steps so that you'll feel confident despite the road you choose to take.

PART 2

Location, Location, Celebration

6

What to Look for in a Community

Community cannot for long feed on itself; it can only flourish with the coming of others from beyond, their unknown and undiscovered brothers.—Howard Thurman

Real estate is, of course, all about "location, location, location," so the choice of a community when considering a vacation or investment property is paramount. Whether you are personally enjoying the use of the property or are looking to derive income from its ownership, where you buy will go far in determining how well you can realize your goals.

Interestingly, the importance of the factors determining the choice of location will differ depending on your plans for the property. For example, when considering an investment property, it's usually better to emphasize locations close to your primary residence. You are more familiar with the qualities of the area, and you can easily look in on your property even if you use a professional to manage it for you. This might not be as important a factor when choosing vacation property or your ultimate retirement residence. For vacation property, the convenience of the property to the type of activities or environment you most enjoy will be very important, even if being in that location requires travel of several hours to reach. For retirement homes, the need for consistent social and medical services often becomes critical, as does the proximity of transportation centers that will allow family and friends to come for a visit or in an emergency.

There are two aspects to selecting a community in which to invest or vacation. The first of these can be done in the relative quiet of the home or office, and that is *gathering information*. Here the Internet is a marvelous tool and ally because it can provide the facts about a given community with greater detail and far less effort than would be available or required if you were to seek out the sources yourself. The second part of selecting a community is *personal inspection*. While the Internet can give you a very good overview of the facts about the community, there is no substitute for the personal visit. You must take the time to actually inspect the area. For investment, this means seeing the property at different hours of the day and night. And, for vacation property, it means spending some time in the area and getting a feel for what an "off day" can be like.

In this chapter, we look at the considerations that go into choosing a community in which to buy, either for investment or vacation purposes. These obviously overlap in some ways. A vacation home can be a source of investment if you want to rent it out when you are not using it, or if you are looking to realize a profit when you sell it. We differentiate between the considerations that are most important for investment property and for vacation property, but indicate which considerations are important to both. We also look at the information gathering and personal inspection aspects and suggest how to accomplish these efficiently and economically.

Choosing the Community for a 100-Percent Investment Property

General Considerations

Your ability to maximize the net income you receive from investment property depends on choosing the right property in the right community. Doing so will minimize the amount of time the property is vacant and might also increase the monthly rental you can charge. But your own preferences as to location and building mean very little in this choice; the property and the community must appeal to the renters who will consider your property among all others. So you must look at the attractiveness of the community from the viewpoint of the renter.

What to Look for in a Community

It might be a truism, but the best locations for investment homes are communities where there are a high percentage of renters. This is true at the city or town level as well as at the neighborhood level. This means doing some research into the structure of the population in the community. The best source is the Census Bureau Web site (*www.census.gov/hhes/www/housing.html*), where the results of the 2000 Census are available down to the census tract level, an area of about five square blocks. In the housing section, you will be able to look at the percentage of residents in your target community who do rent and the age and household structure of the community.

Also important is the structure of employment in a community. Different types of industries will bring different housing configurations. For example, consider the recent technological boom that boosted the economies of (among others) the San Francisco Bay area, Northern Virginia, and Austin, Texas. In each of these markets, the rental sector boomed as thousands of twenty-somethings poured into the market to capitalize on all the new jobs created in technology. In early 2000, the bubble burst in the technology sector, followed by the collapse of the job market in these areas. The rental market also collapsed with a glut of unoccupied rental properties on the market. So look at the employment figures for your target market. Determine the number and type of jobs being created or lost; these numbers will tell you what the prospects are for investing in rental property there.

Going to the Census site might be a bit more work than you're willing to do in the investment process, and you might not want to become a labor statistician. What can you do? There are two alternatives that will save you this expenditure of time and effort.

1. *Invest where you live.* If you have lived in a community for any period of time, you should be familiar with the qualities of the different neighborhoods in your area. You know where the students from the local college live; you know where lower-income service workers rent, and you know where the upper-income luxury market can be found. Staying close to home and leveraging this knowledge is a sound investment strategy. In addition, you can drive past your investment whenever you want at no cost and with little bother.

2. *Use a professional.* One of the major competencies of real estate professionals is the knowledge of properties and communities. They spend long hours every day understanding what is occurring in the real estate market. They can point to the best available properties and provide the context (merits, liabilities, rental possibilities) for those properties. If

you don't choose to invest where you live, real estate professionals are even more important. They may be the only (and certainly the most cost-effective) way you can find out about the area in which you seek to acquire property.

Specific Factors

Even if you use a professional, and even if you invest where you live, there are some very specific factors that you need to consider in choosing a location. Each of them can be resolved by answering a series of questions. The factors are presented in order of importance from the viewpoint of the renter.

- *Access*. The most attractive properties will be those that offer the best access to the things renters value. For example, renters tend to want to be close to work or school regardless of space considerations. A location that is near these centers or transportation convenient to them rates higher than one that might be larger or better appointed. Again as an example, a vacation rental property is more valuable the closer it is to the water, the wilderness, or the golf course. So in evaluating a location for investment, ask (and answer) the following questions. You can score each answer on the basis of a 1–5 scale, and then compare total scores for each alternative property.
    1. Where is this property located in reference to major employment and education centers? The closer the better.
    2. Is the property convenient to major transportation corridors? Consider both roads and public transportation here.
    3. How convenient are shopping, amusements, and recreation? Renters often use public space more than private space for nonwork needs.
    4. If the investment property is a vacation rental, how close is it to major recreational sites (water, mountains, golf, etc.)?
- *Safety*. In this environment, safety is a high priority for everyone. For renters, this is even truer than for owners. In part, this is because owners have more direct control over the security of their properties; in part, it's because rental properties tend to be in more densely settled areas with higher crime rates. In either case, renters will rate alternative properties in part on the safety of the neighborhoods in which these properties are situated. So ask yourself the following questions that will rate the neighborhoods in which you seek to invest.

1. What is the crime rate in your target area as opposed to the metropolitan area as a whole? Check it out at *www.robertniles.com/data*.
2. What security precautions have been taken at the property? As a related consideration, think about what you are willing to spend to increase the safety of the property after you acquire it.
3. Is the property fireproofed? Fire is often a greater risk than crime in many areas.
4. If the property is a high-priced or vacation condominium, is the community gated or the entrance tended 24/7?

- *Neighborhood Quality*. There's an old saying that the best indicator of whether an area is on the upswing or on a downward path is the number of broken windows. When there is pride in a community, those windows will be replaced. If there is neglect, the windows remain untended. Research has shown that where the community is strong, house values are high, and demand for living in the community high, as well. Most people, renters included, want to live in vibrant, unified communities. If you are considering an investment property, the quality of the neighborhood is a very important factor. It will go far in helping you maintain strong cash flow and high appreciation on the property. The important factors are listed below. The answers can be found for most zip codes at *www.list.realestate.yahoo.com/realestate/neighborhood/main.html*.

1. How strong are the neighborhood organizations? When a community is progressive, the residents will participate.
2. What is the quality of the neighborhood schools? Even if renters tend to use schools less than owners, they will benefit from communities where education is a priority.
3. Do the commercial areas in the community attract a large volume of street traffic? Busy areas are more vibrant, exciting, and attractive; besides, they tend to be safer.
4. If you are considering a single-family detached house as an investment, what percentage of the population owns in that neighborhood? Traditionally, high percentages of ownership are associated with better neighborhood quality.

Choosing a Vacation Home Community

Jay and Marla Bonfiglio lead very hectic lives. In their mid-fifties, they have both reached the acme of their careers, Jay as an international lawyer and Marla a public relations executive. They loved Washington, D.C. and their town house in Georgetown, but they also saw the toll the pace of their life was exacting. Five years ago, they decided to buy a safety valve in the form of a weekend retreat where they could put the Washington rat race behind them from Friday through Sunday. By temperament, they really couldn't completely leave D.C. behind, and they really wanted a place where they could at least find some connection with the excitement of the capital, but where the pace was slow and being alone a real option.

Given the location of Washington, their options were varied. Both Maryland and Virginia offered beach, mountains, and farmland, with most of these available within two hours of home. They decided to look a little more intensely at Virginia, figuring that the weekend commute might be a little less hectic. "One night, at a cocktail party, we were talking with another couple who were singing the praises of Orange, Virginia," says Jay. "They spoke of the restful beauty, the easy commute, and the lively social scene. It really caught our interest."

That weekend, they drove down and looked at available properties. After several such weekend visits, they settled on a 10-acre farm with a restored nineteenth century farm house, about a two-hour drive from D.C. and an hour from Charlottesville. "At first, it was very strange," says Jay. "Marla and I are both Jersey kids. We love being in the city. I went to college and law school in Washington; I've been here for nearly 40 years. The country is alien territory to us."

"Yes," adds Marla, "but we absolutely love it in Orange. It's the perfect antidote to a hectic week in Washington. We can stick close to home and read and rest, or we can wander around looking for antiques, or we can drop into Charlottesville for some good food and music. And there are always evening gatherings where we can get the kind of stimulation we get in D.C.. In the summer, we come down for a month, and really recharge our batteries."

Jay and Marla might well retire to the farm; then again they might not, and ultimately sell it. With the interest in Orange of professional people similar to themselves, they know that their options are wide open. For now, they're just enjoying it.

In another case, Lonnie and Dan O'Keefe, fiftyish professionals, wanted a getaway place they could use on weekends. But they were not rich people; Dan was a government attorney and Lonnie ran a day care center. So they needed to find a place where their financial outlay was relatively modest. Additionally, they needed to offset some of the costs of their getaway by renting it. They were quite impressed with Bethany

Beach. It was convenient to their suburban Washington home and allowed for a tranquil oceanside location. "We needed a place where we could just be quiet and recharge our batteries," says Lonnie. "We like the beach best in the early morning and late evening, and we don't need the nightlife on the boardwalk to be happy."

"But other people do," adds Dan. "So access to Rehoboth and Ocean City would make the property very rentable." They decided that if they could find a building lot and serve as their own general contractors, they could have their retreat. After a search, they found a lot about three blocks from the beach across the highway. "I basically grabbed all my friends and enlisted them in the construction of the house in return for free weekends at the beach. Even if they had no skills, they could always fetch and carry," says Dan. "The pros did the basic building, and my amateurs finished it off. Surprisingly, it all worked!"

Dan and Lonnie now spend 10 weekends in the house and rent it out about 12 weeks over the course of a year. Thanksgiving with their growing brood of grandchildren is an annual ritual at the beach.

As these two stories indicate, unlike investment property, vacation homes are sought for a number of reasons. Sometimes, they represent a stake in an area where one has fond memories of childhood vacations. They might be seen as retreats where the pressures of the weekday work world can be put aside for short periods of time. Some people see them as "audition" homes, which might become a principal residence when retirement comes around. And in any and all of these instances, they can also be seen as partially a vacation home and partially an investment.

Because there is a diversity of motives connected with the decision to buy a vacation home, the process of choosing a community is less straightforward than it is in the case of a rental property. An investment property can be chosen in a relatively objective fashion because for the most part, you never will live there. The purpose of owning the property is to appeal to others so that you can maximize your return from your investment. With a vacation home, emotion and subjective judgment come into play much more significantly. You will live in the house and participate in the community, so your own preferences will be the guiding factor here.

Clarifying those preferences are the first step in deciding on where to buy. If you can come to a clear understanding of why you're making this purchase, what type of relaxation activities you prefer, and what your ultimate goal for the property is, than the choice of a community becomes a process of matching up community attributes to your own designs.

Choosing a Vacation Home Community: Self-Analysis

The best way to choose a community in which to purchase a vacation home is to begin with yourself and your family. You need to know what you want before you can determine where to look. Work your way through the following process:

- *How much do we intend to use this home?* You have several options with vacation properties. You can use the home two weeks a year for maximum tax benefits (see Chapter 5 for details), use it in peak season to maximize personal enjoyment, or use it in the off-season to maximize financial gain. Deciding how you will use the house will determine two things. First, it will tell you how far away from your principal residence you need to look when evaluating potential vacation homes. If your intent is to use the property each weekend and several other weeks, travel time becomes a significant factor. You probably want to stay closer to home. For example, if you live in New York City, you might want to consider some of the upstate counties, the shore communities of New Jersey, or the Pennsylvania mountains when looking for a weekend retreat. Each of these can be reached in two or three hours by car and are thus reasonable to consider for weekends, just as the Bonfiglios can drive down to Orange or the O'Keefe's to Bethany Beach. But if you want a place just for longer vacations, then your scope of choice widens. When you go to a place for a week or two, travel time becomes less important, and any location that meets your other criteria is possible.

- *What do you do to unwind?* Any choice of a vacation home must center on the vacation itself. No vacation home will be enjoyable if members of the family can do what they find enjoyable. Dad's desire for peace and quiet fishing in a mountain lake might not suit the kids' need for active fun. Remoteness might bring peace but won't work if no one wants to prepare meals or if the kids need to associate with their peers. Before you make any exploration of vacation home possibilities, come to a clear understanding of what type of atmosphere, amenities, and facilities the whole group wants.

- *Is this a nostalgia trip?* If you spent many happy hours on vacation with your family in a particular spot, you might want to return there and buy a home in the same location. This is a legitimate, wish but you should consider how important this is to you. Sometimes, you can't go home again. Prices have risen, congestion increased, and many of the things you fondly remember have disappeared. More importantly, your memories are not necessarily shared by those around you. If the vacation home is to provide satisfaction, it must meet the needs of the whole household. Even a seemingly familiar place requires investigation before you seek to relive old memories. Don't let nostalgia for the past come before the more important considerations of the present, where you live.

- *How long will you own this home?* Plan ahead. If you want to hold this vacation home for the long term, think about how the preferences and needs of family members will change over time. Kids grow up, and the desire for play space evolves into the need to be with their peers. The young and vigorous will age and slow down. Things that you could do, you no longer can. Any successful vacation home choice will reflect a desired holding period. One that stays in the family for generations is of necessity flexible both in terms of its physical capacity and its access to recreational activities. A vacation home that will be sold in a few years must satisfy the investment criteria defined above.

- *Is it just pleasure or business as well?*[1] As the O'Keefes decided, they needed to rent their home out for at least part of the year in order to afford it. Their decision on a location was determined in part by the attractiveness of that location for seasonal renters. Not all vacation homes will be suitable as investments. Those located in beach communities (in fact near any water recreation) are far more desirable both as rentals and for their eventual resale value.[2] The tax laws also come into play here as there are limits to the amount of time an owner can use an investment property before the tax treatment loses many of its benefits. We discuss these considerations in Chapter 4.

Seeking the Vacation Home

The next step is to look at some specific communities and some specific properties. There are three important considerations in this process.

1. *Go where you've been*. Think about places you've visited, either on vacation or for other reasons, and that you think fit your vacation needs. This gives you a leg up because you have a working knowledge of the area, have some information to use in compiling its merits and demerits, and can get a good fix on costs (including travel time and expense) in having a vacation home there.

---

[1] Significantly more second homeowners buy for personal reasons than for investment purposes. See National Association of Realtors, *Profile of Second Home Owners*, 2003, Table II-1.

[2] National Association of Realtors, *op.cit.*, Figure II-1.

2. *Visit again.* This time, look at the whole community through the eyes of someone who will be part of it and not just a short-term visitor. It's important to visit during all the times you intend to be there. The lively, summer, beachfront community might turn into a boring, deserted, dead autumn town. On the other hand, the winter ski community might turn into a summer playground of mountain trails, green forests, good fishing streams, and pleasant golf. The seasonal mood should match your needs, and you should visit often enough to be able to gauge those moods accurately.

3. *Use a professional.* In all likelihood, you will be buying a vacation home at some distance from your principal residence. This makes it even more important to use the services of a real estate professional who will make it much easier to find the best community to suit your needs. There are two good ways to identify a real estate agent to use. First, ask one in your own community that you trust to refer you to a colleague in the areas you wish to investigate. This avoids the shot-in-the-dark approach of simply looking up a real estate professional in the phone book. Alternatively, if you don't have a real estate professional that you can ask, use the Internet. If you search on the areas of interest, you will find a number of real estate Web sites. You can then e-mail a series of questions that will constitute an interview to screen potential agents:

   a. How long have you been in business?
   b. How long have you been doing business in this market? Obviously, experience is a big plus.
   c. Have you had experience with buyers looking at vacation homes from a distance? Specific familiarity with your type of need is important.
   d. Can you give me the names of some of your past customers that I can call? The agent should be more than willing to share this information with you.
   e. Will you work with me as a buyer's representative?[3] It's important that you have the full attention of your agent.
   f. What information will you require from me? You might also want to ask how often your physical presence will be required.

---

[3] Buyer's agents are responsible to the buyer; normally all agents are responsible to the seller. In many states, buyer agency is allowed, and in a long-distance transaction, is probably preferable. To determine the prevailing license law in the state where you are, search (and to verify that a particular agent is in fact licensed in that state), go to *www.arello.com.*

g. What services do you offer? You will be dealing at a distance, so an agent who offers all the services needed in the transaction will be more useful to you.

h. What is your usual pricing for an engagement like this? Price is always the tiebreaker but should never be the prime consideration in a transaction of this magnitude.

You can, of course, add to this list, but this represents the basics of what you need to know before proceeding. Going through this process with a number of agents (three to five is usually the most efficient number) will help you find the best fit for your individual need.

Vacation Homes as Retirement Homes

Approximately one-fifth of all second homeowners see the home as a potential retirement residence.[4] If you are considering buying a vacation home that could turn into a retirement option, there are three considerations that you should put on your list as you assess your options.

1. *What is the quality of medical and social services in the area?* As you age, you will come to rely more and more on the helping professions and your own mobility will diminish. Being close to good community hospitals, elder centers, and recreational opportunities suitable to age becomes more important as time goes by.

2. *Will the home age with you?* Steps become a barrier as you get older, regular door openings are too narrow, regular countertops are too high for wheelchairs, and regular wall studs are often too weak to hold grab bars. Before you decide on a house, inspect its construction carefully not just for now, but also for 20 or 30 years from now. We live longer these days, and you're likely to spend more time in that house than you think you will.

3. *Can your friends and relatives or medical professionals reach you easily?* The visits might be friendly and enjoyable, or they might be necessitated by a crisis, but they will come. Whether you want them to, as a break form the routine of the retirement community, or whether they have to, your friends and relatives will come more frequently if you live near a major airport or train station or bus station. When you select the home, evaluate it for convenience of access.

[4] National Association of Realtors, *op.cit.*, Table II-1

Vacation Homes as Investments

The factors that determine your choice of an investment property may come into conflict when you want to use your vacation home to generate revenue while you are not using it. This alters the process by which you might choose the home. Now you must balance your own needs with the preferences of potential renters because what you want in a vacation home might not necessarily be attractive to others. There are four additional considerations that you want to include in your planning if your vacation home will also be a rental but that you wouldn't think about if the home will be exclusively yours. These are necessary to ensure that your vacation home is also a sound investment.

- *Buy near the water*. In a recent study done by the National Association of Realtors, the top five recreational desires of vacation homeowners all had to do with water.[5] Vacationers most love to swim, boat, or fish, so choosing a place near water will most likely suit both you and your potential renters.

- *Buy within easy reach of a major population center*. While you might love the remoteness of some mountain lake, if it takes a long time to reach your hideaway, not many renters will share your view. In order for a vacation home to make sense as an investment, it must be readily accessible to major population centers, as the Hamptons are to New York City, or Ocean City is to Washington and Baltimore, or as Traverse City is to Detroit and Chicago. This proximity might not completely suit you, but, remember, you're balancing two goals here: vacation and profit.

- *Choose for durability*. If you rent your vacation home, you lose control over the treatment of the house and its furnishings. Choose the house for ease of operation and durability. Similarly, choose the furnishings in a way that minimizes their chance of breakage. Even the best of renters will never treat a rented space with the same care and respect that the owners would.

- *Hire a professional manager*. By now, our emphasis on using professionals might seem like a broken record. But you are making a major investment here, and it is one that requires consistent monitoring. Even if you are close enough for it to be feasible that you do it yourself, it eats up more of your time than you want to sacrifice. It makes sense to hire a professional property manager who can ensure that the four people to whom you have rented your beach house don't turn out

[5] National Association of Realtors, *op.cit.*, Table II-1.

to be 20 people when the weekend rolls around. In some developments, management comes with the monthly fee. If you have to hire your own, you can expect to pay around 5 percent of the rental income for the services of a professional manager.

Accumulating Information

Choosing an investment or vacation property is both easier than it has ever been and more difficult. The difficulty arises because of the increased demand for these properties. There are a variety of reasons, chief among which is the demographic surge we have termed the baby boom and which is now moving through a period of life when additional real estate makes sense for both portfolio reasons and for family reasons. At the same time, the supply of investment and vacation properties has failed to keep up with demand because of a dramatic rise in home ownership and restrictions on land use that have hampered the creation of new housing. So the market remains very tight.

But buying an investment or vacation property is also much easier than it has ever been because of the abundance of information available to the prospective buyer. The Internet is a marvelous tool for researching the housing market and finding out about a community. Local newspapers now have detailed sites that allow you to research community organizations, leisure time activities, and safety factors. From the comfort of your own home, you can find out how it is to live somewhere else. You can also identify and evaluate potential investments and eliminate properties and even whole areas before you physically begin to search for a property.

Searching will also help you understand how rents change with location. For example, on the Outer Banks in North Carolina, a house a block from the beach will generally rent for 10–20 percent lower than one at the beach. Differences will vary from one vacation community to the next, so you need to do some investigating on your own. Here's the key: Do house price differences accurately reflect the differences in rent? If you look at two houses in the same vacation community whose rents differ by 25 percent solely because of their location, the prices of the two houses should also differ by 25 percent. If this is not the case, the house whose rent is a greater percentage of its price is the better buy.

Finally, there is no substitute for actually visiting communities that interest you. That's the only way to gauge accurately the suitability of a house or a community for your purposes. Before you go, though, visit all the relevant Web sites. It will give you a leg up on your decision and will make you feel more comfortable with an area when you actually go there.

7

Where to Roll the Dice?

Second-Home Buyers Share Their Stories

Although it might not be a castle, it is the functional equivalent of a hotel room, a vacation and retirement home or a hunting and fishing cabin.—John Paul Stevens

After all is said and done—after you have sold or leveraged your primary home, or accrued enough equity in a rental property to trade for a prime spot in a retirement area—where do you see yourself ultimately spending the majority of your leisure time?

Right now, what would be your best guess?

As we explained in our previous chapters, The New Second Home can be one property purchased for a specific purpose or a stepping-stone process usually culminating with a retirement-recreational home held for a long period of time. The number of regions from which to choose the "Ultimate" second home —and the type of amenities and topography chosen—are as varied as the persons seeking them. Rolling meadows, waterfront, desert ranchland, golf and tennis—different places and spaces of the country beckon different individuals for extremely personal reasons. While many consumers focus solely on comfort, others have a keener eye on appreciation potential and resale appeal.

In this chapter, we look at the ways in which some folks have made their location choices. We look at several communities that have proven attractive as investment or vacation places for several families. Obviously, you want to buy in a place that is welcoming and pleasant to your family and other families who might want to rent there. Last but not least is the opportunity of maximizing the return on your investment.

Choosing a location for an investment or vacation property also can be a no-choice proposition. There are certain rules that will allow you to maximize the return from investment property, and one of them is to stick close to home—especially in this age where the fear of terrorism has become common. However, if your investment is in a vacation property that you will rent out, the world is your oyster.

Housing prices have risen dramatically in most parts of the United States over the past several decades. This is both good and bad news. The good news is that your home is now worth more (perhaps) than you thought possible. The bad news is that investment properties might seem out of reach. Clearly this price rise cannot continue indefinitely, and if history is any guide, some markets will fall on their faces, sooner rather than later. Others will continue to thrive.

For example, the South Atlantic region is perhaps the broadest and most disparate in the country. It includes the District of Columbia and the states of Delaware, Maryland, Virginia, West Virginia, North and South Carolina, Georgia, and Florida. Despite the geographic breadth of the region, it is clearly identified as one of the top—if not the top—region for vacation, second, and retirement homes in the United States. Most of this reputation comes from the long-standing migration, both seasonal and permanent, of Northeasterners to the sun and warmth of Florida. But while Florida has traditionally been regarded as the poster child for relocation, increasingly the northern portions of the regions have become extremely popular. There are several reasons for this:

- The Maryland, Delaware, and Virginia seashores and the mountains of West Virginia are extremely accessible to the population centers in Baltimore and Washington (and to a lesser extent, New Jersey). For example, over the past decade, as the Federal government downsized, many early retirees have chosen to move to the shore or the mountains, enabling them to reduce their cost of living while remaining close to family and friends.
- Both North and South Carolina have aggressively marketed the advantages of living there. Stressing lively academic communities, the com-

bination of mountains and seashore, excellent recreational facilities, mild climate, and low costs, they have sought to "convert" potential Florida émigrés to stop their journeys a bit farther north.

- "Ricochet" émigrés, bothered by the costs or heat or congestion of Florida, or wishing to experience a change of seasons without seasonal extremes, have relocated farther north where these problems have not yet caught up with them.

What follows are stories about choices. These people share the reasons behind their second-home decisions and why they chose to roll the dice and test the waters in one particular place. (See Figures 7-1 and 7-2.)

Pack the Clubs AND the Kayak

Naples, Florida

Naples is one of the oldest towns in Southwest Florida. But its old town and surrounding residential areas is no longer "the end of the trail." Rather it has been overwhelmed by an expansion of golf course and marina communities that have proven to be a strong lure for both retirees and foreign investors. While Naples still remains a relatively quiet location, it offers a great range of excellent facilities for outdoor activities, including golf, kayaking, and sailing. In addition, there is an active retirement community with a full range of activity, and its climate is extremely attractive, particularly for older Americans.

Ken and Nedda Hamilton had lived in Pennsylvania all their lives. They planted their roots deep and had a large circle of friends and relatives to help them enjoy life. Now things were changing. Both were retired, so there was time to enjoy life, but their friends and relatives were moving away, many to Florida. They went down to visit and enjoyed it but couldn't get their minds around the idea of leaving Pennsylvania. Or at least one of them couldn't.

As Ken put it, "I've mentally been in Florida for the past five years. It didn't take much to get me to leave."

Nedda still resisted, largely because of the presence of her sisters nearby in Pennsylvania.

Enter Fred, their only son. He set out to convince them that they really needed to join the parade south. He skillfully laid out a case for Florida—lower costs, better climate, better health care. The clincher to the argument was Fred's willingness to become a co-investor with his parents in their new Florida home. Reluctantly, Nedda agreed.

But this was only half the process. They still needed to find a place. In January, they visited Florida. At first, they focused on the East Coast;

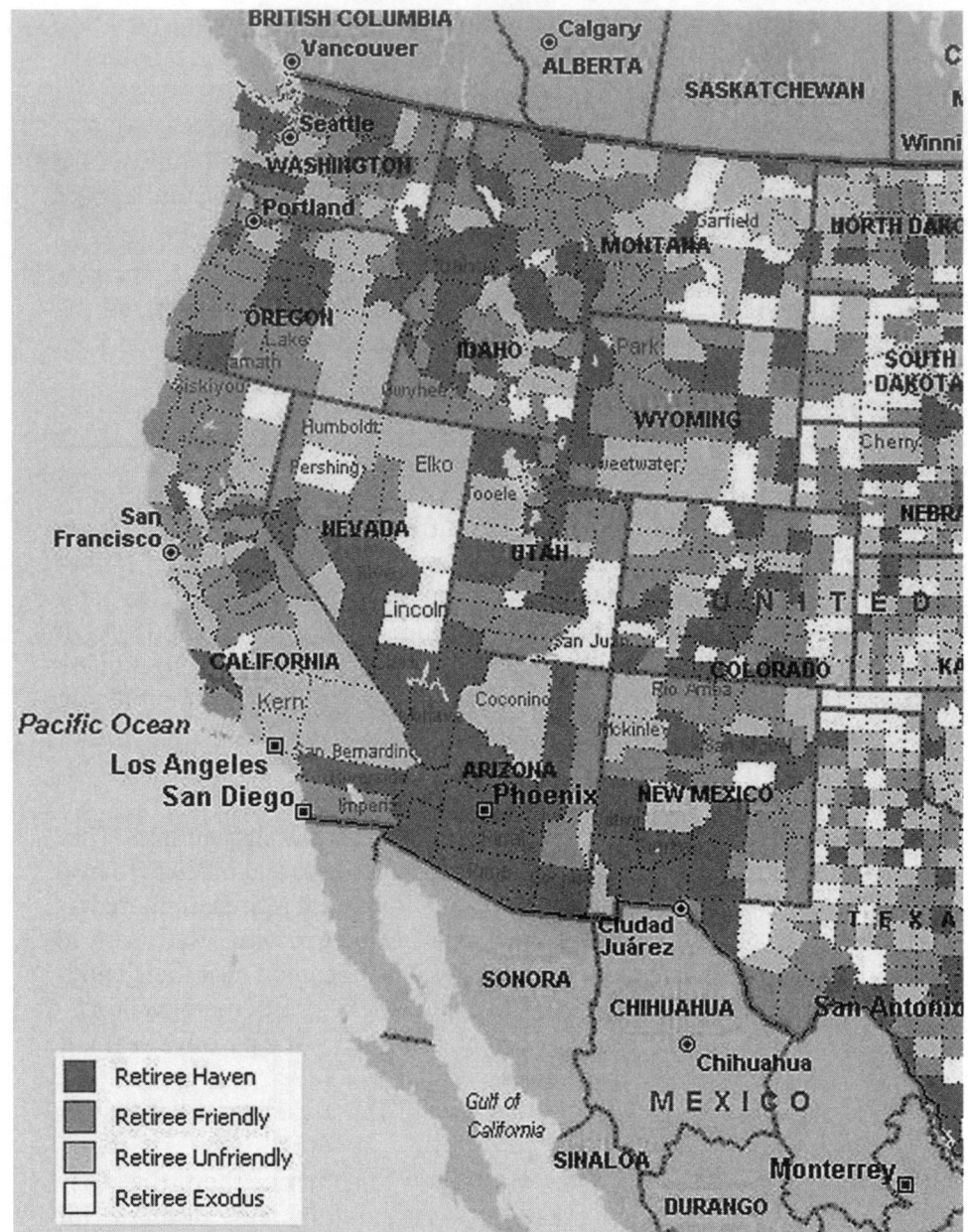

Figure 7-1 Staying close to home. Many second home destinations are within a few hours of a major metropolitan area, allowing consumers to stay close to their family and friends. This trend is likely to continue, especially given the

Where to Roll the Dice?

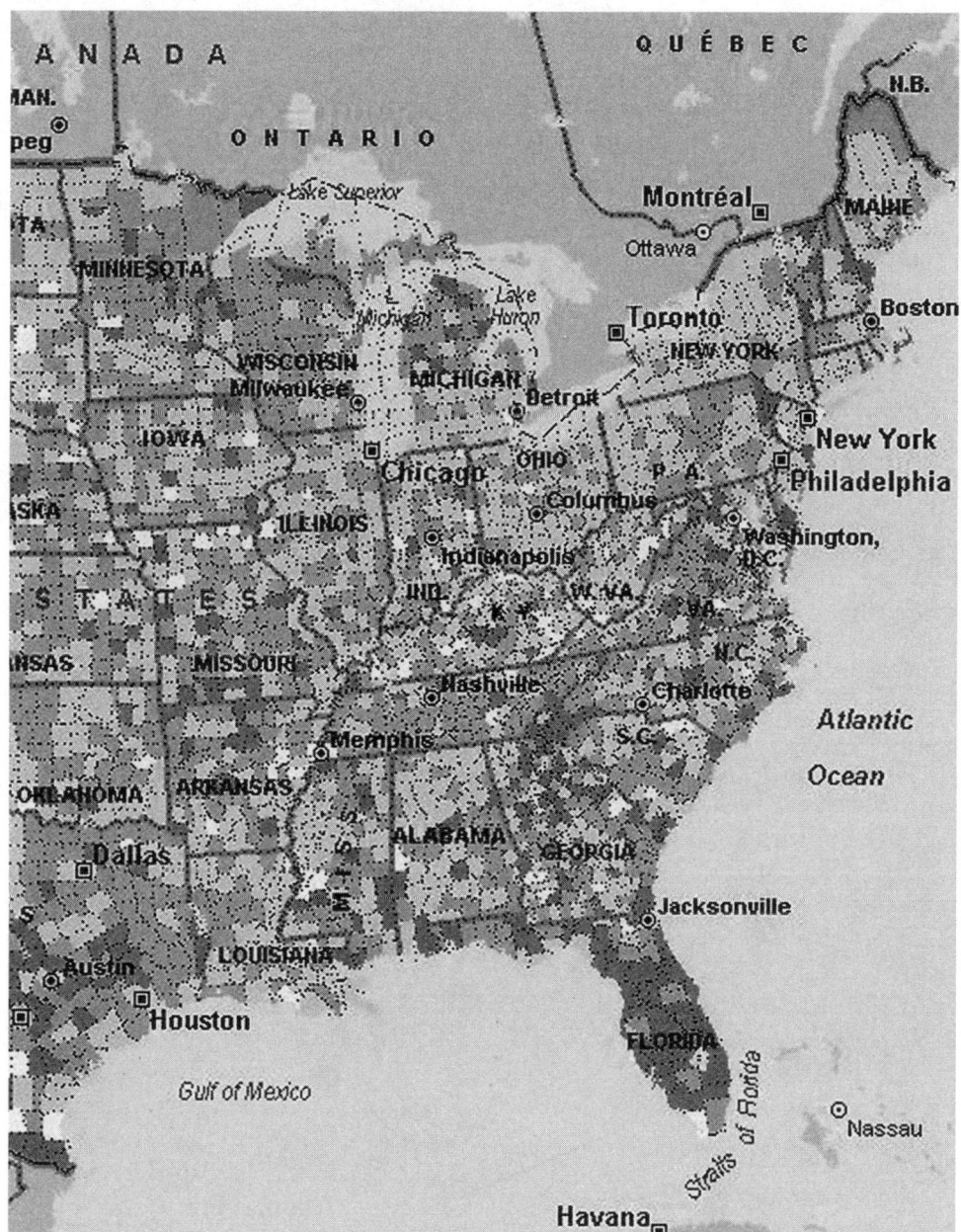

tragic events of September 11, 2001. Notice the high concentrations of retirement areas (dark and gray sections) near many of the most populated metropolitan areas in the country. *Source:* John Burns Real Estate Consulting

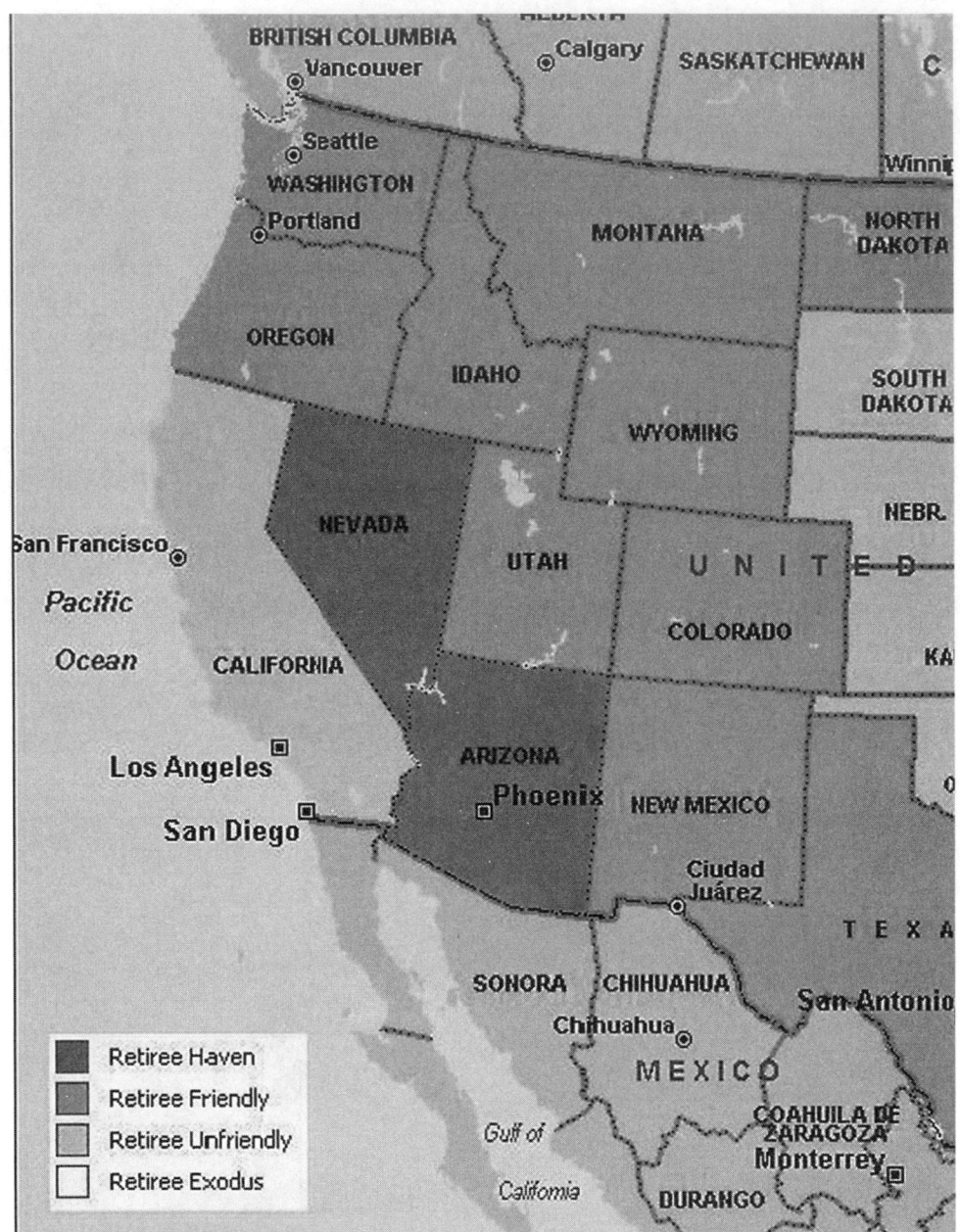

Figure 7-2   Second home zones. The home purchasing trends of consumers over age 55 provide helpful background in gauging the preferences of the "Ultimate Phase" of "the New Second Home" cycle. While Arizona, Nevada, and Florida will continue to be the fastest growing retirement states in the country, the

Where to Roll the Dice?

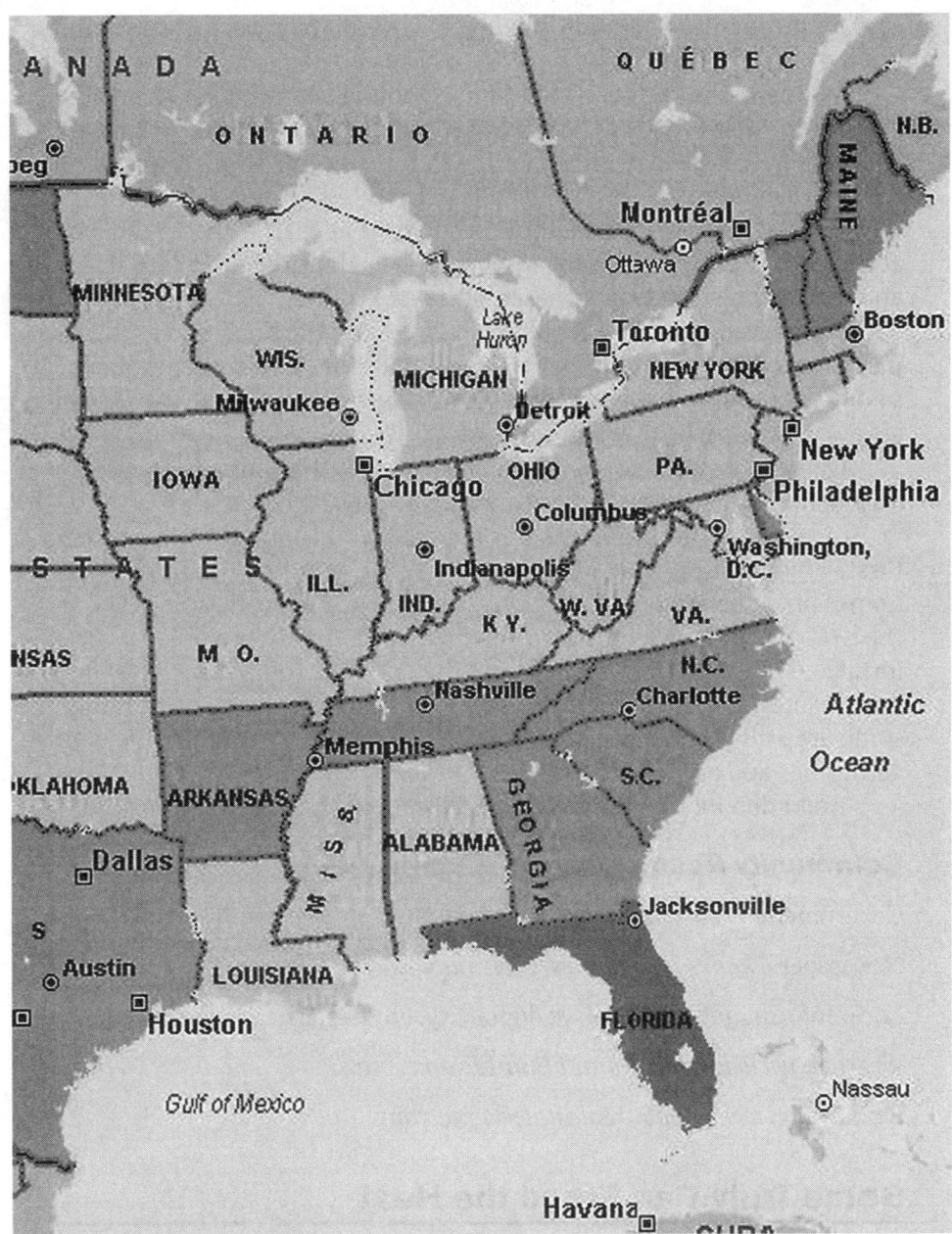

Pacific Northwest, Rocky Mountain region, Texas Hill Country area, Ozarks, Carolinas, and New England will also attract more than their fair share of retirees. Dark states are retirement havens, gray states attract more than their fair share, and light states are net losers when drawing older second-home buyers.

Source: John Burns Real Estate Consulting

spending four days actually staying in a unit they were considering buying.

"We had some relatives and friends living in the Palm Beach area, so we thought that would be the place we'd wind up," said Nedda. "When we visited there, we liked it, except for the degree of congestion. It was really too crowded there."

Fred suggested they take some of the time at their disposal and look at the West Coast, since his fiancée's parents had retired near Fort Myers, and they could serve two purposes with one visit.

This proved more to their liking, particularly the Naples area. "It was just so quiet and friendly, and we really like the developments there," said Ken. "Besides, it's really only a short drive across the state, so we can always visit our friends when we want."

Again they stayed for several nights in potential homes. They were now homing in on several specific places to buy.

The final decision, however, was not made until June, for two reasons. First, Fred, tied up with work, was unavailable to help them hunt for homes until then. More importantly, they wanted to spend some time in the heat of the Florida Spring to determine whether they would be comfortable. They were; they bought, and they're still comfortable. They find that the number of retirees who own units around them, even though some are still "snowbirds," have created a vibrant community life with gatherings and activities to spare.

"And I don't even play golf!" exclaimed Ken.

Community Resources

Government: *www.naplesgov.com*

Newspaper: *Naples Daily News*, *www.naplesnews.com*

Local Information: www.aolsvc.digitalcitycom/naplesfl

Weather: *www.wunderground/US/FL/Naples.html*

Real Estate: *www.naplesrealestateonline.com*

Some Truly Can Stand the Heat

Sarasota, Florida

This oasis on the Gulf Coast offers sea and sunshine, with warm weather and white sand beaches. Activities abound for those who love the outdoors: fishing, sailing, and golf. You'll find excellent health care and many good hospitals. If you're looking for cultural amenities, you'll enjoy the city's theaters, art galleries, and museums. You can drive to Disney World in only 1-1/2 hours. But Sarasota's summer heat might not be for everyone. For some, though, it's perfect.

Kay and Harry Carlson decided to abandon Connecticut winters and relocate to Florida. Harry had grown up there, on the west coast near Bradenton, and they both thought that "partial retirement" to the sun would suit them. They would open a seasonal mail order gift business, operate it from their home, and spend half the year traveling, golfing, and fishing. Their kids were grown and out of the house, so their location requirements were minimal, and they were not yet old enough for full retirement. This seemed like the perfect solution.

Kept at home by business, Kay zipped her "Wish List" into Harry's suitcase and he headed south to fetch a place for them to live. The list, scratched out on a legal pad at 3:00 a.m., included their number-one priority, waterfront!

"After all," said Kay, "he'd grown up on the water, I'd always lived at least within sight of a river, lake, pond, or creek, and there always seemed to be a gnawing tug on both of us to return to the calming effects of water."

But not just any water. Two of their three children were married, and the prospect of grandchildren was real, if not imminent. Although the house would have to have a pool, the pool had to be away from the house and of course, fenced. The house would have to be on the water, but the waterfront would have to have a sloping beach—no dangerous sea walls!

"I wanted a yard big enough for a garden, and I was old-fashioned enough to want a clothesline, so no gated communities with their complicated rules of proper yard etiquette for me!" said Kay. "My mother would eventually be joining us, so we needed a separate in-law suite where she could feel independent yet closely secure. Because she loved to "chew the rag," I knew that there would be times when my ears would need a break from her incessant chatter!"

Kay and Harry wanted a fireplace and wood floors on which to scatter their inherited Oriental rugs. A big family kitchen with a hanging pot rack would be nice, and Kay wanted a separate sewing room. A toilet separate and away from the actual master bathtub and perhaps a couple of fruit trees in the back yard completed the basic list.

And Kay added, "Remembering the winter storms that were propelling us to move south, and the value of my gas stove during times without electricity, I knew I'd need a gas stove down here in Hurricaneville."

When Harry called a few days later, his voice was so wobbly it sounded as if he'd either been out drinking or we had a terrible connection. He whispered shakily, "I found it!"

Forgetting for a split second where he was and the purpose of his "vacation," Kay asked stupidly, "Found what?"

"Our new home" he crowed! "I've e-mailed you a copy of the listing complete with photos. You're gonna love it."

But when she opened the file, she called Harry and told him he was nuts! "It's so ugly," she cried.

"That's just the garage and apartment" he replied, laughing. "You have opened the second file."

She did and gazed upon a magnificent home. Acting quickly, Harry snatched up the house, signing a contract the next evening. The house had more than satisfied the wish list Kay had put together. And the house was just the beginning of the adventure. With a thriving business in a growing community, Kay and Harry made many friends and used the house to entertain on a regular basis.

Oh, yes, those grandchildren did come along and they love the pool and the waterfront.

Community Resources

Newspaper: *Sarasota Herald-Tribune, www.heraldtribune.com*

Magazine: *Sarasota Magazine, www.sarasotamagazine.com*

Cost of Living: *money.cnn.com/.best/bpretire/index*

Local Statistics: *www.co.sarasota.fl.us*

Schools: *www.sarasota.k12.fl.us*

Convention and Visitors Bureau: *www.sarasotafl.org*

Real Estate Site: *www.michaelsaunders.com*

Weather: *www.wunderground.com/US/FL/Sarasota.html*

Trading the Cost of Southern California Waterfront for Airline Tickets

San Juan Island, Washington

The migration of series lookers began as a trickle nearly 20 years ago and now has become quite common: Out-of-state second home and retirement buyers, priced out of expensive West Coast waterfront markets, are investing in airline tickets and traveling to less expensive areas in search of a piece of quiet.

"It took us nine hours to get to Mammoth Mountain for a weekend of skiing and eight hours to get back," said Graham Carr, a Newport Beach, Calif. tax consultant.

"Just trying to get anywhere is ridiculous.

"I live a mile from the John Wayne Airport. It's just as easy for me to come up there than to put up with this."

Carr, 52, is a good example of many of the buyers who seek refuge on one of the largest of the 743-island chain first explored and charted by Captain George Vancouver in 1792. San Juan is one of a handful of islands served by the Washington State Ferry system, and thus property values are higher than the smaller islands that can be accessed only by private boat.

San Juan Island is about as far Northwest as you can get inside the continental United States and is nearly equidistant from Vancouver, British Columbia and Seattle, Washington. Victoria, British Columbia sits a short boat ride across Haro Strait on massive Vancouver Island.

The economic Secret Sauce of the San Juans? Price and accessibility. In fact, before additional airport security measures, visitors from California could get to Friday Harbor—San Juan Island's largest town—faster than Seattle residents on busy summer weekends. A two-hour flight from Los Angeles to Seattle-Tacoma, plus another 50-minute ride on a small plane to Friday Harbor could bring dreams of a fresh air, waterfront retreat to reality.

Seattle residents face a two-hour drive to the Anacortes ferry dock, a boat wait that can stretch to the same amount of time, plus the water crossing than can range from 70–120 minutes.

Although local residents refer to Carr as a "rich Californian," folks from Boston, New York, and Miami are relocating here, too. Like Californians, they come to kayak, bike, and sail, and are able to buy with big bucks, a result of home equity accrued in expensive markets. San Juan Island, the quintessential Northwest destination, has seen its prices leap, too, but they still pale when compared to the expensive retreats like the ones that dot the mile-high Lake Tahoe waterfront on the California-Nevada border.

Carr visited the area during one of his summer breaks from college, remembered the beauty, and returned. Twenty years after his first visit, he purchased a medium-bank lot with 110 feet of waterfront near Roche Harbor and invested in a well, small trailer, building permit, stairs, and mooring buoy, plus paid a backhoe operator to clear a driveway and garden area. He kept an old pick-up truck on the property for trips to the store and airport.

Carr has made friends with many of his neighbors—part-time residents from Washington, Oregon, Idaho, and British Columbia, plus the airplane riders from out of state. He longs, though, for the isolation of a nonferry island. He is now considering selling his island property, stashing a sailboat and small outboard in Anacortes, and commuting to one of the smaller islands in the chain.

"You only go around once," Carr said. "And soon I'll have more time to really spend up here."

Community Resources

Local newspaper—*San Juan Islander* (*www.sanjuanislander.com*).

Community hospital—Inter Island Medical Clinic (Friday Harbor) (*www.islandhospital.org*)

Airport—Port of Friday Harbor (*www.portfridayharbor.org/airport/*)

Chamber of Commerce—San Juan Island (*www.sanjuanisland.org*)

The Value of Making the Best Local Agent's "A List"

Bend, Oregon

Billy McMonigle wanted his piece of rural Eastern Oregon while it was still rural. The region's most popular city—Bend—has boomed past the 50,000-population mark, no longer fits the rural moniker, and expects an incoming peak around 2005. There's no huge urban center, but the lifeblood of forest products has been replaced by tourism, manufacturing, technology, and health care.

McMonigle, a former star running back from one of Philadelphia's "Big Five" colleges, was lured to the open spaces of the Northwest when a New York investment firm needed a bond trader "out west" that knew what he was doing. He was stationed in a downtown Seattle high-rise yet was addicted to the winter slopes and could not stay away from express gondolas on the weekends.

McMonigle liked the convenience of the Snoqualmie Summit, yet the crowds and snow were not as attractive as Crystal Mountain or the Whistler-Blackcomb region two hours north of Vancouver, B.C.

Where to Roll the Dice?

While the journey to Whistler was a bit shorter than the trek to Bend, the roads were less treacherous, especially at night. And, of course, there's that big orange ball in the sky that Northwesterners miss for weeks on end.

What's the quickest way to escape the wet Westside of the Cascade Mountains? Jump in the car and head to central Oregon, where the sun shines at least three times as much than the soggy region flooding the Interstate-5 corridor. If it's raining in Portland 121 miles to the west or in Seattle 251 miles to the northwest, there's often clear skies in the region around Bend—nearly dead-set east of Eugene—especially in the springtime.

The most often heard reasons for buyers wanting to purchase in the Bend region are clean air, good schools, excellent medical facilities, golf, fishing, skiing, and hunting. Approximately 78 percent of Deschutes County is government land (Forest Service, Bureau of Land Management, etc.), so there is an abundance of outdoor recreation close to town. Three are terrific cultural choices with a local symphony, opera, two community theatre groups, and the popular summer Cascade Festival of Music.

The region recently added a four-year college affiliated with Oregon State University that will add to a much-needed diversity of the area.

Many of the expensive second homes purchased during the high technology boom went back on the market and sold again to retired people seeking a sunny last stop or to second-home buyers who might pick up a few rental bucks when their kids are in school during the prime winter ski weeks.

McMonigle, who often frequented his brother-in-law's condo near the Bend Athletic Club, finally settled on a small parcel a few miles up the road near the community of Tumalo. It was clearly a recreation-then-retirement decision. McMonigle knew he could conduct most of his business electronically from home. He chose to make that full-time home in Tumalo while keeping a second home on one of the islands of the Puget Sound. He also chose a spot with room to roam—an old, 2000-square-foot house on 30 acres, 17 of which are irrigated for grass hay that's devoured by llamas and horses.

"We were able to get this place because we were on the best Realtor's A List," McMonigle said. "The trick is getting on the A List of somebody who really knows what they are doing—and what you want."

Community Resources

Local newspaper—*The Bend Bulletin* (*www.bendbulletin.com*)

Community hospital—St. Charles Medical Center (*www.scmc.org*)

Airport—Redmond Municipal Airport (*www.flyrdm.com*)

Chamber of Commerce—Bend Chamber of Commerce (*www.bendchamber.com*)

"Just for the Halibut" and a Lot More

Homer, Alaska

Tim Hayes, 52, is the type of guy who needed a stunningly new blast of nature every few years. He had hiked California's majestic Yosemite Valley, bodysurfed at a secret place the locals called "makihorse" off the west coast of Molokai, and floated the Snake River in the treacherous Hell's Canyon area that separates a desolate portion of western Idaho and eastern Oregon.

So, falling hard for kayak trips in far-off places did not surprise friends or family. The stunner came the day he revealed he had purchased—and planned to retire—in Homer, Alaska. The Nevada accountant had made several trips to Anchorage on business the past two decades and even once spent three days camping on the Kenai Peninsula near Kenai Fjords National Park.

Hayes thought he had found Kayak Paradise when a business associate requested that Hayes come to Homer to meet a potential client on a gorgeous September afternoon. The only time he had ever heard of the place was three years earlier when an uncle had come "just for the halibut"—the summer weeks that surround the city's popular Jackpot Halibut Derby.

The area depends on summer fishing when the harbor fleet, tucked closely against The Spit, a narrow finger of land jutting 4.5 miles out into Kachemak Bay, balloons from 800 to more than 1700 vessels looking for the biggest "slab"—a 300+-pound white bottom fish that could win the $25,000 derby. Its in-city residents number about 4000, with about twice that number in the surrounding area. The spot could be substituted on a picture postcard for the Norwegian fjords and few would know the difference.

Kachemak Bay State Park, with over 30 miles of trails and 375,000 acres of wilderness, provides backcountry hiking, camping, and lake and stream fishing. Also nearby are Halibut Cove, a remote fishing and artists' village, and Seldovia, "The City of Secluded Charm."

Homer, with an excellent community hospital, police, and fire departments, was a boomtown for homesteaders and coal miners in the 1800s. Visitors prefer its relatively mild climate and Hayes, like many others, have successfully found a way to bring some of their workload north.

He's used some of his savings to buy a piece of a commercial halibut boat and often greets the crew in his kayak when the boat arrives back in the harbor on warm summer afternoons.

"Some nights I think it's nuts to be up here," Hayes said. "But then I get back in the kayak the next day and realize it's absolutely an amazing place."

Community Resources

Community Hospital—South Peninsula Hospital (*http://www.sphosp.com/*)

Local newspaper—*Homer News* (http://www.homernews.com/)

Local airport—Homer Airport (*http://www.akohwy.com/h/hom.htm*)

Chamber of Commerce —(*http://www.homeralaska.org/*)

"What to Do When It's a Buck-10 in the Shade"

Palm Springs, California

Bob Howard travels the entire West Coast installing and repairing huge radio and television receivers. He calls himself a roving "communication construction specialist" and spends at least half of the month on the road.

He loves to drive, carries his golf clubs in the back of his car in the event that a meeting or event is postponed at the last minute, and really could live anywhere between Yuma, Arizona, and Bellingham, Washington.

"I actually used to own a lot on a golf course in Yuma," Howard said, "but the NAFTA agreement kind of made the place crazy."

Howard and his wife, an elementary school teacher, chose to make their primary residence in Palm Springs, not far from the old center of town that made the Coachella Valley famous. As the valley grew south and the visitors came and stayed in the communities of Cathedral City, Rancho Mirage, Palm Desert, Indian Wells, Bermuda Dunes, La Quinta, and Indio, the afternoon breeze kept the area relatively free of the air pollution so famous in Los Angeles, a two-hour drive to the west.

"We're backed up against the mountains, so we do get some protection from the elements," Howard said. "However, the air is not boxed in, like in the Phoenix area."

Palm Springs is certainly not new to out-of-state Snow Birds, golfers from all over the world, and tennis players seeking an over-50s tournament in the early spring. Retirees are buying the attractive ranch homes that were sold new in the 1970s, while younger getaway buyers are cashing in home equity to finance the down payment on larger homes with all the bells and whistles. Others, tired of dodging golf balls in exclusive, gated communities, come for the privacy of the horse farms and larger parcels in the east valley near Thermal.

"A home down here definitely has access to golf, tennis, and swimming," Howard said. "The question is how close do you want to be and how nice do your facilities have to be? A lot of guys are happy with the basics, which really can be pretty nice. Others . . . well, they got to have it all because that's just the way they are."

Old Palm Springs still has the Thursday night street fair, and the Eisenhower Medical Center nearby boasts expert physicians. There are parks, restaurants, and theatres always catering to adults. Yet for every negative associated with being a "tired" place, the area counters with something new and inviting. Such as the Palm Desert Campus of the California State University San Bernardino, the new satellite of the Cal-State system, which opened offering a B.A. in Liberal Studies plus a Multiple Subject Teaching Credential, where 37 percent of the student body is age 40 or older. Not only will the school be home to successful professionals seeking a third or fourth career, but it will also be one of the largest employers in the valley.

"A lot of these people want to go from the classroom to the golf course," Howard said. "That's simply how they want to spend their time some days.

"The problem is finding what to do when it's a buck-10 in the shade."

When it's 110 degrees, it's time to hit the Southern California beaches, less than three hours away. Or it's back to the more pleasant summer environs like those of Wisconsin, Michigan, Idaho, and Washington. The Palm Springs exodus begins before Memorial Day and typically lasts into October. That's because the average high temperature for June (102), July (106), August (102), and September (102) is not conducive to golf and gardening.

"We're looking for a part-time place on Puget Sound, just north of Seattle," Howard said. "We'll hang out there, do some traveling during the summer, and then head on back to the desert about the time school starts. It's deserted in the summer, but there's no mystery while people still go there during the other months of the year."

Community Resources

Community hospital—*http://www.emc.org/*

Local newspaper—*http://www.thedesertsun.com/*

Local airport—*http://www.palmspringsairport.com/*

Chamber of Commerce—*http://www.palmsprings.com/frames/chamber*

Cost of Living Can Make Paradise Tough on a Fixed Income

Kihei, Maui, Hawaii

Tommy Carter met his future wife, Carolyn, in the bar at Lahaina's Pioneer Hotel. It's the kind of place that, if you sit there long enough, you could almost touch some of the famous characters that have graced the establishment since it opened in 1901. The large, open-air main room with lazy ceiling fans waits eagerly for the reappearance of Bogie, resplendent in a white skimmer pulled low over his brow and a gorgeous woman on his arm.

Mark Twain and Robert Lewis Stevenson were among the first famous tourists to publicly marvel over Maui. Local legends abound, including one that brings Maui to the forefront of island lore. According to ancient legend, the Hawaiian islands were created by Maui, the "god of a thousand tricks," who pulled the islands from the ocean with his magic fishhook. This mythical demigod also lassoed the sun god "La" from atop Haleakala, releasing it only after it promised to move slowly through the sky, thus providing abundant daylight and warmth for the islands.

This warmth and friendly spirit brings millions of visitors to the islands every year. Carter, a marine equipment supplier from San Diego, was part of a Transpac sailing team that took a few extra days after the 1972 race. He returned for the sun and bodysurf near Kahana several times in the next two decades before leasing a small home Kihei for a month in 1995.

"Lahaina is still a terrific place, but the crowds seemed to stay instead of filtering away. There seems to be no downtime there anymore, especially since the first big cruise ships came and tossed anchor."

While Carter is leery of the commuter traffic that has steadily grown on the Piliani Highway that links Maalaea, Kihei, Wailea, and Makena to the Mokulele Highway and the Kahluli Airport, his love of nearby golf, snorkeling, and tennis offset the congestion of the main roads.

"The master plan is to come and stay four to six months a year," said Carter, who sold his San Diego home and moved to the mountains outside of Reno. "We love the church here, and my wife has become involved in a tutorial program at the local elementary school. The house is close enough to a great swimming beach that the rent we receive nearly pays the annual mortgage and taxes."

The cost of living in Hawaii can be a huge drawback for persons on a fixed income. Basic staples—milk, cereal, meat—can be far more expensive here than in any other state. Carter balances expenses by repairing outboard motors in a neighbor's garage.

"I don't do it every day, but I can't go too long without tinkering with something," Carter said. "Besides, one of the locals might come in with a new snorkeling spot I haven't tried on another part of the island. That's really the kind of stuff I'm after."

Community Resources

Community hospital—*http://www.hhsc.org/*

Local newspaper—*http://www.mauinews.com/*

Local airport—*http://www.state.hi.us/dot/airports/maui/ogg/index.htm*

Chamber of Commerce—*http://www.mauichamber.com/*

How do you plan to use your New Second Home? If you are like most people, the needs and wants of a second home change over time. A rental one year, personal use the next . . . plans are altered by situations beyond our control. In the next section, we will provide you with some money-making ideas that you might not have considered—practical wrinkles that can really pay off over time.

PART 3

Income-Generating Strategies for the New Second Home

8

Turning Your Vacation Home into a Cash-Cow Rental

When I was kidnapped, my parents snapped into action. They rented out my room.—Woody Allen

The down payment has been made. Your financing is in place.

Now, how do you want to handle potential renters—perhaps family or friends of friends—who would really like to occupy your property when you are not there? Should you even rent it out at all? The income would help offset mortgage and tax payments, but is it really worth moving all of your personal belongings, including your favorite bathrobe and slippers, back to your primary residence?

In this chapter, we will offer a few creative ways to crank significant rental dollars from your New Second Home. If your New Second Home is only in the Interim, or investment stage, you probably need full-time tenants to inhabit the property, pay rent, and thereby reduce your mortgage while the place appreciates (hopefully) and/or fulfills any rental time-period obligation. (To avoid IRS scrutiny, tax advisors say consumers should rent out the property for at least two years before occupying it as a primary residence.) For example, if you purchased a small rental home with the idea of trading it down the road for a property in a more desirable area where you plan to spend more time, you need to screen applicants carefully and choose the ones who stand the best chance of safeguarding your investment.

However, if your New Second Home is now in the Cocooning Stage—a family cabin, golf-course fairway home, beach retreat, ski condo—a property you don't foresee selling—then your rental decisions are very different and definitely more personal. There are a number of considerations to ponder before letting strangers—or casual acquaintances—use your place. Do you mind the hassle of leaving? Will the renters really honor your request for no pets? Will your favorite water ski be dinged even though you stowed it in a private place? Do you have the time, patience, and people skills to deal with people who do not consider your home their prized possession?

One way to defray the costs of owning a second home is to rent it out when your family isn't using it. Here are some steps to consider:

- *What "R" the CC&Rs?* Your group of cabins, luxury homes, or condos may limit—or prohibit—renters. Research any association restrictions before you rent.

- *Are you patient with people?* Do you have the time, and patience, to field inquiries and calls from potential applicants? Check the costs of hiring a local rental manager who often arrives with solid, reliable leads. Good managers can be worth an entire season's commission by quickly handling an emergency.

- *What are friends for?* To serve as good renters. Rent to friends (or friends of friends) whom you know. They'll usually treat your place with care—and often in better condition than strangers.

- *Lock and load:* Don't forget to keep a locked closet, or storage area, for your supplies and favorite possessions—like a prized water ski you want no one else using. It's also a good idea to load up on cozy comforts like large televisions with DVD and VCR, top-of-the-line gas grill, and all kitchen essentials. You want renters to return, and nothing's a bigger turn-off than having only three plates and two forks.

- *Longer rather than shorter:* Rent by the month, or season. It will lessen cleaning, maintenance—and extend the life of your favorite Berber carpet.

Turning Your Vacation Home into a Cash-Cow Rental

Many traditional recreational property owners have come to depend on seasonal rental income to ease mortgage payments, county taxes, and repair costs. The big question is: Do you want the depreciation and maintenance benefits of a rental home or the mortgage-interest deduction of a residence? A personal residence may not be depreciated. A home does not have to actually be used to qualify as a residence. If there is no rental or personal use of a residence for an entire year, it can be designated as a "qualified residence," and mortgage interest can be fully deducted. If it is rented a majority of the year and used just two weekends by the owner, no interest can be deducted under the personal-residence rule.[1]

If you deem your second home as an investment property (full-time rental) and use it yourself for 14 days or fewer a year, or not more than 10 percent of the days you rented it at fair market value (known as the 14-10 Rule), you can deduct expenses for maintenance, repairs, utilities, and depreciation. Days spent painting, repairing, and maintaining the home don't count as personal use, even if your children are with you. So if your all-weather getaway is rented for 300 days a year, you can take 30 days of personal time PLUS whatever time is necessary to paint and scrape. There is no deduction for depreciation, utilities, or repairs unless interest and taxes allocated to rented time are less than rental income. And be careful of the number of days used by family. If your long lost Prodigal Son wants to hole up in your magnificently manicured Maui mansion for a month—even if he can be coaxed to paying some rent—the use can be considered "personal." If you occupy the property for more time than the 14-10 Rule allows, this is considered use of a personal residence. If you are feeling you are in jeopardy of blowing the 14-10 Rule, shrink your personal time so that you can take the maximum possible deduction. It's a good idea to postpone maintenance and repair expenses to the tax year in which you can get the most bang for your buck. The deductibility of rental expenses and mortgage interest enters a gray area when you alter the cut-and-dried, 14-day or 10-percent guideline.

Regardless of how you designated the property, history has shown that it typically will appreciate in value. So if you want that getaway all to yourself but find you can't afford the mortgage payments after you buy it, go ahead and rent it. You can juggle rental and personal use status

---

[1] Here's another timeshare whammy . . . some consumers are under the impression that as long as they rent their timeshare out for fewer than 15 days each year that the income is tax-free. No so. Their share is only a slice of the 14-day pie. Rental days for ALL owners of the unit combined must be fewer than 15 for the cash to be tax-free. In a timeshare, the more difficult part is fulfilling the 14-day personal use rule.

from year to year. As stated in previous chapters, well-planned tax strategies and fluctuating conventional financial markets have changed how we look at second homes. The getaway that was once viewed only as a luxury is now a great place to stick your savings. And in a few years, you may even be able to retire into what has become the best investment you ever made.

So, you have decided to give renting a try . . . the next question becomes full-time or part-time? If you deem a second home as a full-time rental property, you can deduct up to $25,000 of rental expenses in excess of rental income. On the part-time side of the ledger, if you rent your second home (or even your primary residence) for fewer than 15 days a year, the rental income is tax-free as long as your personal use days exceed 14.

Is There a Tiger in Your Rental Future?

Let's start with some underutilized—and much-needed—ways to pocket part-time rental money without moving out for months at a time. A terrific example of a short-term rental is a middle-aged couple with a golf-course home that they rent to players or fans during big tournament weeks. The owners vacate the premises, hook up with a touring professional or corporation seeking to entertain executives or important clients, and rent out their home for tournament week without having to worry about reporting the income on a tax return. According to one Pebble Beach, California family, it's another reason why Tiger Woods is often smiling walking up the eighteenth fairway. Not only can he see that there are no reporters and photographers at the private home he rented near the finishing hole, but he also knows he will not have to drive through a traffic jam to get to his temporary home!

Short-term rentals have become common practice at the Olympic Games, NCAA basketball tournaments, Super Bowl, and World Series. While this tax-free luxury is always a hot topic for Congressional revenue raisers, it has not been shot down. The concept is not new, but it has been often overlooked. For example, when the 1983 men's NCAA Final Four basketball tournament was held in Albuquerque, New Mexico, (the famous Jim Valvano-North Carolina State year) seven San Francisco Bay Area buddies rented a gorgeous Spanish hacienda with five bedrooms and four baths just outside of town for $700 for five nights—big money in those days. While the cash came as a bonanza to the homeowners, it did come at a price. The group started a fire in the fireplace of that beautiful hacienda only to discover the flue was closed. The smoke went everywhere, and the home reeked for days.

Turning Your Vacation Home into a Cash-Cow Rental

Before the 1984 Olympic Games in Los Angeles, rumors were flying that all hotel rooms were booked and that anybody who offered a home for rent would receive at least $350 a night. It turned out that after the initial Olympic panic period, things really slowed down. The demand for hotel rooms and absentee homes did not come close to the supply. Regular convention bookings, generally made three to four years in advance, had gone elsewhere because of the Games. However, some of the world's largest financial institutions did rent blocks of homes to accommodate their executives. For example, Citicorp guaranteed five families $1200 to $1500 a night for three weeks to rent five exclusive residences in Hancock Park, an upscale Westside area. The owners were told to take everything that was irreplaceable, and Citicorp took pictures of every room in every house before and after the Games so that nothing was missed. In the end, the only private homes that were rented around Los Angeles for the 1984 Summer Games were the ones with special amenities and locations or the elegant residences with huge spaces and secure, private yards. There were simply too many average homes for rent.

Renters for homes and condominiums at the 2002 Olympic Games paid some Salt Lake City residents—especially those ski slope-side owners—up to $700 night. Basically, the owners chose to swap the chance of being close to world-class athletes for television viewing in another locale —and a big rent check. And, Salt Lake City is not Los Angeles. There were fewer hotel rooms and private homes—from the common to the extraordinary—and most received a ton of interest. The top locations and expensive abodes received the most attention. Rental agencies found that given a choice, the average person will splurge and select elegant over ordinary for a short period of time. It's simply human nature, and it's especially true when you are on vacation or a corporation is picking up the tab.

Take a few moments to think about the 14 days that would bring the biggest bucks at your place. Is there a popular water-ski tournament that lures the best performers in the region to your lake? Is it a good year to pass on the traditional winter carnival, thereby freeing up your slope-side cabin to a family very willing to pay top dollar for ski-in, ski-out accommodations? For example, residents near Mount Vernon, Washington, eagerly await the annual Once Around Lake Cavanaugh Footrace, an 8-mile fun run circling a crystal clear lake in the north Cascade Mountains. When the race date is chosen, families with homes near the lake plan their vacations. The days before and after the event are jammed with picnics, Hobie Cat regattas, and fundraisers for the volunteer fire department. Lakeside cabins are scarce during "race week" and bring more rent than any other week during the year.

What is your prime rental time? First consider the number of possible conflicts—family reunions, weddings, and can't-miss business trips—on your upcoming annual calendar. If these events will keep you from spending your traditional weeks at the beach, let your neighbors know that your place would be available "to the right family" for that Sensational Seashell and Balloon Blowout in August.

And, speaking of neighbors . . .

Friends Are Wonderful, but They Don't Fly Free

The best way to ensure your sanity, and your second-home's safety, is to first consider renting only to family, friends, and neighbors. In a capsule, you USUALLY get the renter that you know and hopefully trust, who will give you less hassle and who is most likely to leave your getaway in good condition. Think about it—how many weeks do you realistically have available? Wouldn't you want to fill your available weeks with somebody that you know? Why rent to a stranger who has contacted you off the Internet when the McMonigles from the parish church known for their altar-boy kids would die to have the week you can't use before Labor Day? Second-home owners often underestimate the large pool of potential renters created by the number of neighbors and friends near their primary residence and second home. These two separate and independent areas can produce more than enough folks to fill your rental calendar. And it's a huge advantage to have personally witnessed how potential renters keep their own home. You'll rest easier knowing they probably will keep your place in much the same condition that they keep their own home. Conversely, your visit to their home might be the primary reason NOT to rent to them!

Remember, friends know the going rate and usually *expect* to pay—so charge them. If your place clearly is on a resort's 50-yard line, has the best dock, crab pot, and feather beds, your friends and neighbors will be prepared to pay top dollar for your top spot. (Family sometimes can be totally different matter, but . . .) If the getaway is in the middle of nowhere with no obvious amenities (besides serenity) and you have never rented it out, at least consider covering your utility and cleaning costs even if "nobody would be using it during that time anyway."

If you are renting to someone you already know, the chances are you probably won't sign a rental agreement. One of the most important things to do is to try to set some ground rules before they move in. Discuss any issues (broken pipes, best place to park the boat trailer, nasty lifeguard at the pool) that you think could arise while they occupy your place. Preparation always helps prevent some awkward situations down the road.

Underestimated Need for Home Offices Can Mean $$$

It seems everybody now wants—or needs—to work at home. That also is true in second homes, as the number of telecommuters who take at least some work with them wherever they go continues to rise every year. The numbers will continue to soar. According to the Small Business Association, the number of entrepreneurs will rise—and most of these bright people will not spend more than they earn. They will not get another corporate job, but they will work—in more than one home. Home businesses, pushed along by a sluggish economy, the ton of white-collar layoffs that came with it, and a corporate move toward outsourcing also have to move from time to time with their owner operators. Approximately 20 million home-based businesses are now operating in the United States, and the space many owners use for business in their primary residence might not exist in their second home.

And more and more home-based business owners with children will often seek quieter confines to field important client telephone calls when the family is on vacation. You know the drill . . . the kids come in and scream "Who is taking us to the beach . . . you or mom?" while you are attempting to speak with a client who has taken three months to return your call. That's why a second home with an extra room or storage space adjacent to the garage that can be converted to a home office can pay significant daily, weekly, or monthly dividends. It's not that difficult to at least do the research to obtain high-speed Internet access, purchase a fax machine, comfortable chair, and a versatile desk.

The Mary Kay (or was that Max?) Factor

If a woman driving a large pink car suddenly introduces herself while you are pulling weeds from your golf-course retreat, she might be getting ready to ask you to buy her lipstick—and also about a place to stow it. A moneymaking cousin of the home office is a simple residential storage space, typically a large garage that neighbors have come to know is rarely used during specific times of the year. With an often-skittish economy pushing more and more individuals into independent sales positions, friends, neighbors, and friends of friends often need extra room to house their supplies and are not afraid to part with a few hundred bucks a month for the space. The need has become especially keen in second-home and retirement areas where major sales companies are welcoming new representatives to corral a demographic that is huge, healthy, and wealthy—and largely wanting to stay young. And Mary Kay Inc., one of the largest direct sellers of skin care and color cosmetics in the world (and the most famous company providing its top salespersons with pink automobiles for achieving lofty goals) is just one of the home-based business kingpins often seeking space. When you consider the company's 950,000 sales force and nearly $2 billion in sales, then toss in local residents who represent Avon, Tupperware, and Amway, you start to get an idea of the potential your garage—or unfinished basement with its own entry—can bring.

The need for space is not always about sales. For example, a second-home owner near Truckee, California, rents out her small cabin to snow skiers during the winter and kayakers during the summer. The home is very close to the Squaw Valley ski area, site of the 1960 Olympic Games and just steps away from the Truckee River, a favorite Northern California spot for rafters, fishermen, and hikers. While all renters of all seasons have use of the mother-in-law unit above the garage, access to the two-car garage is reserved for a local man who repairs kayaks for a nearby float shop in the summer and stores the kayaks in the garage in the winter. The repairman keeps an electric garage-door opener in his van for exterior access and has the key to a special deadbolt lock on the interior door leading from the garage to the cabin.

And, speaking of deadbolts . . .

"Lockoffs" Provide Space and Distance

While we have not been terrific fans of timesharing for a variety of reasons stated earlier, one concept that industry has helped to popularize is the "lockoff" unit, enabling two different renters to occupy one traditional dwelling at the same time. This idea is wonderful for owners who want to stay in a getaway during popular times of the year yet don't want to give up all of the potential for rental income. Lockoffs, usually a smaller unit with its own "lockable" entry, are common in Europe and now are included in many destinations operated by Marriott and Disney. These units come in several configurations, including a standard hotel room, a studio suite, or one-bedroom suite.

The flexibility of the lockoff is especially appealing. Parents and grandparents can have their own area away from the chaos of a large family while young couples can have their privacy at a fraction of the cost of a larger home. Owners can rent the entire house to the same party, rent both units simultaneously, netting at a slightly higher rate, or use one and rent the other. They are particularly useful when there is an all-day amenity nearby, like a popular ski hill, golf course, or beach. Owners often can easily convert two-story or daylight basement vacation homes into lockoff structures by sealing off one floor from the other with a soundproofed, double-lock door. Separate entries also are a must, yet many basement homes already contain their own "cellar" entry that can be upgraded and improved for increased foot traffic. In recent years, the most common lockoff unit for residential dwellings has been a living space about a detached garage and is known as an Accessory Dwelling Unit (ADU) in some jurisdictions This space, separate and independent of the main house, has become versatile in its own right. For example, owners in Southern California beach cities have rented their garage lockoffs to vacationers during the summer and to college students during the academic year.

Homesharing–Singles Find Income, Companionship

How do you supplement your income after you lose a partner and you love your vacation home? Often, a divorced or surviving spouse does not want to leave the dream place designed, purchased, and occupied by the couple several years ago. Some residents near college towns have opened their homes to students or visiting professors, renting them a vacant room, basement, or space above the garage. Now, more and more single owners in vacation and retirement atmospheres are doing the same. The need for inexpensive shelter in upscale resort areas is legendary—marinas, hotels, and casinos continually find it difficult to retain service workers when local rents continue to leap. While advertisements for "homesharing" are common in most local newspapers, United Way has begun sponsoring several pilot programs around the country designed to match people for mutual benefit and compatibility. The amount of rent charged is up to the homeowner, and amounts vary depending upon the region. According to program officials, the average renter usually pays about $350–375 per month. The tenant can reduce that amount by doing household chores, yard work, or running errands for $10 an hour.

A big booster of the program is Sisi Sedgwick, 90. She's not your average landlord. She takes in all sorts of renters in her large Seattle-area home, usually only one at a time and enjoys intellectually stimulating conversations, free thinkers, and people who spend little time in her kitchen. "You know, I don't even ask for references anymore," Sisi said. "Nobody is going to say that they cheat or steal. Besides, I like to solve the world's problems." Not all of the second-home owners are seniors; some are thirty something, providing shelter for folks 55 and older. While retirees often need additional monthly income, young investors also need cash to offset mortgages and taxes. With quality, affordable rental options continuing to be in high demand and short supply in many areas of the country, home sharing makes a lot of sense. Home equity often is the primary asset for consumers. Sometimes, especially after the loss of a spouse, older folks are forced to sell and seek less expensive housing. And the number of seniors—both landlords and tenants—will continue to increase.

According to housing industry projections, senior population growth rates will outpace national population growth through 2030. The United States Bureau of the Census's projections show the age 75-plus segment will grow at a rate 1.25 times the average through 2010. Sisi, and other women who are retired and/or widowed, are the most common candidates to become landlords in the home-sharing program. She learned about the setup while having lunch at her local senior center, and she's had so many housemates in 10 years since then that she can't recall all of them.

One renter, a woman in her early 40s who was attending nursing school, became as close as a family member.

"She was just wonderful," Sisi said. "She would give me suggestions for gardening and was helpful in so many ways. I ended up going to visit her in Vermont on Thanksgiving. Now, she's married and has a daughter who is about to graduate as an architect. Such an interesting person . . .

"Some stay for two months, some stay for two years. That's just the way it is. It keeps it interesting."

Time . . . How to Get It on Your Side

One of the most difficult things to handle—and the biggest obstacle to your bottom line—is when Uncle Miltie wants to use your getaway for two nights, midweek, during the peak rental season when you could book the place for top dollar for 30 consecutive nights. If there is no way around Uncle Miltie's two-day presence, ask if he can move his dates to the beginning or end of the rental week when you still could salvage four–five nights of prime rental income. If that's also impossible, call the renters on both ends of Miltie's dates and ask if they would like additional days at a reduced rate. You could turn out to be a real hero to both groups, especially if they are arriving by car and don't have to alter their airplane dates.

If that strategy produces no takers, see if you can take off work and surprise your family with a few days of vacation. You might even be able to paint the bathroom while they are enjoying the ice rink or afternoon matinee. You also will be able to halt any statements from family members such as "our place is always rented at the best times of the year." (If such statements continue, ask the speakers to help donate their allowances to help you pay the mortgage.)

While many owners choose a weekend day for comings and goings, adjust your start-end dates with the most common mode of transportation. For example, if most of your visitors will have to arrive by air, the least expensive days to fly typically are Tuesday and Thursday. Depending on the region, Saturdays can be inexpensive, too, and also in line with your competitors. That fact often surfaces when friends are staying in the same area yet at another property. Friends like to vacation with friends, and common arrival dates make for happier campers.

Remember, many of your decisions to accommodate unorthodox requests like Uncle Miltie's must be made with cleaning in mind. If you have booked renters before and after Uncle Miltie, make sure you have made arrangements with your cleaning folks to get the job done before the new people arrive. Altering a cleaning company's routine during a busy resort season can be nearly impossible—making Uncle Miltie's visit all the more difficult to approve.

You Never Get a Second Chance to Make a First Impression

It's no mystery . . .The key to a successful, moneymaking second home is satisfied renters who want to return because of the special experience they enjoyed at your place. And if they were impressed with their time and accommodation, they are going to tell their friends and acquaintances. While you often can't be there to place a rose in every room every time a new visitor arrives, make sure you take the time between cleanings to scoot back to your property and make certain your people are getting the kind of dwelling you want them to enjoy.

The goal is to provide a relaxing environment. Help ensure that goal by investing in great bedding—especially in the largest, or parents', bedroom.

Kids are resilient and can curl up in a sleeping bag in the most curious of places. But go out of your way to pamper, and even indirectly coddle, the people most likely to write the check. A great night's sleep brings people back. If they don't receive it, it's often downhill from there. They'll find fault with the inefficient corkscrew, comment on the poor water pressure, or complain about getting a splinter while walking on the deck.

At least once or twice a year, put yourself in the renter's shoes. What would you expect to have in a vacation home at the rental price you are charging? When compared to your competition, are your rates fair and in line with the rest of the pack. When it pours rain for three straight days, is there enough to do to keep your renters from harming themselves? While cable television is the scourge of many vacation-bound parents, some owners have found cable has really made a difference for some of their customers. What could be done right away—perhaps deeper cleaning than you are getting from your service—that would make your stay more enjoyable? During the high season, what could you accomplish with $20, one helper (your loving husband?), and four hours dedicated to intense elbow grease? Be sensitive to smell, aware of color.

A couple of times a year, substitute the throw rugs in the kitchen with inexpensive, colorful new rugs. Not only do they help give the home a clean and fresh look, but such moves show renters that you care about the condition of your home—and that you expect the same from them.

Now, before we roll into our next chapter and outline some ways of coaxing people to your getaway, here's a quick honey-do list you can complete with that 20 bucks, one helper, and four hours. Never underestimate the renter's first up-close look. Remember, these people are on vacation! Make it memorable from the start.

1. Clean the front door and make sure the doorknob and lock work and look sharp. It's a pain to wrestle with a difficult lock in the dark.
2. If the street numbers are dirty, paint or clean them. If you have a screen door, repair any holes in the screen and wipe the metal frame. Clean all cobwebs from the light fixtures and fingerprints from the entry.
3. Pull the grass from any cracks in the steps and trim trees and lawn. Make certain your shrubs don't look like grubs. If you have sprinklers, see that they actually spray and not merely trickle. Coil the garden hose and rake any leaves.
4. Buy a welcome mat if you don't have one. This will save you time and effort cleaning interior rugs and also gives a good impression.
5. Don't make the backyard the dumping ground just because most people probably will come and go from the front of the house.

6. Always look twice at the gutters and downspouts. A bent gutter can slow the flow of water, collect pools, and cause rusting. Realign the gutter by repositioning nails or gutter hangers. It can often save you from moisture problems in the basement.

7. Make sure your deck doesn't take anybody for a surprise slide ride. Clean the deck of moss. If your tulips have toppled, place a potted flower or two on the deck to add color.

8. Clean all kitchen appliances, and don't let the refrigerator resemble a bulletin board. Save the kid photos for home. Replace Teflon pans if the scratches resemble golf divots. Make sure drinking glasses shine.

9. No mold—anywhere—especially in the bathrooms. If necessary, replace the toilet seat. A new oak unit, with brass fittings, can be purchased for less than $15.

10. Never apologize for the condition of your home. Offer a clean, comfortable home for rent and hope for the best.

Now, it's on to marketing and advertising.

9

Seven Methods for Marketing and Advertising

Advertising is the greatest art form of the twentieth century.—Marshall McLuhan

So you can hear the cash cow mooing in the pasture. The question is: How can you market the milk to make it work? That's what this chapter is all about. It might be trite, but you can't make money on a rental property unless someone rents it! And no one will rent it unless they know about it and it attracts them. Let's face it: Much of life is about marketing. The best ideas, the most marvelous inventions, the greatest medical breakthroughs, and even the most worthy politicians would have little power to enrich and change our lives if it were not for marketing.

We take the approach that you have a product—your investment property—that consumers want. Your job is to inform the general public of the benefits that this product offers to them and thus attract a consuming audience for your product. The objective is to match the needs of the renter to the features of your property in such a way that the property stays rented as long as you want it to be.

In this chapter we present seven marketing ideas that will help you achieve this end. In the process, we give an idea of the relative cost, difficulty, and effectiveness of each method in marketing your product. Choosing the right marketing program for your product will involve a trade-off between cost and effectiveness. It's rare for a single marketing strategy to give you both low cost and high effectiveness; you will often need to choose which of these two—low cost and high effectiveness—you value more and act accordingly. So here they are: seven ideas for marketing your property.

Number One: Sell the Sizzle, but Make the Steak

Marketing is all about informing the public about how wonderful your investment property is. If it's a vacation rental, then the house will be the best experience for the vacationer who likes (pick one or more) the ocean, fishing, golf, hiking, the mountains, peace and quiet. When you show the slides of your vacation, your friends will swoon at your luck in finding such a perfect spot (just before they nod off from boredom). If it's a full-time rental, then your house is most convenient to (pick one or more) transportation, work, shopping, recreation. The tenant will have the most attractive address in town and be the luckiest renter in the whole city.

Before this happens, however, your house must really *be* that great place. In Chapters 5 and 11, we describe how to find the location and the house that most appeals to both full-time tenants and vacationers. But once you have that great property, you need to make it into the perfect place. This means painting, repairing, and generally cleaning the house. We talked in other chapters about how you need to choose an investment property with the desires of the renter in mind. Once you get the house, you need to prepare it for rental as if you were going to live there.

If the place is rented furnished, then choose furniture and equipment that is sturdy and useful—after all, the renter will probably not care for your things like he would his own, but he still needs a functioning place. New paint, especially in bright colors, makes the house look clean and attractive. Repair everything that needs repair: no holes in the screens, working blinds, holes in wall covered, all lights working, etc. Is the roof OK? How about the water heater and the kitchen appliances? How old are they and when will they need to be replaced? When the potential renter is attracted to the house, it must be in a condition such that it then sells itself.

The cost of this marketing tool might be low or it might be high, depending on the physical condition of the property. You can control the cost to a certain extent by doing much of the work yourself. It's a trade-off between your time and your pocketbook. Painting, for example, is easy but time-consuming; replacing broken screens and blinds is easy as well. For major work, you probably want to use a specialist. But the total cost of bringing the property up to standards, whether high or low, is irrelevant. You simply *cannot* attract rental business to your investment property unless that property is in the best condition it can be and shows as well as it can.

Number Two: Outsource, Outsource, Outsource

Do you really need a property manager? Jake Farnsworth, a successful attorney in a Washington, D.C., suburb, felt his time was worth more than money. He is also a civic activist in the area of planning and housing. Over the years, he has blended his occupation with his avocation by using the money he made from his law practice to finance the acquisition of a number of investment properties, mostly individual units in condominium buildings that he offered as full-time rentals. At first, Jack was able to manage his properties by himself. But as the demands of his business grew, his family increased in size, and his rental portfolio increased, he found that his time was too limited to both be a lawyer and a father and manage property, too. He set out to find a property manager, so he could devote more time to both his family and his practice. After interviewing a number of potential managers, he found a local real estate company that specialized in property management and outsourced the marketing of his properties and their management to the real estate company. It cost him a bit, but the cost was worth it in terms of the time liberated by using a professional management company.

Perhaps you don't want to be in the marketing business. You bought your investment property as a source of income and capital appreciation, and you'd rather do the things you really enjoy. In your scale of values, dealing with renters is not very high. Sometimes you really don't need to do it yourself. It is possible to hire someone to manage your property, market it, collect rents, and arrange for necessary repairs.

Property managers are pretty easy to find. If you've purchased a vacation home in a development, the management of that property will probably come along with the purchase. Either the developer will have an on-site manager, whose job it is to represent the owners in all these matters, or a local real estate firm will have the franchise on marketing and rental management for the development. In many cases, except for specific rentals that you would like to carve out (say for friends or relatives) and the time you will be using the property, you will be required to use the on-site property management.

For your individual full-time rental unit, you might want to hire your own manager. The phone book will be a good source for developing a list, which can then be whittled down through interviews. Be clear on the services that the property manager offers and the cost to you of these services. You should expect that the property manager will send the rents to your specified location (lock box, bank account, etc.) within a certain number of days of the rent due date and ensure the enforcement of any late penalties for unpaid rent. The manager should be available to tenants and responsive to their requests within a (short) specified time period. The manager should also maintain a reference file of reliable tradesmen who can be used to fix anything that goes wrong with the house. Check on references not only to assure yourself that this property manager is a reliable and effective one, but also that the property manager has the experience in managing your type of property—single-family house, high-rise or garden apartment, condo, high-rent, low-rent, etc.

This might not seem like marketing, but it actually is. Using a property manager can ensure that you have as few gaps as possible in the rental period for your house. For this peace of mind, you can expect to pay about 10 percent of the rent for the property management service. This is one of those trade-offs—you're paying a specialist so you have time. As we illustrate in the story above, hiring a property manager to keep your rental property filled makes more sense the more property you own.

Number Three: I Get by with a Little Help from My Friends

Sometimes the easiest way to market your property is to look to those closest to you, your family, and friends. This is especially true if you have a vacation home that you only want to rent part of the time. Simply mentioning the possibility of a vacation rental to your immediate circle can take care of all the marketing you need to fulfill your rental goal. In Chapter 8, we cover many of the details of this type of rental. There are emotional pitfalls and tax consequences that you must avoid in rentals. Please avoid them and make sure that whenever you rent to a close friend or a family member, you do it with a contract that would be identical to that you would give to a complete stranger. The phrase "arm's-length transaction" is a valuable one to remember when dealing with family and close friends.

So we don't mean rent the property to family or friends. Rather, we are talking about using your family and friends to spread the word that you have a certain property for rent for a certain time period under certain terms. Be as specific and as limiting as possible. Don't give your family and friends the impression that this is an open invitation to come and enjoy your investment property. But make sure they understand that you are asking them to help you rent the property. You might even want to throw in a free weekend, if it's a vacation house. Certainly some sort of finder's fee is appropriate if they do lead you to a tenant.

Then let them be your market force. Everyone knows someone (or knows someone who knows someone) who is looking for a rental. The advantage here is that you will probably get a tenant who will do right by your property, or at least better than a perfect stranger, because there is a personal link to you, the property owner. This does not negate the need to check out the prospective renter, but it should give you a head start on the process. This is perhaps the most inexpensive method of marketing your property—all it costs is an evening eating Aunt Edna's dreadful fruitcake. Of course sometimes you get what you pay for, so don't expect too much from this approach. This marketing strategy might not be a consistently reliable way to keep your house rented, but it can be a great help to fill in the bare spots on the rental calendar.

Number Four: Think Globally, Act Locally

You can reach plenty of potential renters by using local marketing techniques. The power of these is that they can be focused to have the greatest chance of reaching those whom you wish to attract. When you do advertise locally, be sure to list a phone number or e-mail address that you can use as a message drop, particularly if the rental market is tight. You might be deluged with communications to your inconvenience if you use your main numbers or addresses.

Regarding techniques, consider Jim and Marsha Tosca's experience. They live in the Washington, D.C. area and have an investment property in New England. Marsha, a high-school teacher, stays in the house all summer and Jim visits there for four weeks each summer. During the school year, they rent the house to students from the local college. When they bought the house, they knew that this was the way they wanted to use it, but they had to think a bit about how to market it to the student audience they sought. They decided to use a three-pronged approach. They created an attractive flyer with pictures of the house and a description of all the benefits it afforded student renters and tacked the flyer to bulletin boards all over campus. Most importantly, they advertised the house with the university's housing office. (Jim now says that this was never really effective, but he had to be there, and would still do it even now.) Simultaneously, they placed an ad in the student newspaper to run during the months of February and March, the time period during which most students were deciding where to live in the next school year. Finally, they used a local real estate professional in marketing their house. Their relatively limited marketing campaign has paid off: The house has been rented by students during each school year they've owned it.

Consider the following local marketing techniques:

- *Bulletin boards*. This is an almost ancient form of communication, but one that is very effective. Bulletin boards are literally everywhere: on the streets, in the supermarket, at the post office, etc. They are read and they are effective. To use them, create an attractive ad for your property, like the Toscas did in the story above. The ad should emphasize the advantages of location as well as the amenities of the property and should contain a color picture. All of this is very inexpensive. Your cost consists of the time it takes you to compose the ad, the paper it is printed on, and the time you need to post it. It helps if you have access to a digital camera, but given the power of the word-processing software that is standard on most personal computers, this is a relatively easy process (and you probably know a 10-year-old who can do it for you in minutes). Likely locations:
  - Common areas of local colleges. This will catch the student audience, if that's the rental market you hope to tap. These include cafeterias, bookstores, and the lobbies of dormitory buildings.
  - Supermarkets. Everyone shops for groceries, so the audience here is composed of locals. This is a good place for ads about your vacation home because the family traffic here is strong. Given the volume of ads on supermarket bulletin boards, you might want to take care that your flyer stands out.
  - Coffee shops. These are today's town squares, and they serve the same gathering function. The crowd that loiters here tends to be younger, somewhere between college graduation and first-time home buyer, so the demographics are good for someone offering a place to rent.

- Local government offices. You might want to investigate the possibility of using the bulletin board in your local housing office to advertise your rental property.
- *Merchandising circulars. The Penny Saver* type merchandising newspaper is everywhere. It reaches a geographically targeted audience and generally is read by people who are motivated to find something they need—a car, a boat, or a place to live. Unlike bulletin board ads, merchandising paper ads will cost you something, with the cost varying with the size of the ad and the length of time the paper carries the ad. Yet given the readership of these merchandising papers—interested in buying and local—this might be a very cost-efficient strategy. Finally, find out if the specialty real estate books that feature homes for sale and rent are open to advertising by individual property owners. Mostly, these books are used by large property owners and real estate professionals, so it might not happen, but it's worth a try.
- *Local newspapers.* Moving up the food chain a bit, local area newspapers offer an effective way to reach sub areas of a metropolitan area. For example, in the Washington, D.C., metropolitan area, *The Journal* newspapers publish editions for each of the suburban counties. Because each concentrates on what is essentially local news, the readership drawn to these papers is looking for information about the local area. The readership is interested in those specific areas, so the ads will be viewed by a part of the population that comprises the highest probability of potential renters of your property.
- *Church bulletins.* This is an old standby, and one glance will tell you about the concentration of real estate advertising in church bulletins. Marketing your property in the church bulletin gives you an automatic bona fide status with the readers. If you are advertising there, you must be like them, you must be honest, and you must be good-hearted. Who wouldn't want you for a landlord? Your vacation home must be a sheer delight! The downside here is that you don't really reach many people, except in the large, "corporate" churches that boast of thousands of members. In addition, you're competing with real estate professionals who are themselves seeking clients from among the congregation. Of course, it's also cheap to advertise in the church bulletin, and who knows what other benefits you might reap from being on the side of the angels?

The bottom line here is that local advertising offers the opportunity of reaching high-probability prospects for very little cost. It's well worth thinking about.

Number Five: Roll Out the Welcome Wagon

Harry Taylor was retired and lived in a condominium ideally located on Long Island Sound. He could walk across the cul-de-sac to the marina where he kept his boat. His wife, however, was still working, and she was transferred to Pittsburgh. Harry decided to rent the place on the Sound, figuring that soon enough they would be back there, enjoying the site and the boat (which was now placed into dry dock). But he wanted to make sure that his condo was kept in good order. He used his old work contacts and identified the perfect candidate for the rental. An executive from Massachusetts was being transferred nearby, but for reasons of schooling, needed a place during the week, since he would return to his own home on the weekends. The contact was made and the deal was struck without the need for any advertisement of the property whatsoever.

Corporations move their people all the time. They move them short-term (which we'll call three months to a year) or long-term (three to five years). For the most part, corporate relocation will tend to involve the sale of one residence or the purchase of another, but not always. Some employees with short-term assignments might prefer to rent rather than uproot their households (see the story above) only to have to resettle them later. The growth of long-stay hotels and motels—*The Embassy Suites* of the world—over the past several years is a testimony to that.

There's another class of corporate employee whose transfer might also include a rental. In this technological age, many of the programmers and computer experts who make up the backbone of the company are young and somewhat rootless. They don't necessarily want to be tied to home ownership, especially at a stage where their career has not yet taken definite form. For example, when the tech bubble burst after April 2000, employment in the tech sector in Northern Virginia fell dramatically. Shortly thereafter, the rental market softened noticeably. This is negative proof but strongly suggests that corporate relocation and expansion might well lead to opportunity for owners of rental property.

Where is this going? Well, it's another marketing strategy that might help you make money from your investment. Learn about the companies that maintain facilities in your market area. Make inquiries with their corporate human resources or corporate relocation office about any plans for expansion in the area, including both transfers and new hires. Then arrange for your rental property to be placed in their information base, so that those who are relocating to your area have access through their employer to information about the property you are offering for rent.

Beyond this, read the business news carefully. Find out if any new companies are expanding into or relocating to your area. If you find one that is, contact the human resources or corporate relocation departments at those companies and arrange for your property to be displayed to their employees. We might add here that a variation on this strategy, namely offering your home for rental during major events, was discussed in Chapter 8. What was said there holds here.

This strategy is costly only in the time it takes for you to do the research necessary to identify the employment plans and the right contacts in the companies you target. For the most part, they will be glad to channel your information to their employees, although they might require some inspection of your property to be able to "certify" it. The effectiveness of this strategy is hit-or-miss. If the event—corporate expansion or relocation—occurs, the strategy is highly effective. If no event occurs, then the strategy is a nonstarter.

Number Six: Go Digital

There is no piece of information ever recorded in all of human history that is not now on the Internet. So why shouldn't your rental property be there as well? The Internet is particularly useful for vacation properties where the owner and customer are usually widely separated and the majority of the negotiations are done via telephone, e-mail, or (horrors!) even snail mail. But, given the degree to which younger people are tuned into operating on the Internet for everything from communications to shopping to finding a restaurant to go to on Saturday night, it can work wonders for your year-round rental. The age group that is most likely to rent is the age group most comfortable with the Internet.

Ideally, your Internet advertising should be as painless as possible. You could create a Web site for your property. If you have the computer training (or know someone who does), it is a fairly simple proposition to create the property Web page and then place it with any number of popular search engines (*Google, AOL,* etc.) The problem with doing this is that it's very easy for your property to become lost in the traffic jam of the information floating around in cyberspace. The number of people who would reach your site would likely not be worth the time, effort, and money necessary to place the Web page on the Internet.

Once again, we have the trade-off of effort and effectiveness. You could do it yourself, but why? There are a number of sites that can be used to list your property and whose processes are by and large easy. For example, *www.apartments.com* gives you the facility to list your year-round rental on a national site for a relatively low cost. As this is being written, a rental listing with picture can be placed on *www.apartments.com* for three months for $95. The advantage is that this site will give you national exposure. The disadvantage is that it gives you national exposure. You really want to target your marketing to the most likely renters, and these are people who will be looking at more local sites. Each metropolitan area has such a site, essentially a local marketing utility for local properties. Alternatively, you can just type the information you need into a search engine and find that localized Web site.

Conversely, for vacation properties, a national Web site is probably desirable. There are three reasons for this. First, and most simply, the property is not local. When you own a vacation property, you are no longer being a local landlord. You are absentee. Second, the potential clientele for your vacation home is national in scope. It's not confined to the local area, as is the audience for your year-round rental. So you want the value of a national name to bolster the credentials of your property. You're likely to be dealing with renters whom you will never see and who live a considerable distance away from you.

The final reason for preferring a national site is that the information you are offering is not necessarily time-sensitive. One of the major criticisms of national real estate sites is that the properties listed are often sold or rented before the viewer can contact the seller or landlord. In other words, it's stale information. This is not a problem with vacation property because vacation planning is done well in advance of occupancy. So a national site makes sense.

A typical site is *www.worldwidevillas.com*. This site allows you to list your property by location so that the potential renter can home in on a particular area and then search listings in that area. The search process is easy for the customer, and ease of use usually means that repeat visits will occur. This gives your property an even better chance of discovery.

Of course, if you prefer a local site, many vacation destination areas (Orlando, Scottsdale, etc.) have sites oriented to vacation listings. In any case, the use of established sites on the Internet is a key marketing strategy that will become increasingly important as time goes by.

Number Seven: Extra, Extra, Read All About It!

There is, of course, the traditional newspaper advertisement as a marketing tool. We left it for last not because it is least, but rather because it's not what it used to be. Until the emergence of the Internet, newspapers held the monopoly on advertising for vehicles (we can't say cars anymore because Americans don't drive cars; they drive urban assault vehicles), employment, and real estate. If you had a property to sell or rent, you would either place an ad in the local paper or you would instruct the real estate professional with whom you were dealing to do so.

As the Internet grew, the newspapers' position in these key advertising areas eroded. The success of *realtor.com*, *monster.com*, and any number of vehicle sales sites drew business away from the newspaper. Print was increasingly viewed as an old medium and therefore lost the allegiance of the new generation of "technorati." And because newspapers were slow to react to this, their positions were weakened even faster.

This is all history. It did, however, cause a change in the manner in which newspapers deal with their traditional advertising business. One of the most notable developments over the past three years has been the development and improvement of newspaper Web sites and the cooperation between newspapers and other media, most notably television.

Newspaper sites and television sites have been linked to leverage their ability to report on local news and to offer information on local weather, schools, entertainment, civic activities, and, oh yes, real estate. You can go to a real estate site and get significant information about properties for sale or rent, but it's hard to place those properties in the kind of context that can be developed by a newspaper site. The newspaper site will give you all the information about the location of the property as well as the physical and financial details about the sale or rental offer.

If you use the newspaper—that old reliable, unsexy medium—to advertise your investment property, you can now list that property not only in the print part of the paper, but also list it online at the newspaper site, where the prospective renter can look up crime rates, school quality, transportation routes, and local entertainment opportunities. The marketing potential of the newspaper establishment has grown significantly over the past several years.

There are two caveats that must be offered here. The newspaper can often be the most effective form of marketing for your property because the public is conditioned to reach for the newspaper as the first point of information about real estate. But it might also be the most expensive form of marketing. If you don't want to spend a lot of money to rent your investment property, then the newspaper is probably not the marketing vehicle you should use. The second caveat is that not all newspapers have made the linkage described above. If you are going to use the newspaper to market your product, ask about the possibility of listing your property in several media—print and electronic, most notably. If the paper cannot do this, then the marketing becomes even more expensive relative to its effectiveness.

In the End. . .

If there really are 50 ways to leave your lover, then there are at least that many ways to market your investment property. We have focused on the seven that we think sum up all those ways and that can prove to be the most effective. You must market your property. Except in rare cases, renters are not going to amble up to your door and ask about properties for rent (unless of course you live in the field of dreams, but this is not heaven and it's not even Iowa we're talking about). How you market (or more precisely how you choose to market) your property is the question.

Each of these ideas and strategies is a good one. Each, however, comes with its benefits and drawbacks and its cost-effectiveness. Choosing will really be a matter of three factors. First, your budget will determine how expensive a strategy you are able to choose. There's a lot of room between telling your family and friends and advertising in the newspaper, and you will fit financially somewhere on that line. Second, your target population will help determine your choice of marketing strategy. The young renter, working in a technological occupation, might live on the Internet but never open a newspaper. Finally, your level of comfort will guide you toward a market strategy. If you feel ill-at-ease before a computer or with e-mail, the good old flyer or newspaper ad backed up by your telephone might well be better for you than an electronic strategy.

So consider the alternatives and, as the Old Knight said to Indiana Jones, "Choose wisely!"

10

Minimizing the Hassle Factor of Your Investment

A market is never saturated with a good product, but it is very quickly saturated with a bad one.—Henry Ford

There was a movie several years ago called *The Money Pit*. It depicted the adventures of a young couple remodeling an old house. Murphy's Law guided their efforts, and what could go wrong, did. They suffered through complications and expenses that they never considered and never foresaw. Currently, we have cable television shows—like *This Old House* and *Trading Spaces*—that show the other side of home adventures, the side where everything is a breeze if you think it through and apply hard work.

Which of these models applies to investment in real estate? Both do, and unfortunately, it's impossible to tell which will be the case for any specific investment. In fact, your first investment home might be a breeze and the second a nightmare—or vice versa. So the patron saints of investment real estate are Job and Martha Stewart (prescandal).

Owning an investment property should be a profitable venture, but it will be loaded with hassles and require work to maintain. Tenants will not pay on time, they will wreck the house, the property will stand vacant for long time periods, systems will fail, and appliances will break down. You will be lucky if only a few of these things happen and downright blessed if none of them do.

But, like a visit to the dentist, the more prepared you are for the worst, the better the experience will seem. And like most things, it will be easier the second time than the first, and easier the third time than the second. If you're just starting out, there are some rules to follow that will make the process go more smoothly. They don't guarantee smooth sailing; they just guarantee that the hassles you encounter can be handled efficiently and effectively. Here are the major things you can do to minimize the hassles that will invariably arise when you own investment real estate.

Be Clear on the Terms of the Rental

At the time of occupancy, tell the tenant in writing what your responsibilities and theirs are. You will be grateful later on if the tenant does something you forbade or doesn't do something you specified and a disagreement ensues. Unless you are clear at the outset who will do what, you open yourself up for a lot of headaches.

Use a printed lease, even if you're leasing the family farm to Aunt Tessie. This might sound like a burden for you, but it will minimize the hassle of disputes that can resolve themselves into a "he said, she said" type of argument. Spell out all the terms that are important to you, like:

- How much of a deposit is expected on the property? Usually, the landlord requires the first and last month's rent as well as some amount for damage.
- When and under what conditions will that deposit be returned or kept? Increasingly, the law requires landlords to hold the deposit in escrow and to return it with some form of interest accrual attached.
- When, where, and how will the rent be paid? The last day or the first day of the month is traditional, but you need to specify whether that day is for postmark or for receipt. You might specify a grace period, but be specific as to how long and any penalties that will be incurred if the grace period is exceeded.
- Who will be responsible for utility hookups and payment? This can be either you or the tenant. Putting the account in your name ensures continuity of service when a tenant leaves. Because utilities are requiring large payments to reestablish service, continuity is a considerable benefit. Even though you will put some estimate of utility costs in the

rent, having the account in your name puts you on the hook for more outlays, whether your tenant pays the rent or not.

- Can the tenant sublet the property? Subletting can reduce the gaps you might experience in tenancy, but it will also decrease your control over who is in the property.
- Will the property be furnished or unfurnished? This also includes the appliances that might be part of the lease and should specify the condition of the furnishings as agreed to by both owner and tenant.
- What restrictions will you impose on the use of the property? This will cover things like the number of adults who can live in the house, any pets that are allowed or banned, or any age restrictions on occupancy.[1] It can also cover whether the premises can be used for other than residential purposes.

There are three potential sources for a lease document. First, you can simply draw one up yourself or get a generic form on the Internet or at a stationery store. For most property owners, who have a single investment property or whose needs are simple, this is the most cost-effective and efficient way of creating a lease document.

If you have a number of rental properties or if there are some complications attached, you might want to consult an attorney who will draw up the lease for you. In general, it is probably a good idea to talk with a real estate attorney before you launch into the investment just in case there are local ordinances that will affect your ability to rent your property or your flexibility in its use. For example, Florida imposes a tax on any rental of less than six months in duration, treating such rentals as the state treats hotel rooms. Using annual (or semiannual) leases will avoid that extra cost.

The third source of lease documents is the management company if you own an investment or vacation unit. In many cases, condos are built with the expectation that owners are investors and will seek to lease their property. Generally, the management company will use standard documents that cover all local requirements.

Check Your Tenants

Federal, state, and local fair housing laws are quite clear. There are certain categories that cannot be used to screen tenants or buyers. We are not attorneys, and neither are most of you. So before you invest and before

---

[1] Increasingly, new communities in resort areas are deed-restricted to adults over 55, with further restriction on any presence of younger individuals. This will only grow as the baby boom reaches its seniority in large numbers.

you rent, check local laws to ensure that you are in compliance with them in your advertising and in your application process. It would be very helpful to get an attorney's opinion, although most municipalities maintain housing offices that are more than willing to help you understand the requirements of the law as they apply to landlords. But the state of the law does not preclude you from checking on certain aspects of your renters' credentials.

For example, Jane bought a rental property, a three-bedroom house in a residential neighborhood in Sarasota, Florida. She advertised for tenants and asked each respondent to fill out an application form giving previous addresses for all adults who would live in the house, employment, and income and references. She then checked the application information through the Tenant Verification Bureau in Bradenton. Her first two sets of tenants, married couples, worked out beautifully. Unfortunately, the second couple divorced and eventually both moved out. She went through the process again, and discovered that her next two applicants had a history of bad debts and a spotty employment record. She is certain that taking the precautions she did saved her from the headaches of late rents, defaults, and the need to expend her time and energy just to get what was her due as a landlord.

People are occasionally not what they seem to be. Accepting a tenant who will be chronically late on the rent, or will simply not pay and disappear, will cost you money and dramatically reduce the return on your investment. You will have significant gaps in the cash flow from the property, and you will spend significant resources in the form of your time and money in order to track down your rental payments. *In order to protect your property, use a printed application form that is in compliance with federal, state, and local housing laws*. This is a simple matter for any word-processing program. If you don't want to draw up your own form, you can find specimens on the Internet or at your local stationery store.

When you get the application, do background checks on potential tenants. There is likely to be a service in your area, like the one mentioned above, that has gathered information about a large database of individuals from public records available over the Internet. As scary as this sounds— yes, you're in there, too—it can be a great help when you are renting your property. Also check with the local law enforcement authorities. Both of these sources can furnish reports on any variety of public records concerning your applicants. If you are buying a resort or vacation condo, ask the property manager what process they use to validate renters. It should be sufficiently stringent to provide security for your property and the cash flow you expect from it.

Keep Enough in Reserve

It would be nice if every month the rent on your investment property hit your bank account one day before your mortgage check was mailed. And it would be nice if the property were occupied continuously. And it would be nice if nothing ever happened to the property unexpectedly. In other words, it would be nice to live in a perfect world. But we don't. Unfortunately, the cost of ownership goes beyond the payment of the mortgage and the utilities. It also encompasses all the outlays you need to make, even in anticipation of the cash flow that comes from rental income.

In order to maximize the return from your investment, you need to keep a financial reserve that can be used to close the gap between expenditures and receipts and cover unexpected expenses. This reserve ought to be on the order of one year's rental receipts, together with any planned expenditure for scheduled maintenance.

There are two ways to create this reserve. The first is to liquidate other assets and place the funds in a segregated account to be used to support the investment.[2] There is, of course, a cost in doing this because you will presumably be sacrificing yield to buy security. But the loss in return is probably less than the cost of any borrowing you might need to do to cover expenses.

The second way to create a working capital reserve is to tap the equity in your current primary residence through a home-equity line of credit. This is a relatively low-cost loan and has the advantage that it only generates costs if you need to use it. If you do happen to live in a perfect world, you will never pay a cent in interest or sacrifice any return on assets.

Rely on Good Trades People

Things will go wrong with your property. Some of those things will be predictable and you can plan for them. Appliances, plumbing, furnaces, air conditioning systems, and roofs have an expected life. When you buy the property, you should be told by the previous owners the age of these systems (most states now have laws that require that the seller disclose to the buyer both the age of, and any problems with, major components of the property). This will allow you to develop a maintenance and replacement schedule for the property. In turn, the projected expenses for these will enter into the calculation of your expected rate or return to the investment.

---

[2] All funds—income and expenditures—related to the real estate investment ought to funnel through a dedicated account, and separate accounts for the investment should be maintained.

There will also be things that will go wrong and require attention that are unpredictable. Some of these will be major—a windstorm damages the roof, water gets under the eaves and requires that a wall or ceiling be replastered and repainted, etc.—and some will be minor (the tenant's kid clogs the toilet with his pet frog), but they will happen. When they do happen, the tenant will want immediate attention. The odds are that you have a day job, and you don't really want to drop everything and become Sam the plumber.

Additionally, you might want to make some renovations on the property either to make it more attractive to renters or refit it to serve as your own vacation retreat or retirement house.

To illustrate, consider Hope and Jeff . . . They lived in New Jersey and owned a rental property near Ft. Myers, Florida. After several years of renting, they decided the place needed a facelift. Says Hope, "We knew pretty much what it was that we wanted to accomplish and hired a company that specializes in renovations. For the most part, they did a good job, but I subcontracted out a few things myself, and that did break the flow. Also, doing it long distance was a nightmare, but all in all, the outcome was great. Even though we went over budget, we are very happy with the new look. Now we only want to rent it to people that we know because we put too much of ourselves into the renovations and I am now very attached to it." The odds are that they started out to create a better rental and ended up with a vacation retreat and potential retirement address.

If you own a resort or vacation property, you probably pay a management company that will see to any repairs necessary to your property. But most real estate investors own one or two properties. They don't have management companies and must see to property maintenance themselves. Unless you are a full-time real estate investor, it will help greatly if you have some reliable workers to see to property maintenance. A general handyman is most useful, but you should maintain a file of roofers, plumbers, etc., who can be called upon to provide repair work. When you buy the property, create that list and keep it close by for emergencies. If you buy a property close to your principal residence, you probably know the reliable repair people in the area, especially those who provide emergency service. If you invest in property that is located far from your principal residence, asking around with other investors or consulting the local Chamber of Commerce or Better Business Bureau will get you the answers you need. The real estate professional who helped you with the sale also has a list of reliable trades people that she uses and will probably share this with you to get your list started.

Drive by Often

One of the most significant threats to your investment is physical damage to the property. Repairs cost money and, in the worst case, complete destruction is devastating, even with insurance. The two major culprits in this damage are Mother Nature and your tenants. Now, you can't fight or control Mother Nature. But you can control your tenants to a certain extent. And you can see that whatever they do is neither significant nor irreparable.

If you are remote from your investment, rely on your management company. Insist that they inspect the property between every tenancy, and during them as well. They can advise you as to the condition of the property at frequent intervals. If you live close to your investment, there is no substitute for being there. Don't try to micromanage your tenants, but visit the property periodically to see how they are maintaining it. Driving by will give you a sense of whether the exterior of the property is holding up to your standards. Arrange for periodic visits as well. You can't tell how the interior paint, carpeting, and appliances are being treated unless you look inside.

Remember, It's a Business

The fact that a house is a physical object causes us to believe that it is different from other investments. Any real estate professional will tell you that buying a house is an emotional decision. There is just something that feels "right" about this particular property. But owning an investment property is the same as owning any other asset. It's a business decision. You have to do the math as you do with other assets, and when it's time to sell, it's time to sell.

Owning investment real estate is different from other investments in one very large way: It requires interaction with people. When you own a share of stock, and its price falls, you don't need to confront your broker, or the management of the company (although going to annual meetings can be recreational and therapeutic). You just dump the stock. In fact, most of us who own stock have never met the management of the companies we "own." Because most of our ownership is through pension plans and mutual funds, we barely even know what we own.

With investment real estate, it's a different ballgame. We get to know the tenants; sometimes we get to like them. In any case, it's personal. It's even more personal when the renter is a family member or close friend. Now our kith and kin are a little late on the rent. Or they miss a month altogether. It's harder to simply cut and run here because it requires that we confront a real human being. That's hard for most people.

Delivering unpleasant news and enforcing the terms of the lease are the most stressful parts of owning investment real estate. Yet they account for most of the hassles that investors, particularly small-scale investors, face. There are ways around this. If you are uncomfortable playing "bad cop" with a late-paying tenant, hire a property manager. Your local Realtor association is a good source of information about property managers and can usually provide you with a list of companies in your area. Hard decisions and hard conversations are often necessary in the rental business, and property managers do this for a living. Remember, though, this service comes at a cost and you will need to factor that into the rent you charge.

Conclusion

If you reread this chapter, it might occur to you that there are a great many things that can go wrong in a real estate investment—and you would be right! This has been, in effect, a primer on how to play defense in investment real estate. Most of the rest of this book is in the nature of teaching an offense: We try to show you how to execute effectively. This chapter tells you how to protect yourself against all the things that can go wrong. Unless you were born under the unluckiest of stars, only a few of these things will occur. But if you take the steps we suggest in this chapter, you will be prepared for the worst. You will minimize the hassles that accompany investment in real estate and whatever happens will be easier to handle. One final caution: Just because your first investment is a breeze, doesn't mean the second or third or fourth will be as well. You still need to take these precautions with each subsequent investment to ensure a limited-hassle experience in all your real estate investments.

PART 4

Appreciation Strategies for the New Second Home

11

Choosing a Location That Will Appreciate over Time

Imagination is more important than knowledge.—Albert Einstein

By now you should have gotten the plan that drives this book. Investment in real estate can be a lifelong journey that allows you to reach the destination you've always sought. It's likely that the destination represents a dream for you and a place that is better than where you live now. The plan we present allows you to enjoy rental income while you move toward your dream. In order to make all of this work, you need to invest wisely, in properties that will increase in value. Now we can't guarantee that this will happen, and we certainly don't think that the price increases that have characterized the real estate market of the late 1990s and early 2000s will continue unabated. But you don't need that to happen for the plan to succeed. Over time, real estate will appreciate at different rates (some negative), and ultimately will be worth more than you paid. You can then use the tax system to cash out and buy the place you finally want to inhabit. Your task in the interim is to find those properties that will track or beat the market over time.

In Chapter 6, we talked about how to choose a community to maximize your investment by maximizing your cash flow from rental income. There we focused on the needs of renters, rather than your own tastes and preferences as the controlling factor. In this chapter, we home in on choosing the property that will move you fastest toward your dream from the viewpoint of investment potential. Remember, you don't need to plan to live in or even like this property. In fact, it's better if you don't, so you can cast an objective–investor's–eye on the properties you are considering buying. The only thing necessary is that you choose a property that has a high chance of increasing in value during the time you hold it.

Let's draw an analogy. In the 1950s, the New York Yankees won world championship after world championship. During the decade, they were in the World Series eight times and won it six of those times. They did it by acquiring players late in the season (and often late in their careers) that could help them win the pennant and the Series. Often these players were gone before the next spring training. It didn't matter: They had served their purpose, namely to provide the missing element that would assure the championship. It might seem like a cold attitude, but it was focused and it was effective. This is the attitude you should have toward your investment real estate. Use it, don't love it.

What Is Most Likely to Appreciate?

Real estate is a marvelous asset if you look at it from 30,000 feet. No building looks shabby, no farm unproductive, and no office unfilled. And every one looks like a terrific investment that will do nothing but increase in value. For houses, this has been largely true, and we're not just talking about the past five or six years when home prices have jumped dramatically in all parts of the country. For the United States as a whole, the price of houses has done nothing but increase for 35 years! This is quite a record, but misleading. During those 35 years, whole metropolitan areas have seen price declines, and individual properties have sunk in value. So when you go hunting for that investment property, you need to take a rifle and not a shotgun. The more you know about choosing an area where appreciation is most likely, the further along you will move toward your dream.

The factors we described in Chapter 6 will point you toward communities that will be attractive to renters, whether they are long term or vacationers. Within those communities, the key to choosing a specific property is to find houses that are undervalued relative to the rest of the community. These will be the properties that will have the greatest chance to track the market or even beat it. Properties might be undervalued for a variety of reasons, and some might require additional investment to become income producing. Rest assured, though, that they are always there. You just need to do some digging to find them. Let's look at the map to see where to dig.

Vacation Properties

As we pointed out in Chapter 6, water is the single biggest attraction in the demand for vacation homes. Most people want to be on or near some body of water that can be used for recreation. Unfortunately, the amount of shorefront land is limited and largely inflexible in supply. Land use controls being imposed for environmental reasons have even reduced the availability of what supply exists. Moreover, in long-developed areas water-accessible property is not only taken, but probably overpriced. Trying to buy these properties is like buying into the stock market in March 2000: You can get them, but their upward potential is nil. Their value has probably peaked and will not keep up with the market.

Trying to buy property that is off the water but within reach is a little better, but here, too, you need to consider the history of the development. In most areas that have long been known as vacation locations, you need to go a good distance from the water in order to find a property that will track or beat the market over time. Investment here—or for that matter away from the main attraction in any well-developed vacation spot—is likely to be a low-yield proposition.

Where should you look, then? There are two types of areas where you will most likely find the best prospects for investment in vacation housing. The first lies on the edges of popular locations. For example, Orlando is a hot destination for vacationers, but it is full of attractions and densely populated with vacation condo developments. Yet the area keeps expanding, and new developments on the periphery are always springing up. Some of these even have man-made water, thus enhancing their appeal. Investment in a new development in a popular area will likely allow you to get in relatively cheaply and yet position yourself for appreciation as the subdivision grows and matures. Obviously, the earlier you get in, the better. If you can get in before the local infrastructure is developed, so much the better. Eventually, roads and commercial development will be put in, thus increasing the value of your property. This type of purchase requires a bit more due diligence, however. Because the subdivision is not fully built, you need to consider the financial strength and reputation of the builder. Make sure that your "bargain" doesn't go bust with the majority of the houses planned, but left unbuilt.

Appreciation Strategies for the New Second Home

Speaking of bargains, Jim Paduano thought he had found the perfect place. Following the dissolution of his long-term marriage, he had been renting. He found a new development on a spit of land near an old industrial area. It had everything he needed. Now retired, he enjoyed sailing and flying. The new development was on the water and had provision for docking space a mere 100 yards from his front door. Next to the development was a small, private airport. To top it off, the golf course was a five-minute drive away. He would have all this plus a water view for a very affordable price. Unfortunately, his builder was underfunded, and the project languished. Forced to leave his apartment, but without anyplace to move into, he moved in with his son and the son's family. The process dragged on for nearly two years (during which time his welcome began to wear thin) until the project was finally finished. He has what he wants now, but it was a struggle.

The second area where you can find that upwardly mobile property is in places that have not yet been "discovered" as getaway destinations. Sometimes, the area can develop gradually as more and more people find it to be a pleasant bargain. In the late 1980s, you could have purchased property cheaply on the Gulf coasts of northwest Florida, Alabama, and Mississippi. This is an area of white sand beaches, ample sunshine, and calm, warm water. The setting is comparable to the outer banks of North Carolina but the prices were about half as much. The states involved began a publicity campaign to attract tourists to the area and it became increasingly popular with Midwesterners who were tired of the crowded resort communities of Florida's west coast. The number of visitors gradually increased, as did the number of property owners. New developments sprouted up along the shorefront. Those Gulf coast properties are now very popular, development has increased, and prices have soared. The setting of the movie, *The Truman Show* in Destin, Florida., and the creation of gambling casinos on the Mississippi coast have only fueled the growth.

Sometimes people are drawn to a region by the glare of publicity and the area is "created" as a vacation destination. The Flathead valley of northern Montana was undiscovered country a decade and a half ago. Situated near the Canadian border, it features quaint western towns, recreational lakes, golf, skiing, and easy access to Glacier National Park. Again, the prices for housing were far lower than the area's amenities would have suggested. But for the most part, it was inhabited by locals and visited mostly by skiers seeking to avoid the crowds of Colorado and Utah. But in the 1990s, the valley was "discovered" by Hollywood and a number of celebrities bought up ranches there. This generated publicity and interest on the part of developers who built condominium complexes and publicized them to a general audience. The Flathead Valley is now a very well-known and popular spot.

And sometimes vacation areas become popular because major resort developers move into areas that had previously been known only to a few people. Southwestern Missouri is a fine example of this kind of growth. For years, Lake of the Ozarks had been a vacation destination for families from some parts of the Midwest. In the late 1980s, several resort developments and their attendant advertising began to draw more and more Midwesterners to the lake and its surroundings. This was capped by the recreation of Branson, Missouri, as a country and western music destination rivaling (and in some ways, surpassing) Nashville. Following the business news about the plans being made by Disney, Marriott, and Hilton might lead you to a spot that you had not previously considered for investment, but that might be the next tourist Mecca.

In all these cases (and in many others), a relatively modest investment would have paid off handsomely. This is not a "shoulda, coulda, woulda" argument. Everyone wishes they could have bought IBM at 4, or Berkshire Hathaway at 40. Rather, it's a pointer. To find the next Flathead Valley, remember these examples and do some research into the travel patterns of people you know, the investment plans of large companies, and even the homes of the stars. Ask yourself the following questions:

- Where do people who live in my area go to vacation?
- Where do they own vacation homes?
- Of these places, which seem to be modestly priced relative to other popular areas?
- In those areas, has there been any significant development recently?
- Which of these areas, if any, have received national publicity recently?
- What areas are the large developers looking at?

Online searches will help tremendously here. Once you've nailed down the area, choose the development that appears to be the most attractive and buy into it. You might have to be a bit patient until the rest of the world appreciates your wisdom, but it will happen.

Investment Properties

For investment real estate that's not in vacation areas, the process of choosing a house is somewhat different. New developments, which tend to be away from the urban center and from transportation lines, might be good prospects to increase in value, but they tend to be poor candidates for rental income. They will not be attractive to most types of renters. As we pointed out in Chapter 6, renters tend to value ease of transportation and access to jobs, shopping, and entertainment. Being out in the "burbs" will often not cut it for them.

There are two keys to finding an investment property that will at least track the market. First, after you choose an investment area using the criteria in Chapter 6, find a house for sale whose price is lower than the average price for the entire neighborhood. These properties have the greatest potential for appreciation. In most housing markets, all the properties in a given area will eventually move toward the average, so the lower-priced houses will be the ones most likely to appreciate the most. Granted, these houses might be underpriced because they need some work, but ultimately, they will pay off.

A new tool can help you evaluate alternative properties for their appreciation potential. Professor Edward Leamer at UCLA developed it, and it is a variation on how stocks are evaluated. When analysts look at stocks, they often focus on the price-earnings ratio as a measure of whether the stock is overvalued or undervalued. The higher the number (especially relative to either the market as a whole or to historical averages), the more likely the stock is to decline in price over time. At the peak of the technology boom of the late 1990s, for example, most tech stocks not only had high price-earnings ratios relative to more traditional stocks, they were trading at historically astronomical price-earnings ratios. It was really no surprise that the market tanked when it did.

Leamer's suggestion is to look at the same measure for real estate. In this case, though, the ratio is the price of the investment property to the annual rental it will earn. This calculation, simple to do, will give you a standard by which you can judge the relative potential for appreciation of different properties in different neighborhoods and even in different cities. In other words, it helps to make sound investment decisions by giving you a tool to measure alternative investments against each other. Here's how it works.

- *Step 1.* Suppose that you're looking at a $200,000 property that will rent for $1200 per month, or $14,400 per year (We can assume that there is no vacancy period, but you can figure in whatever you deem to be a reasonable.) You are also looking at a $100,000 property that will rent for $700 per month, or $8,400 per year. The price-earning ratio for the first property is approximately 14, and the second is approximately 12. The second property appears to be a better candidate for appreciation since it has the lower price-earnings ratio.

- *Step 2*. For a truly effective comparison of the two properties, you need to make a second calculation. You need to look at the price-earning ratio average for both properties relative to those properties in the same neighborhood. If the ratio for the neighborhood of the first house is 20 while the ratio for the second house is 10, then the first property might be the better buy. It is underpriced relative to its surroundings, while the second property is overpriced.

While all this might sound complicated, it's really quite simple. After all, you already know the prices being asked for the properties you are evaluating, and you should know what rent you can charge once you own them. All that's needed is to find out the averages for prices and rents in the immediate neighborhood, and you're done. Any local real estate agent or property manager should be able to help you out with these two numbers.

This is a very important process to go through if you want to choose a property that will propel you on the path to your dream. We can't stress too often the fact that you are using the investment real estate-tax system connection to get you where you eventually want to be. You don't have to love what you own (it's better if you don't), but you do have to evaluate your investments with a cool, detached eye.

The second strategy for finding the most promising investment property is similar to the one developed above for vacation properties. Only instead of looking for the next hot vacation spot, this involves looking for the next hot neighborhood. Like vacation properties, these can evolve in different ways.

The area around the U.S. Capital in Washington, D.C., is a good example of how this strategy can pay off. Until the early 1980s, Capitol Hill was a mixture of rooming houses, low-income properties, and slums. The housing stock was basically sound but had fallen into disrepair as middle-class families moved to the suburbs in Maryland and Virginia. Then the new Washington area subway system (Metro) reached the Hill and the area became more convenient for urban professionals, who decided that living in town was far more interesting than being in the suburbs. Gradually, the properties on the Hill were renovated and upgraded in a pattern fanning out from the Capitol to the east and north. Some of the houses were owner-occupied, and some were rental properties, but all appreciated far faster than the rest of the market. Now the area is filled with restored town houses that sell for well into six figures, and the process continues to spread.

A similar story happened up the road in Baltimore. The Rouse Company revitalized the Inner Harbor by creating a festival park consisting of open space, shops, and restaurants. It served as the centerpiece for tourism to what had been a rather dingy industrial district. But it was definitely a tourist area, with few new residents. When the Baltimore Orioles, and subsequently the Baltimore Ravens, chose to relocate to the Inner Harbor, the area took off as a residential area. Hotels, more restaurants, and more tourist attractions followed, and then the high-rise apartments were created and town houses renovated. The same kind of development, centered on sports occurred in Cleveland with Jacobs Field, the new Municipal Stadium, and Gund Arena (together with the Rock and Roll Hall of Fame), and also in Denver with Coors Field. In all these cases, previously neglected housing that sold inexpensively was suddenly in the center of the action, and prices soared.

The early entrants to the gentrification process in D.C. reaped enormous gains, but they are no different from anyone who buys into neighborhoods that become hot. How do you find them? There are several ways to determine which will be the next hot neighborhood:

- *Visit City Hall.* Much of what happened on Capitol Hill could have been forecast with a review of publicly available information. One of the major drawbacks of the Hill was its separation from the downtown business district. Public transportation was inconvenient, it was too far to walk, and cabs were an extravagance. With the coming of the Metro, all that disappeared. Now the entire city was only a short, inexpensive, and comfortable ride from Capitol Hill. Those subway construction plans were public information; all it took to profit from them was to connect the dots. Take a look at the plans for your town or city.
  - What major employment, transportation, or development projects are on the drawing board?
  - How is the municipality using federal and state grant money to place new facilities?
  - When will these come online and begin to change the location of jobs and residences?

    Answering these questions would have led you to developing neighborhoods in Washington, Baltimore, Cleveland, and Denver, among other places. All of these questions can be answered with some easy research. Besides those directly involved, few people pay much attention to plans drawn up by their government. Yet these can be a roadmap for successful real estate investment for you.
- *Read the newspaper.* Electronic media do a very poor job of reporting the news that is of interest here. At the national level, local detail is lost: You might find out how much money HUD is distributing in

Community Development Block Grants, but not how much is going to your community. At the local level, sensationalism prevails: Robberies, murders, and fires crowd out announcements of new development projects. Use the newspapers as your source of record. If you look at the business pages, you'll get a good sense of what new things that affect the value of housing are happening in your community. It will also give you a good sense of the time frame within which you should be thinking for your investment.

Newspapers will also tell you about trends among young professionals. In any urban environment, these are the folks who will set the trends in entertainment and residence. The random story in the features section of the newspaper about what new clubs are the most popular or where the "urban homesteaders" are living will tell you a lot about where prices will be rising and where they will not.

- *Ask the professionals*. The people who best understand the housing market are those who are in it every day and who depend on it for their livelihood. If you are interested in where prices will rise the most or where the best rental property buys are in your area, seek out Realtors, developers, builders, and city planners. They have a feel for the market and will be able to point you in the direction of the bargains. Try this. Interview a number of the top people in each of these fields and ask them about the future of the community. Try to understand who is now living in the community and whom they think will be living in the community in the near future. Find out which neighborhoods they think are the best values and which neighborhoods will be boosted by the development going on in the community. From their answers, you should be able to form a clear picture of where the opportunities for investment are in your area.

One last thought about investing in real estate in evolving neighborhoods is in order. Remember the old Western movies where Roy Rogers or Gene Autry fought the bad guys (or "evildoers" as modern terminology would name them)? In many cases, the bad guys had gotten the secret plans for the new railroad and were trying to run off the farmers and ranchers along the right-of-way so they could make a huge profit when the railroad company had to buy the land. There's a lesson in that for real estate investment.

In some cases, profit will come from destruction. In other words, sometimes you need to look at buying real estate that will literally be destroyed in a short period of time, property you will not rent out seriously for very long. We mentioned the Metro system in the D.C. area above. In many areas, the train line was built through areas of older housing that had very little attraction as investment property. The maintenance was high, potential rents low, and the neighborhoods lacking most amenities. The neighborhoods along the Metro line in Arlington, Virginia, are a case in point. For the most part, these were old areas with modest houses built in the 1920s and housing low- and middle-income families. They were both low and accurately priced.

Yet, as the Metro arrived, new development was sparked virtually everywhere it went, including Arlington. This dramatically increased the value of the properties in these areas, not for the rental value of the houses, but rather for the value of the land as a development site. Those older properties now disappeared. Whole blocks of houses were torn down to make way for high-rise condominiums, office buildings, and other commercial development. The effect spread as well, with all property within accessible reach of the Metro system increasing in price consistently.

The lesson here is simple. If you can stay a step ahead of public infrastructure development and buy the properties that will disappear to make way for the development and its consequences, you can profitably invest in urban real estate.

Conclusion

We said at the beginning that making money in real estate is a very straightforward process, but one that requires some hard work. In this chapter, we have laid out some of that work, namely the process of selecting the properties that will track or beat the market in appreciation and thus add the most to helping you reach your dream. If you follow the steps laid out here, you have optimized your chances for a successful real estate investment career.

12

Improvements That Will Pay for Themselves over Time

Decorate your home. It gives the illusion that your life is more interesting than it really is. —Charles Schulz

Finding the perfect house is a dream we all share, but it is also a goal that few of us realize. As is the case with most Americans (especially baby boomers), if what we find is imperfect, we work to make it perfect, whether that be people or things. When you find your vacation or investment home, it will meet the criteria we described in Chapter 6 (location, amenities, income potential, etc.). It might not necessarily be the complete house. The kitchen might be too old or too small or the appliances too antiquated. The bathroom might be cramped and lacking in storage space. The bedrooms might not have good bathroom access or privacy.

So what will you do to make it perfect? Or, more pragmatically, which changes offer the best potential for increasing the value of the home by more than those changes cost? That is the topic of this chapter. In it, you will find the best estimates from professionals in the field, as well as tips that will make your renovation as easy as possible. We begin by looking at the process of planning for renovation and improvement. Because costs tend to increase dramatically during the project, getting a firm grip on it from the beginning serves as a protection for you. Secondly, we look at average returns nationally for typical improvements, as well as cost and return figures for specific projects in different areas of the country. Finally, we consider what you really might want to do, indoors and out, to improve the attractiveness of your property for either rental or sale.

There is no set rule as to house size or amenities. The bottom line on any decision to change your vacation or investment home is your own satisfaction and the attractiveness of the home to potential renters. In any investment property (or in a vacation home that you intend to use for retirement), however, you need to balance three important aspects:

- What features most appeal to potential renters?
- What features appeal most to you?
- What features will provide the most yield with the least bother?

The trade-offs here are not necessarily easy. You might value a carefully landscaped yard, but this might be of no value to potential tenants and might require considerable outlay to maintain. Yes, it will provide pleasure to you in retirement, but until then, it's simply a drag on your profitability. Conversely, you might not see the need for more than one "master" suite. But if you want to rent to groups of unrelated individuals, they might value privacy and independence and be attracted to a property that allows this. So, in choosing how to amend your property, be careful not to be swayed by your own preferences. Try to think about what renters want, and then balance that with what you might need should you live in the house later in life.

This chapter provides you with a guide for deciding upon and executing renovations to your investment or vacation home. Take the information presented here—the planning process, national statistics about renovations, and practical advice on what to do—and place it within the context of your own house, market, and personal situations.

The First Steps: Planning the Renovations

Any renovation of an investment property will cause you to spend resources. Whether you hire someone or you do it yourself, there will be both time and money involved. As with any expenditure, you ought to work through a decision process *before* the project starts. No matter what it is that you will be doing to the house, ask yourself the following questions:

1. *How long do I intend to own this house?* The payback you receive for any improvement depends on the length of time you hold the property.

The longer you plan to own the house, the lower the annual rate of return, and the more you will spend to maintain the improvements. If your time horizon is shorter, these conditions are reversed. Answering this question will not only help you decide what to do to the house, it will, more importantly, affect the quality of the labor and material you choose to put into the improvement.

2. *Will I ever live in this house?* The type of improvements you make to the property will largely be dictated by whether you are seeking to please a tenant or yourself. Even if you use the property two weeks a year as a vacation home, you will still want to create a house that attracts renters, while reserving some private, secure space where you can keep your things. In addition, the degree to which you use the house will also dictate the quality of the renovation.

3. *Who will do the work?* You might want to do some or all of the renovations yourself. The extent to which you will do this determines the ambitiousness of the project as well as the choice of an outside contractor. Not all trades people will abide by the participation of an amateur. (The old construction joke goes: "My fee is $50 an hour if I do the work, $100 if you want to watch, and $500 if you want to help.") Remember that the amount of time the job takes is important. The finished basement on your own home can take a year or two; on an investment property, time truly is money. If you are going to do any of the renovations yourself, make sure you have the skill and the time to do it as quickly as possible.

4. *How will I pay for the improvements?* Your payback from any improvements to an investment property will come over time from rental income and any appreciation in the value of the property *attributable to the improvement*. That means your money will be tied up for a considerable period of time. The cost of committing these funds must be minimized if you are to realize the maximum benefit from improving the property. Consider these three options, which represent the most usual methods of paying for improvements:

   a. Transfer assets from other uses. If you have savings, they can be tapped to pay for the improvements.

   b. Take out a line of credit secured by your primary residence. This gives you the convenience of borrowing funds only as you spend them.

   c. Roll the costs of the improvements into the financing of the investment property. In this way, you can amortize the improvements over a 15- or 30-year period.

In each case, the cost of financing can be measured by the interest rate either paid on the mortgage or line of credit or foregone by transferring assets. It might also be effective to compare this cost with the rates of return cited below for specific improvements to determine whether it's worth doing at all.

5. *Do I have dependable help?* When you employ construction help, it's important to find reliable, honest, and efficient workers. If you have used outside help in the past, you probably have a roster of dependable (and a list of undependable) people. Then you need to ask whether they have the requisite skills to do the job you need done. If you don't have experience in using outside help, there are a variety of ways to choose good help.

- Your primary source, of course, is friends who might have used others in the past. The local Chamber of Commerce can also help.
- Ask for references and contact them to assure yourself that you have someone who can complete the job on time, charge reasonable fees, and produce quality work.
- Be sure to match the job with the experience. Most tradesmen can do a variety of tasks, but invariably, they are better at some things than others.
- Make sure that whomever you use is bonded. This is not a catchall, but it does offer a reasonable protection against any problems.
- Determine who will actually do the work. Will the owner of the company or his most experienced help do the work, or will it be farmed out to relatively inexperienced workers?
- Work as closely as possible with the contractor. Be clear about the plans for the improvement, have a common understanding of materials to be used, and jointly agree on the projected costs and timetables.

When you have answered these questions to your own satisfaction, you have a plan to renovate your investment property. And you need to stick with the plan. Any home improvement project carries with it the danger of spiraling out of control; discipline prevents that from happening. The next step is to evaluate alternative improvement projects.

The Value of Investing in Your Investment Property

The two greatest concerns facing any homeowner considering improvement or renovation are the utility of the change and the ability to recoup the investment. For investment property, we add a third concern, the ability of any improvement to attract rental income and thus improve the return on investment. The impact of any home improvement on rental income and ultimate sales price is not the same in all cases. Rather, it depends on the state of the house, the location of the house, and the profile of the rental market.

- Some changes are absolutely necessary. A defective roof might render a property unrentable and therefore must be repaired.
- Climate might make some changes more valuable than others. A vacation rental property might be more lucrative with a pool, while a residential rental investment in the Northeast might never return the money the pool would cost.
- Making improvements that move the house out of line with the neighborhood might never return their cost. Adding a $100,000 addition to a $75,000 house where all the other houses in the neighborhood are also worth $75,000 is usually not a good idea. But making the same change to a $500,000 house will usually yield as much or more than the cost in ultimate value.
- The same project done in two different metropolitan areas might cost different amounts and thus yield different returns. For example, identical master suite additions would typically cost 42 percent more in Minneapolis than in Tampa.[1]
- Adding a second master suite to a house in a market with groups of singles might pay off, but doing it in a family-dominated market might not.

As they say in the weight loss infomercials, "typical results might vary." Before you look at the statistical results for the return on home improvements, understand that they must be adjusted for your own circumstance in property, location, and market. Table 12-1 shows the national averages for the rate of return for 15 potential investments in vacation or investment properties. In the case of kitchens, bathrooms, master suites, and kitchens, two levels of expenditure, midrange and upscale are identified. In later sections, we define these. A value of 100 percent means that the investment is fully recouped in the sales price.

These figures are derived for renovations done by homeowners on owner-occupied houses. They represent the considered opinion of real estate and construction professionals in markets throughout the United States. Notice that none of the national averages indicate that

---

[1] *Remodeling Online, 2002 Cost vs. Value Report.*

TABLE 12-1. Percentage of Cost Recouped from Various Improvements (national averages, 2002)

Improvement	Percentage Recouped
Bathroom Addition, midrange	94
Bathroom Addition, upscale	81
Bathroom Remodel, midrange	88
Bathroom Remodel, upscale	81
Major Kitchen Remodel, midrange	67
Major Kitchen Remodel, upscale	80
Master Suite, midrange	75
Master Suite, upscale	77
Two-story Addition	94
Basement Remodel	79
Family Room Addition	79
Siding Replacement	79
Window Replacement, midrange	74
Window Replacement, upscale	77
Roof Replacement	67

Source: *Remodeling Online, op. cit.*

the investment expenditure can be fully recovered by the sale of the house. As we indicate in later sections, this is not necessarily the case for all sections of the country; in many, average results are consistently above 100 percent.

For vacation and investment homes, however, the total return from the investment must come from both the impact of the renovation on the sales price and the ongoing return during the holding period. If the property is held as an investment, the extent that the rent on the house can be increased because of the improvement increases the cash flow from the property and thus increases the return from the improvement. More subtly, if you buy a vacation retreat, any improvement that increases your enjoyment of it is a nontangible but real return to investment in the property.

To illustrate, let's say Jane decided she needed to diversify her portfolio and bought, for $125,000, a three-bedroom, two-bath, single-family house to use as a rental unit. She put $20,000 down and took out a mortgage for $105,000. To enhance the attractiveness of the house as a rental, she spent $6000 to renovate the kitchen, expanding it and increasing its utility as both a food preparation area and as a gathering place. She knocked down a wall between the kitchen and the family room/living room and replaced it with a long island containing a sink so that the island could be used for both food preparation and dining. She also replaced the appliances, increased the number of electrical outlets, and painted. In addition, she spent $2000 to repair a roof over the sun porch that had been leaking. The renovation of the kitchen allowed her to charge an additional $25 per month rent, thus paying for the kitchen over a two-year period.[2] Three years after buying the house, she sold it for $145,000. The real estate market at the time was good, so it's unclear how much the kitchen and the roof added to the sales price, but it can reasonably be argued that these improvements more than paid for themselves over the three-year holding period.

Specific Changes

In this section, we break down the national averages into regional cost and return factors for specific types of renovations and improvements. In this section, we look at bathroom additions and remodels, master suite additions, kitchen remodels, and roof replacement. In each case, we have chosen a particular metropolitan area in each of four areas of the United States, corresponding to Census Bureau regions: East, Midwest, South, and West. In each case, two figures are cited. The first number represents a midrange bathroom addition, the second an upscale project. The cities chosen represent a midrange for the region; for example, the cost percentage recouped in the West ranges from 205 in Los Angeles to 61 in Denver for a midrange bathroom addition. The estimates are not meant to be definitive, but are presented to give you an idea of what you can expect generally in the way of cost and return from any renovation project.

Bathrooms: Additions and Remodeling

Bathrooms have, in recent years, become multifunction rooms. While serving their basic purpose, they are, especially in new construction, quasi-gathering places as well as important individual space. There has

---

[2] If you consider the time value of money, the payback period (at 2002 interest rate levels) is about three years.

been a tendency in new construction to build the bathroom bigger and include more fixtures as well as more space. Older bathrooms suffer in comparison to newer houses, and the attractiveness of a vacation or investment property can be crucially affected by the way its bathrooms stack up against others in the neighborhood.

Bathroom additions tend to be the most profitable of all discretionary house projects. (Obviously, a leaking roof has more urgency.) Regardless of the use of the house, there never seem to be enough bathrooms! Adding additional bathroom facilities will clearly increase the value of an investment property. If it is a residential rental, another bathroom increases the flexibility you have in attracting tenants, whether they are families or groups of unrelated individuals. For vacation homes, the convenience of additional bath facilities, especially in beach areas, makes the house more attractive. Table 12-2 sets out the costs and rates of return for the addition of a bathroom, at two levels. The first is a full 6-×-8-foot bath added to a home with one and a half baths. This is a midrange bathroom. The second number represents the addition of a full bath to a master suite, which includes separate shower and whirlpool tub. This is the upscale bathroom.[3]

TABLE 12-2 Bathroom Addition Project Cost and Cost Recouped in Selected Metropolitan Areas, 2002

Metro Area	Project Cost	Percentage Recouped
Atlanta	$13,615	94
	36,329	96
Cleveland	16,098	81
	38,562	74
Philadelphia	16,178	103
	38,756	93
San Diego	16,216	100
	38,726	94
National Average	15,058	94
	37,639	81

Source: *Remodeling Online, op .cit.*

[3] A full description of these and the other changes we consider can be found in *Remodeling Online, op. cit.*

Improvements That Will Pay for Themselves Over Time

National patterns for rates of return are quite interesting. Returns tend to be higher in larger metropolitan areas, even though costs are seemingly unrelated to city size. In part, this is a result of higher prices in larger metro markets, where small percentage changes in value can result in large dollar returns. Because rents tend to be higher in these areas as well, the addition of a bathroom can yield a relatively high rate of return when the additional cash flow through rental is included in the calculation of return.

The second impression that comes from the statistics is the large degree of intraregional variation among metropolitan areas. In the East for example, Philadelphia might represent a midpoint, but returns range from 195 in Fairfield County, Connecticut, to 58 in Pittsburgh, Pennsylvania, for the midrange bathroom addition. The range is similar for the upscale bathroom addition and also within the other regions from metro area to metro area. This last factor reinforces the need to look closely at local conditions when considering a renovation project.

The returns to bathroom remodeling tend to be lower, as a national average, than those for adding a new bathroom. This is sensible considering the fact that a remodel, even if it expands the existing bathroom, adds less capacity than a new room addition. Table 12-3 displays the results of *Remodeling Online*'s 2002 survey for our selected cities. The top figure,

TABLE 12-3 Bathroom Remodeling Project Cost and Cost Recouped in Selected Metropolitan Areas, 2002

Metro Area	Project Cost	Percentage Recouped
Atlanta	$ 8,980	99
	21,394	119
Cleveland	7,984	76
	23,649	62
Philadelphia	10,486	118
	23,941	104
San Diego	10,314	80
	23,730	105
National Average	9,720	88
	22,639	91

Source: *Remodeling Online, op. cit.*

the midrange remodel, updates and replaces the fixtures in an existing bathroom at least 25 years old. The upscale version expands a 5-×-7-foot bathroom to 9-×-9 and replaces the fixtures as well.

Once again, the intraregional variation for bathroom remodeling is large. Here, the age of the housing stock is an issue. In areas dominated by older stock, newly remodeled bathrooms can stand out, while in other areas, where new construction is the norm, even a remodeled older bathroom carries little appeal in terms of house value. Thus, for the midrange remodel, the return percentage is 115 in Los Angeles, but only 56 in Phoenix.

Master Suite

The master suite offers space and privacy that greatly enhances the enjoyment of a home and the attractiveness to renters. In fact, in the case where the house will be rented to groups of unrelated individuals, multiple master suites might be a requirement for profitability. Creating a master suite is a major undertaking in both time and money. It represents not the addition of a single room, but also of a bathroom. In many cases, wiring must be upgraded to support an entertainment or work center, and closet space tends to take on the dimensions of yet another room.

Clearly, creating a master suite for your own use might take on a different meaning from creating the space for tenants. In the latter case, costs will be less and the design simpler, and perhaps smaller. But if you are even considering living in this house eventually, you will want to take care either to design it to your own tastes or create a space than can easily be further renovated when you want to move into it. These decisions need to be made before embarking on the project; after the job is started, any changes will require extra expenditure, often at higher rates than you might find comfortable.

Table 12-4 lists the average costs and returns on the addition of a master suite to a two- or three-bedroom house in different areas of the United States, for both a midrange addition and an upscale addition.[4] In both cases, the suites include sleeping area, walk-in closets, and bathroom with separate shower and whirlpool tub. This project represents, by far, the most ambitious renovation that you can do to a vacation or investment property. In addition, the return on this change ranks in the lower half, nationally, of all potential projects. In part, this is because of the cost. Embarking on a project of this size, even in a relatively high-priced

[4] As noted earlier, descriptions of each of the projects presented can be found at *Remodeling Online, op. cit.*

TABLE 12-4 Master Suite Addition Project Cost and Cost Recouped in Selected Metropolitan Areas, 2002

Metro Area	Project Cost	Percentage Recouped
Atlanta	$ 62,650	91
	124,835	91
Cleveland	73,526	61
	136,529	60
Philadelphia	72,960	84
	138,838	83
San Diego	73,769	80
	136,685	88
National Average	69,173	75
	131,471	77

Source: *Remodeling Online, op. cit.*

house, represents an addition that the market cannot bear as well as smaller changes. Thus the percentage return will be lower.

But, in part, this low ranking is the result of the idiosyncratic nature of master suite additions. By their nature, they are designed to suit the owner of the property (whether the owner will live in it or not) and thus will vary widely in their attractiveness to either renters or prospective buyers. It is more the case here than it is with bathrooms or kitchens.

Interestingly, as the table suggests, returns to the addition of a master suite tend to be markedly lower in the Midwest, with the high percentage return being in Chicago at 83 and the low in Columbus, Ohio, at 40 for the midrange master suite.

The magnitude of the commitment to a master suite addition is great and thus requires more careful scrutiny than other potential changes. Gauging the market is very important here, not only in choosing to undertake the project, but also in deciding how much to put into it. Creating a house that is significantly at odds with the market, either by underinvesting in the property or overinvesting in it, is a recipe for disaster. Building a master suite that makes your home more elaborate than its competitors will reduce your profitability. Either potential renters will be unwilling to pay rents that make sense given your expenditure, or buyers will be unwilling to pay the price you require to make your expected rate of return. This is the both the most expensive and the trickiest of renovations to undertake.

Kitchen Remodel

Like bathrooms, kitchens have become more than just for cooking and eating. They are, increasingly, gathering places where entertainment accompanied by food takes place. In addition, after the attacks of September 11, 2001, Americans have sought entertainment closer to home or in the home. This has made the size and amenities of the kitchen even more important. A flexible, up-to-date and well-appointed kitchen is an extremely attractive feature to prospective tenants, vacationing families and groups, and, ultimately, prospective buyers.

The numbers presented in Table 12-5 represent averages for a particular pair of remodels. The first number is a "midrange" remodel of an out-of-date 200-square-foot kitchen, bringing design, cabinetry, appliances, and fixtures. The second is an "upscale" remodel in which the quality of all the components is higher. The two specifications are used to give a basis for comparison across areas of the country. But they also show the range that is possible in the remodeling of a kitchen. Various quality levels are far more available in kitchen appliances and fixtures than, for example,

TABLE 12-5 Kitchen Remodel Projects Costs and Costs Recouped in Selected Metropolitan Areas, 2002

Metro Area	Project Costs	Percentage Recouped
Atlanta	$41,201	88
	68,181	98
Cleveland	44,546	68
	71,715	64
Philadelphia	45,111	91
	72,272	96
San Diego	44,971	69
	72,333	84
National Average	43,213	67
	70,368	80

Source: *Remodeling Online, op. cit.*

in the construction of a master suite or in bathroom fixtures. You can thus choose to move along a design and construction spectrum and do more or less than is indicated in the reference remodels.

Population density appears to be related to return here as it was for bathrooms. In each of the four regions of the United States, the highest returns are in the most populous metro areas and the lowest in smaller areas. In the South, the highest return percentage to a kitchen remodel is in Washington, D.C. at 111 and the lowest in Richmond, Virginia, at 41. This is again a function of numbers. Remodeled kitchens are attractive but somewhat specialized. Having a larger market increases the potential that some renter or buyer will find the new kitchen irresistible.

Roof Replacement

Roofs are sneaky. They are not obviously amenities, nor do they lend themselves to advertising. No one has ever bought a house or rented one because of the roof. Yet, if quality is not a selling point, stability is. A bad roof will make even the best of houses unlivable. So it is a necessary evil and one that the owner of an investment or vacation home must heed.

In that sense, the rate of return on a new roof is infinite, because it means the difference between any return on investment and a significant loss. Thus the numbers in Table 12-6 simultaneously overstate and understate the return from a new roof. If you don't need one, any expenditure is wasted; if you need one, no expenditure is unjustified. Not surprisingly, the return to investment in a new roof falls relatively low in the spectrum of potential changes to the investment or vacation house. This represents the lack of "sexiness" that characterizes new roofs.

TABLE 12-6 Roof Replacement Project Costs and Costs Recouped in Selected Metropolitan Areas, 2002

Metro Area	Project Cost	Percentage Recouped
Atlanta	$ 8,955	62
Cleveland	13,008	62
Philadelphia	14,832	66
San Diego	12,576	84
National Average	11,399	67

Source: *Remodeling Online, op. cit.*

The interregional variation here is more striking than the intraregional variation. Roof replacement yields more cost recoupment in warmer areas than it does in colder areas, with Los Angeles having a percentage cost return of 137. It's unclear why this is so, but if accurate, suggests that paying attention to the roof on your vacation house might in fact pay off for you.

Outside the House

Possibly the most dangerous improvements to consider are those outside the structure itself. Unless your investment or vacation house is a condominium, you will be torn between conflicting feelings. Your pride of ownership will pull you toward sinking money into landscaping so that the property you own will be a showplace. Your practical side, though, will realize that landscaping in an investment property is money wasted. No renter, either regular tenant or vacationer, will place any real value on landscaping. For the most part, their attention will be centered on the interior or the location of the house, not its immediate surroundings.

How you resolve this dilemma will help determine the profitability you will derive from ownership. You can spend all you want on the exterior decor of the house, but there are only two things that pay for themselves.

- *Clean up the grounds*. No one wants to live in a sty, or in a jungle. Spend the money to create and maintain a clean, neat lot. Cut back overgrown bushes and trees, plant a continuous (i.e., bare patch free) lawn and remove all eyesores. If you want to go further, hire a regular maintenance company and/or install an automatic sprinkler system.
- *Create accessibility*. Widen the walkways approaching the house and pave them over with concrete or stones. Also add sufficient exterior lighting to promote safety. This gives the property eye appeal and the attractiveness of being a safe place.

Other Ideas to Consider

Besides the standard types of renovation and improvement, it might be profitable to look ahead, especially if your holding period is long. Consider these four aspects of how people live.

- *Americans are aging*. In the future, access ramps, wide doors and entryways, wheelchair-accessible counters and workspaces, and grip bars will be regular requirements of the housing market. If you are building a vacation home or investment property, think about designing it in such a way that these features are built in. If you are remodeling or adding to your house, you can do the same during construction. As a practical matter, none of these changes will significantly affect the cost of construction. Ensuring that these features are part of your house will enhance the appeal of your house for both rental and sale and protect your investment.

- *We are a wired people.* Increasingly, there is a demand for housing that is capable of supporting Internet usage, home offices and home entertainment centers. When you renovate a kitchen or a bathroom or add a master suite, take the opportunity to upgrade the wiring in the entire house. It will be a significant selling point now and a required feature in the future.
- *Nesting is in.* More and more Americans are centering their lives on the home. Entertaining there is becoming more important than going out, and spending money on the house and its capabilities is eclipsing that vacation in Europe. So add a deck onto your vacation or investment house if it lacks one. There are no hard figures on the return it will produce, but expert opinion seems to feel that it will pay for itself. This is particularly important, of course, in vacation homes.
- *We are security conscious.* Urban dwellers have always been concerned about their safety, and now terrorism has been added to street crime and burglary as a concern. Adding a security system to the house will enhance its attractiveness to potential renters. The cost of the system can be added back into the rent without much tenant resistance; they'll understand its value.

Conclusion

Regardless of what you buy, you're going to have to work on it. It's in our nature to tinker, or pay someone to tinker, with the houses we own. In the case of an investment property, the process of altering the house is complicated. It's complicated by the confusion between our tastes and the things that will attract tenants. It's complicated by the end use to which we plan to put the house. It's complicated by the variations in what makes sense by location and market conditions. And finally it's complicated by the budgets we set for the investments we make.

Perhaps the most important things to take from this chapter are these:

- It's crucial to plan before you act. Laying out all the factors that will affect your decision, weighing them for their importance relative to each other, and then gathering information that allows you to flesh out the alternatives will short-circuit a lot of problems and save a lot of money. The five questions we lay out in the second section of this chapter are your guide to creating your plan. Use them in whatever renovation decisions you make.

- Renovating and improving your house is not an all-or-nothing process. For every area that you consider, there is a range of expenditures that you can make to increase both the cash flow and long-run value of your investment or vacation property. Phasing improvements or choosing components of a renovation offer a lot of possibilities to spend more or less. The numbers we cite in this chapter are reference numbers only and are intended for comparison purposes. They do not represent any amounts that must be spent.

13

Tips for Subdividing Your Property

The Bible tells us to love our neighbors, and also to love our enemies, probably because generally they are the same people.—Gilbert K. Chesterton

If you have purchased a traditional second home or are moving through any of the stages of The New Second home—Interim, Cocoon, Ultimate—you could be sitting on a gold mine without even knowing it. How and when you mine for this gold could increase your chances of striking the mother lode. However, if you have the vague notion that the value and potential of your property has risen in the past few years but have done nothing to ascertain that value, you could turn out to be a big-time loser whose nest egg is now resting near Humpty Dumpty at the base of the wall.

In previous chapters, we examined conventional methods and explored new avenues for increasing income and equity by maximizing the potential of your second home's actual structure. In this chapter, we will step back and take a broader view of the lay of the land—the dirt that holds or adjoins your Cocoon or Ultimate spot. How you manage that land could provide you with significant current or future income you never have considered.

The keys to potential success are understanding what you originally purchased, staying current on ever-changing land-use legislation and communicating civilly, politely, respectfully, and amicably with neighbors and local county decision makers. The "how" can be absolutely as valuable as the "when."

For example, let's say your 5-acre waterfront cabin retreat has been rezoned so that 2.5-acre parcels now qualify for a building site. You sell your home in the city and move into the cabin and use it as your primary residence. You might not wish to divide your property, but it usually makes sense to research what is possible. That way, if you decide at some future date to sell all or part of the parcel, you can show the potential buyer that your property is/can be two separate and independent pieces of property. Remember that local zoning ordinances can change faster than federal tax guidelines. What is dividable or adjusted today might not work tomorrow—for a variety of reasons ranging from too much or too little water, endangered species, and basic lot size. For example, under an old California law, landowners could use old records suggesting their property had been subdivided differently at one time and use those records to force a jurisdiction to issue a certificate of compliance. This "loophole" in the law, according to the state, "has enabled speculators to reap excessive profits on properties financed in large part through state parks bonds and federal funds." Even though a new proposal, aimed at halting the practices of one large corporation, makes it nearly impossible for property owners to make lot line adjustments that are necessary for them to sell, lease, or obtain a mortgage on the property, the bill was passed into law. If you do choose to divide, and are successful in the subdivision process, you could easily find that the market value of your 2.5-acre second lot far surpasses what you originally paid for the entire five acres.

So you did decide to sell your extra 2.5-acre lot . . . what would be the best way of maximizing your profit? Once you subdivide your property, the portion without the house on it can no longer be considered part of your principal residence. Hence, it will be subject to capital gains tax, probably at the relatively new rate of 15 percent (which easily could change the day this book is published!). The profit on the newly created 2.5-acre parcel would be the sales price less the cost. Your cost of the new lot would include all the subdivision expenses involved to create it. Plus, you have to calculate what portion of the cost of the original five acres you have allotted to the new 2.5-acre piece. That number will be your cost basis. However, the amount you allocate to the new parcel of land does not have to be equal to the value given to the other 2.5-acre piece. If the

10 Questions

Before you pull out your checkbook and begin paying for professionals to help subdivide your property, here are 10 basic questions to ask any planning department:

1. Will the proposed division require a public hearing or planning board approval?
2. How does an applicant get on the agenda for the next meeting?
3. Will the jurisdiction require a survey of the entire lot prior to any divisions?
4. How many months does it take to receive subdivision approval?
5. What are the minimum lot requirements?
6. Where would you obtain a water availability letter? This indicates where the water source is (public water source, individual well, or community well).
7. What is the minimum (square feet) buildable lot area?
8. What areas are not allowed to be counted in a buildable lot? (easements, wetlands)
9. What common restrictions will be imposed by the jurisdiction on the proposed new lot?
10. If the proposed new lot is not adjacent to a public road, what is the minimum right-of-way width required to access the new lot?

new parcel has a far superior beach, better waterfront access, a more sweeping view of the water and mountains, the new parcel could be worth far greater that its partner with the rundown cabin. In fact, you will want the basis of the new property to be as high as possible so that you can offset the proceeds from the sale. Remember, because you created a separate tax parcel, the new piece is no longer included in your primary residence exclusion. If Uncle Sam challenges you at tax time, you will need to show how you arrived at the cost basis for the new parcel. In this case, maximizing your cost reduces your taxable exposure. The eventual sale of the 2.5 acres with cabin would be tax free (up to $500,000, $250,000 for a single person) because it qualifies as your primary residence.

In many popular rural areas, buildable land has become so scarce that both big-time developers and small builders are hiring real estate professionals to scout potential sites for them. Older subdivisions—those that were platted decades ago but have remained untouched—often have dodged most growth management limitations for building. These sites, quite common in Florida, Nevada, Maryland, Idaho, and other states, have been "grandfathered" in to the previously relaxed development codes. Owners with land in these areas might be pleasantly surprised to discover that their property fits the criteria for subdividing when other parcels in the immediate area do not. And, if your lot has been on the books long enough and the local zoning allows for additional units, then it might be possible to divide it even if there are environmental concerns. Sometimes environmental guidelines restrict the placement of future dwellings but not the number. Homes can be "clustered" away from a sensitive area without curtailing the number of structures.

Obviously, the best way to increase your chances for a profitable sale of a portion of your land is to offer a builder a "no risk" situation. The current landowner takes on the chores and expense of subdividing and pays for a building site application (or approved septic design). The owner also makes sure that there is adequate access to the site, adequate water available, and power close by. These items, plus a sunny, easily staged site and good soil conditions (no threat of erosion) make the property an easier sale to a new owner or builder. Be prepared, however, to wait months—sometimes years—for your project's approval. New legislation scrutinizing the permit process, coupled with an increased number of applications, have overwhelmed many planning departments, stretching simply short-plat subdivisions to waiting periods as long as two years. Depending on location and the need for a separate onsite septic system (no public sewer available), a proposed four- or five-parcel split could take up to three or four years.

New Friends at Your Local City Hall

If you decide to enhance an outbuilding, build on a newly created lot, or attempt a simple subdivision, you will be spending a lot of time at your local city hall from the beginning of the subdivision process until the end of the building process. Therefore, it is crucial that you educate yourself on their processes and identify the most helpful players.

For the initial information-gathering process, you can do two things that are both equally illuminating. First, you can take a local developer to lunch. Bring a legal pad, and ask a lot of questions. What are some pet peeves of the city? Who is the REAL decision maker? Are there any new codes or changes coming along in the next year or two that would affect

In the Zone

Zoning regulations govern the type of structure that can be erected, the dimensions, and even the material used on the exterior. If you want to subdivide, and then eventually build in a rural setting, check the availability of public utility services and the cost of bringing those services to the site. Local planning and zoning boards can provide information about proposed development that could change your quiet country lane into a busy street. Here are our Top 10 Zoning Terms to assist you with a building-department language you might have never have spoken:

Subdivision

Generally, the division of land, lot, tract, or parcel into two or more lots, parcels, plats, or sites, or other divisions of land for the purpose of sale, lease, offer, or development, whether immediate or future. The term shall also include the division of residential, commercial, industrial, agricultural, or other land whether by deed, metes and bounds description, lease, map, plat, or other instrument.

Short Plat

In some states, small subdivisions usually divided into four or fewer lots. Number of lots could be extended to nine in some incorporated areas.

Variance

Permission obtained from governmental zoning authorities to build a structure or conduct a use that is expressly prohibited by current zoning laws; an exception to the zoning laws.

Cluster Development

A development design technique that concentrates buildings in specific areas on a site to allow the remaining land to be used for recreation, common open space, and preservation of environmentally sensitive areas.

Density

The ratio of land area to improvement area (structures). Typically stated as the number of units per acre.

Easement

The right of a person, government agency, or public utility company to use public or private land owned by another for a specific purpose. A grant of one or more of the property rights by the owner to, or for the use by, the public, a corporation, or another person or entity.

Setback

The required minimum horizontal distance between the building line and the related front, side, or rear property line. The minimum horizontal distance between the lot or property line and the nearest front, side, or rear line of the building (as the case might be), including terraces or any covered projection thereof, excluding steps.

Transfer of Development Rights

The conveyance of development rights by deed, easement, or other legal instrument authorized by local law to another parcel of land and the recording of that conveyance.

Zero Lot Line

The location of a building on a lot in such a manner that one or more of the building's sides rests directly on a lot line.

Zoning

The regulation of structures and uses of property within designated districts or zones. Zoning regulates and influences the use of land, building height, and setbacks.

your project? Most importantly, which planner does the developer recommend using to guide you through the actual subdivision process? Individual planners have reputations of being helpful, accommodating, and great mentors in the process. Others have the reputation of being adversarial. The planner you use can save you thousands of dollars and months of time. Learn from someone else's experience instead of recreating the wheel. The second method of gathering information is to go to city council meetings and any other public planning meeting. The hearing examiner specifically addresses individual issues that need resolution. If you have limited time (as we all do), just attend a handful of hearing examiner meetings to determine what issues frequently come up and how the city resolves them. This gives you the benefit of foresight so that you can avoid the obvious landmines.

Once you have determined which city planner you want to steer you through the process, cultivate that person like a delicate flower. While most city employees cannot accept gifts or special favors, go out of your way to let them know how much you appreciate their time and expertise. Stated appreciation for city employees always is lacking and a few kind words at city hall—especially in the presence of other workers and consumers—never hurts. A handwritten personal note every now and then, just a few short sentences, often paves the way to a fruitful relationship. You know you have the genuine appreciation of a city employee when you receive an unsolicited phone call offering information that has just surfaced that the employee knows would benefit your case. If you treat city employees as the crucial keys to your project, they could open many doors.

Beyond The Great Divide: Will They Still Be Neighborly?

Friendly neighbors are valuable assets. They can offer their experiences at city hall, point you toward, or steer you from, specific officials in that often-overwhelming place. However, it might be wise to refrain from discussing any possible subdivision until you have done all the research you need. Neighbors will naturally be very curious about what you are doing and how it will impact them. Getting as much information as possible from the city first will help you when discussing the details with your neighbors. By the way, the city *will* post a public notice when the subdivision is pending. Therefore, it is wise to talk to your neighbors before this step. Otherwise, the natural response will be a negative—they could compare your goal of creating an extra residential building lot with bringing a busy strip mall to their backdoor. Unless you are open and above board, they will think you were trying to pull this off while they were away for a family wedding. When the public hearing rolls around, be prepared to hear every conceivable reason why you should not proceed with this property division from angry people who lack information.

Once you have your ducks in a row, have a casual barbecue or a little dessert party at your home and inform the neighbors of your plans. Continue to emphasize that you will retain the character of the neighborhood, or even improve it. Your intent is to keep all privacy intact and to increase future property values for all. Have a preliminary drawing for each neighbor attending and encourage their questions. If they pose questions you can't answer, let them know you will be forwarding the information when it becomes available. Be prepared—remember that most people detest the idea of change. No matter how conscientious you are, there will still probably be some grumpy responses. Remain calm, ensure them that you are working through proper channels, and tell them you will be around to make sure the project has the least negative impact on the neighborhood. And don't be surprised that some of your neighbors have contemplated doing this themselves. You might have done all of their research for them! They will want all your advice as they explore a similar process. Follow this casual gathering with personal, handwritten notes to thank everyone for coming. Even send out notes to those who could not attend, and let them know that they can contact you at another time to ask any questions. Lastly, be sincere. When you tell your neighbors that the subdivision design has the least impact on the neighbors as possible, mean it. Be the neighbor that keeps his word, follows through—the kind of neighbor you would like to have. You've heard it a million times—to have good neighbors, you have to be a good neighbor. That involves becoming active in the community, meeting other people with similar interests, and offering a helping hand.

ADUs spell G-O-L-D

Accessory Dwelling Units, or ADUs, are pure gold. They can add rental income, increase property value, or provide additional family space without the time and red tape accompanying a full-blown subdivision. These typically are detached living spaces (similar to the usually attached "lock-offs" in Chapter 8) on properties that already have a primary dwelling. Even though these secondary units often appear to be on their own parcel of land, the ADUs do not require an actual property division yet provide excellent rental opportunities and generally increase the value of the entire property. A slick way to increase the value of your property is to convert the old tool shed, barn, or garage into a livable space. Depending on where you live, you might find that your zoning already allows two dwellings on the same lot, or you might find that you can get the necessary approval through a special application.

Newly constructed ADUs come in different forms. Carriage houses have become extremely popular, as have cute cottages and narrow two-story townhouses with a small footprint. Depending on city codes, ADUs are usually limited to a specific size, height, and footprint. For example, some jurisdictions might allow an ADU to contain 800 square feet of actual

Becoming a Convert

Converting an existing building from a nonoccupied use (garden shed) into residential living space (carriage house) typically requires several things to meet the building codes. Code requirements vary from area to area, but here's a quick look at five basic considerations:

It's All About Energy—Windows and exterior doors typically have to meet certain minimum requirements for efficiency, and attics, walls, and floors will all need to be insulated. If the present building won't allow some areas to be insulated to code, the building department might "trade off" for heavier insulation, or upgrades, elsewhere.

Warm and Cozy—You will need to research and implement a proper heating system to adequately warm the building for occupancy.

Coming and Going—Also known as ingress and egress. The windows in your sleeping areas will need to meet minimum "egress" requirements so that an occupant can get out in the event of an emergency. You'll be required to have at least one main exit door.

Cranking up the Juice—Your upgrade must include additional electrical wiring outlets, including two 20-amp circuits in most kitchen areas. The placement of the main panel needs to meet specific clearance guidelines. Sleeping areas will need smoke alarms.

Bathroom Movement—If you have to go outside to change your mind, your bathroom is too small. Make sure you know the standards for bathroom clearances—the expectations will be greater than you think.

living space (not including hallways or closets). While a very large deck can increase living space during warm weather months, the deck might also reduce the size of the building given the allowable dimensions of the footprint. Why an ADU? A simple subdivision can sometimes take up to two years in some regions. During this time, you create added value to your primary lot (appraised value goes up, thereby increasing your equity stake) while pulling in immediate rental income. An ADU also permits you to show your mortgage company an additional income stream when determining your maximum loan amount. When determining the size, style, and placement of the ADU, keep in mind the future placement of property lines, potential expansion of the main house, utility lines, and neighbor privacy. The city has open space requirements, as well as setback guidelines, so be aware of how the ADU will affect your bigger picture.

Too Many Miles, Too Little Interest

Some folks move away and have management firms look after their holdings. While such services are more common for in-city apartment houses and commercial buildings, they also range to remote getaways and vacant land. While competent managers can usually solve most problems regarding improved property, keeping current with the potential of vacant land can be another story. In many areas of the country, growth management regulations have flip-flopped the past two decades. Building restrictions that were absolutely taboo 10 years ago might now be acceptable, and vice versa. To compound the problem, some jurisdictions have not been very communicative regarding current building codes. Most of the time, it's up to the consumer to ascertain how a specific site can be developed, and when. For example, there are forested areas in the many states that cannot be developed during certain months of the year because of bird migrations and nesting patterns. Eagle, falcon, owl, heron, and other habitats are common, curtailing and sometimes even eliminating the possibility of building during specific seasons—if at all. Attempts to protect other animals from development in a variety of environments have been well documented.

When it comes to personal residences—the primary assets of most people in this country—part-time occupancy can have good and bad aspects. Perhaps you welcome the break from your neighbors, yet you often miss out on important local assessment votes and explanations, personnel changes in local businesses and restaurants, and critical gossip. Like new federal income tax guidelines, property laws change all the time. Local zoning, land use and restrictive covenants need to be checked periodically so that property owners can determine what effect those conditions might have on their real estate.

While landowners often bemoan a seemingly unfair change in property use, they sometimes blow a golden opportunity in situations they clearly can control. For example, a retired couple that spends winters in Arizona and summers in Southern California wrote regarding their 76 acres of forested land in Idaho that they've owned for 27 years. The property had appreciated greatly in recent times due to a growth boom and a zoning change, but the couple thought it was still limited to 20-acre minimums. The couple did not discover this until after they had entered into an agreement to sell the 76 acres that five-acre lots were now permitted in the area. According to the couple, an agent representing three investors had put the deal together. The investors planned to divide the property and sell parcels. The agent already had several potential customers interested in purchasing the smaller parcels and stood to make sizable commissions on the sale and resale of the same property. Under the terms of the purchase and sale agreement, the purchase price would be $200,000, with a down payment of $50,000 paid at closing. The balance of $150,000 would be paid in annual installments of $50,000 together with an interest rate of 6.5 percent per annum. All this looked acceptable to the couple, but there were also some questionable requirements deeper in the agreement that would have been contested by an objective agent or real estate attorney:

- There was no cash offered for earnest money. The purchasers "tendered a note" for $5000 to be paid at closing. This means the purchasers signed a document stating they would pay $5000 when the deal closed, but no money was going to change hands until the deal was done. When so many unknowns are involved, it's usually best to require cash as the earnest-money deposit.
- The date of closing was 120 days after acceptance of the purchase and sale agreement. The purchasers asked for this time period so that they could start, and hopefully complete, the division of land. The purchasers have now tied up the property for 120 days with no cash.
- The transaction was to close in the offices of a closing agent selected by the real-estate agent. The closing agent (typically a title company, attorney, lender, or credit union) should be familiar to the seller or at least a recognized name.

The most difficult discovery for the sellers came after the agreement was signed. The couple contacted other real-estate agents in the area and learned that property similarly divided was selling for two and three times what the couple was offered. The couple had spent a great deal of cash on attorneys trying to determine if the agent was truly representing only the buyers. A potential nest egg had turned into a nightmare. A great deal of anxiety could have been saved by showing the agreement to a real-estate attorney or checking with two or three agents about comparable sales in the area. Be particularly careful when you live a distance from the property and are unable to monitor what is going on around it. The value might have risen or fallen significantly since your last visit, and it's best to seek several opinions before making any major decisions.

A Tree Falls in Your Wallet

You probably have heard the awful stories of despicable landowners who divide their property, clear-cut all or a portion of the land, sell the timber, and then quickly move out of the territory. Those stories become more and more common as the price of timber goes up and more private owners purchase more public land. An alternative to clear-cutting is a selective, "thinning" cut that not only can protect homes from precariously perched trees but also can help prepare and show a site for a potential building while netting several thousand dollars. In fact, some woodsy lots are so thick that a very lucrative thinning often can go unnoticed. Many timber companies, especially smaller ones working in the immediate area, are willing to dispatch "cruisers" to determine if your lot contains enough (at least one truck load) of marketable timber. On single-family lots, owners can even flag the specific trees to be taken so that only designated trees are harvested. Landowners can also contact a local lumber mill and ask about minimum loan requirements, price estimates, and contractor referrals.

The amount that a landowner realizes after selling timber is called the stumpage price. It represents the value of the trees "sitting on the stump" after all costs of harvesting and hauling are considered. Many variables affect the price paid for standing timber. On larger tracts, too much is at stake to sell timber without having accurate information on the process, products, volume, and value of the timber and efficient methods for protecting the environment. Prices fluctuate widely given worldwide supply and demand, and seasonal fluctuation. There are no daily market price reports for stumpage and smaller landowners must rely on the estimates provided by local mills. In many states, landowners must file a timber harvest plan that is monitored by a licensed timber operator. As always, preparation pays higher dividends—even in a small-time timber sale.

Before You Take the Timber . . .

Trees are a precious, valuable commodity that should be handled with extreme care. When removing trees to create an access to newly subdivided land, make sure you get a reliable timber contractor with a solid reputation to harvest, market, and replace your trees and who can make suggestions on how to plant new trees to replace the ones taken. Here are five basic questions for consumers who have never cut or sold a tree:

- What is the timber volume?
- How is the volume measured?
- What is the value of my timber?
- Are timber market prices going up or down?
- Are property and cutting boundaries well marked?

Cashing in by Playing the Variance Card

If you want to subdivide your property but it doesn't exactly fit the subdivision mold set by your municipality, take a moment to consider playing the variance card because you could easily take the pot. As mentioned above, a variance permits an owner to build a structure, or conduct a use, not otherwise allowed. Variances often are granted when peculiar properties make it impossible to meet local zoning guidelines. For example, Uncle Bill's lot is oddly shaped. The community's zoning laws call for all homes to be 15 feet from all running trails. No matter how Uncle Bill's house is designed, it's impossible to build his home 15 feet from a running trail. Uncle Bill applies for and is granted a variance to build his home 12 feet from a running trail.

A variance must not alter the character of the area or reduce the value of surrounding properties. In addition, the owner must show "undue hardship." Most of the time, a public hearing is held to discuss the merits of the proposed variance. While you might become unpopular with a couple of neighbors, you are well within your rights to seek a variance—especially when a few total square feet keep you from creating an additional legal lot. For example, Oly Olsen owned a large, wooded lot that contained 46,240 square feet. His family had built a weekend cabin years ago, and

Oly wanted to subdivide the lot so that his children and grandchild could enjoy an "annex" cabin behind the main cabin for vacations and reunions. However, the local county code stipulated that any new building lot required a minimum of 25,000 square feet. Oly applied for a variance, and several neighbors opposed the application at the public hearing. However, Oly did his research and produced the dimensions of all the lots from the original plat of the area. The two lots that bordered the cabin were less than 15,000 square feet, and 16 in the original plat contained fewer than 25,000 square feet. The county granted Oly the variance because it said a smaller lot would not alter the character of the neighborhood. Oly created value, and a family compound, by playing the variance card.

Take the time to research all of your options. Cashing in by dividing your property often comes from going the extra mile. Sometimes the possible solution is not found in current county codes. However you divide, keep your neighbors in mind. Plan your approach, follow all laws, and respect the land at all times.

In our final chapter, we explore just who is holding the cards in The New Second Home game. The odds of getting the getaway you desire might soon be getting shorter as millions of potential buyers enter the picture.

14

Understanding the 75 Million Boomers Who Will Buy or Rent Your Second Home

In the business world, the rearview mirror is always clearer than the windshield.—Warren Buffett

Between 1946 and 1964, 75 million babies were born. Right now, an American turns 50 at least every seven seconds. While there are enormous business implications for this (making money will increasingly mean dealing in products desired by this crowd), the real estate implications of a maturing population are most significant.

Baby boomers are looking at vacation and investment homes in increasing numbers, creating a very competitive market. Regions that were once pristine and quiet will be the victims of sprawl. Areas that once were rundown and unacceptable will be reborn as trendy boomer-compatible places to settle. In other words, the aging of the baby boom will transform the real estate market as it has transformed just about every other aspect of the American economy.

In this chapter, we analyze the demographics of the investment and vacation home market, primarily by baby boomers, but also by those following the boom that have leveraged the prosperity of the 1990s into the ability to own second homes. We look at the scope of the market, current trends in location decisions, the demand for second homes, and the reasons for these choices. Our objective is to indicate the potential size of this market for the benefit of both those seeking second homes for their own use and those who would buy these homes as investments.

Aging in Place

On May 24, 2001, Bob Dylan turned 60. Sixty! To many of us who grew up to the nasal, atonal sound of his marvelous poetry, that hardly seems possible. Dylan isn't 60; he's still the 20-year-old hick from Minnesota who wrote the anthems that drove the adolescent rebellion of the baby boom. But he is indeed well over 60.

There is a tendency in human nature to freeze acquaintances at the age they were when we first encountered them. It helps us place perspective on our own lives. So we hardly see the aging of those around us until it's too late. This can be true with business as well. We tend not to see what is really happening around us because we have frozen our assumptions about the world at the time that they were formed.

Thus the demographic glacier that is the baby boom is invisible to us. We express surprise at the vibrancy of the housing market in the early twenty-first century. But it's really quite simple when the boomer factor is taken into account. The largest numbers of boomers are reaching the stage of their lives when they move into the best house they will ever own. Ironically, they will also want to stay there for a long time, because they're also at the stage of life where root planting is important. High demand, restricted supply, good market—no mystery. Beyond this, they are looking for second homes, in some cases to shelter wealth and generate cash flow, and in some cases to enjoy as a vacation retreat. So let's look ahead and try to skate to where the puck will be. Who are they and what will they be seeking? Who will you compete against when you buy that investment house? Who will you sell it to when you want to get out of the ownership business?

Population Structure and Housing Markets

The housing market has set records for sales activity in every year between 1996 and 2002. That means approximately 42 million American households (about 42 percent of the total number of households) either bought or sold a house (or did both) during a seven-year period. That frenetic activity marks the maturation of the baby boom generation.

Understanding the 75 Million Boomers Who Will Buy or Rent

The boom peaked in 1957. In 2003 there were more 46-year-olds than any other single age cohort. It is traditional behavior to move into the best house one will ever inhabit during the 40-50 year-old decade. Thus this surge of housing demand reflects the boomers doing what comes naturally. This ought to come as no surprise. As we saw in the introduction, the American economy and American society have reflected the impact of the boomers during all their ages. Now their major impact comes in the housing market.

Masked in these housing statistics is the growth in sales of investment and vacation homes. During this great housing boom, the number of second homes sold increased from 296,000 in 1995 to 415,000 in 2000. Between 1980 (when the leading edge of the boomers was 34) and 2000, the number of second homes in United States increased from 1.7 million to 3.6 million, rising from 1.87 percent of the housing stock to 3.09 percent. Moreover, the buyers of second homes during this period were younger than the average second home owner and had higher incomes.[1] This suggests that the boomers used the good economy of the 1990s as a boost to buy a bigger and better principal residence *and* indulge their desire for investment and vacation homes.

More importantly, this expansion of sales and ownership of second homes will only grow in the future. As we discuss in the next section, the number of older Americans will grow, and with that growth will come the demand for second homes as investment and vacation retreats.

Who Are These Guys?

The United States is an aging country.[2] The reason, of course, is the great population surge we experienced after World War II. Although there has been a second surge since 1979, the dominant demographic fact in this country is that the baby boom is getting older. Table 14-1, showing the projections used by the Bureau of the Census based on the 2000 Census, indicates the speed with which Americans are aging. By 2020, there will be as many Americans over 65 as there are now over 55, and nearly twice as many Americans over the age of 85.[3]

[1] National Association of Realtors.
[2] But it is not aging as quickly as other developed, and even some developing, countries. Most of Europe, Japan, and even China show populations aging faster than that of the United States between 2000 and 2050. See *Fortune,* October 28, 2002, p.169.
[3] This narrowing of the population distribution is sometimes referred to as "the pig in the python."

TABLE 14-1. U.S Population by Age, 2000–2020

Age	2000	2005	2010	2015	2020
Total Population	275,306	287,716	299,862	312,268	324,927
55 and over	58,836	66,060	75,145	85,878	95,841
65 and over	34,835	36,370	39,715	45,959	53,733
85 and over	4,312	4,968	5, 786	6,396	6,763

Numbers in thousands
Source: *U.S. Census Bureau, Middle Series Projections*

Even in 2000, the number of Americans over 55—the preboomers—constituted more than a quarter of the population. By 2020, when the baby boomers reach 65, that percentage reaches nearly one-third. By 2050, it's over 40 percent. This is a major and growing market for second homes, not only in the future, but also now. If the recent numbers are any indication, the number of second homes sold should increase by about 30 percent by 2010 and 60 percent by 2020. That projects to a market of 650,000 sales by 2020.

Like all projections, these depend on a lot of "ifs." While the Census numbers appear to be reasonable and reliable, the market projection will be affected not only by demographics, but also by interest rates, prices, and alternative consumption choices. The reliability of any projection over time will be subject to prevailing conditions. That said, the underlying base of demand for second, retirement, and vacation homes—established by the structure of the population—is very strong. So the high points in the market will be high, but the low points will be relatively mild.

Why the Current Surge in Second Home Sales?

Although the current population numbers are beneficial to the second home market, there are other reasons why the numbers for second home sales have been up so dramatically. Clearly, the prosperity of the 1990s gave reality to the desires of younger boomers to own a vacation getaway house. With unemployment low, and productivity up, discretionary income was sufficient to carry the cost of two houses. Additionally, interest rates have been low by historical norms and therefore the cost of owning, as expressed in the monthly payment, is low.

But there are some more significant forces at work in the marketplace. These forces have pushed demand for second homes and will continue to do so as the baby boomers age. These are the factors that you need to consider when thinking about purchasing a second home. Which of these are important to you and how do they figure into your decision? What are they and what will they mean for the future?

Double Incomes. One of the legacies of the 1970s has been the growth of two-income households. The women's movement to a degree eliminated the economic discrimination facing half the population and made success in the marketplace possible for all adults. The great inflation that sprung up in the 1970s made participation in the workforce by all a necessity. For these reasons, boomers and their older brothers and sisters now typically (53 percent) live in households with two or more adult earners.

This has increased the disposable income available to the typical household and thus enabled them to expand their consumption.[4] It has also contracted the time they have available, making time the most scarce and most valuable commodity in the modern economy. In a two-earner household, there are often three full-time jobs. The stress of the last is often the most intolerable. Thus, leisure time is extremely valuable.

The two-earner household and the stress related to a shortage of time have produced a new kind of second-home buyer. This buyer wants a retreat, a place where the activities of the job and the neighborhood cannot intrude, a weekend hideaway. This means a house that is not only secluded but also can be reached with ease.

When looked at from a macroeconomic perspective, the getaway buyer is driving demand in nontraditional areas, usually those within an hour or two drive from a large metropolitan area. Thus, residents of New York City are looking to Rockland, Putnam, and Dutchess counties upstate, as well as to Cape Cod and Nantucket. This pattern is repeated across the country. This is not a passing trend. The pressure on households to generate income to maintain lifestyle will continue, as will the accompanying time pressures. As the boomers age, this will enhance demand for second homes close to metro areas.

---

[4] It has also expanded the need to spend, often to replace labor that would have been available in a one-earner household. But declining birth rates have reduced average household size, leaving the two-earner household on net somewhat better off than the single-earner household.

Tax Benefits.[5] The compact that the U.S. government made with home-owning Americans in 1949 has never gone away. The tax deduction for mortgage interest payments embedded in the tax code still remains one of the major tools available to the American public for sheltering income. The recent change in the tax treatment on capital gains from home ownership in effect ended all taxation attendant to the sale of a house. The impact of both of these is the same: The cost of owning a home is reduced and the return on investment in home ownership is enhanced.

In a normal financial environment, this might not be enough to foster investment in housing, particularly the purchase of a second home. Traditionally, equities carried with them a greater return on investment than real estate. But the first years of the twenty-first century have hardly been normal financial times. The bursting of the tech bubble has reduced the value of most investment portfolios and severely damaged confidence that these values will be restored. This has pushed many investors out of the stock and bond markets and into second homes.[6]

This shift has been made more convenient by a reduction in underwriting requirements for mortgages on second homes. Lenders have traditionally required equity investment of 30 percent (as opposed to as little as 3 percent for some loans on principal residences) on second homes, reflecting the increased risk of second homes. This worked to retard demand for second homes. But, under the influence of the secondary mortgage market, lenders have gradually reduced their down payment requirements to the point where buying a second home is less financially constrained.

Taxes are also driving another form of demand for second homes. In contrast to the U.S. system, most European countries enforce high rates of taxation without providing any convenient tax shelter, except for overseas investment. This has boosted foreign demand for vacation homes in the United States. This is particularly true in Florida, the site of 13.5 percent of all second homes in the United States.[7] While the conventional wisdom holds that second-home demand in Florida is driven by "snowbird" retirees, a great (and increasing) portion of second homes in Florida are owned by foreign investors, primarily Europeans.

[5] In Chapter 5, we detailed the financial and tax aspects of investment and vacation homes. This section serves as a summary of the financial and tax motivation behind the demand for second homes.

[6] And they may be right. See Daniel Akst, "In the Long Run, Residential Real Estate May Beat Stocks," *New York Times*, May 5, 2002, p.B4.

[7] See John Carroll, "My (Other) House," *American Demographics*, June 2002, p. 44.

Technology. The improvements in communications technology have created the opportunity for large-scale telecommuting, allowing workers to operate away from the office as effectively as if they were there. And while the growth of telecommuting has been consistently overestimated, it now clearly appears on the radar of the American economy.

All this has added to the appeal of the second home. One young second homeowner has found that his intended beach getaway has changed into a second home and second office. He says, "It just morphed into this. In my world, it's real easy. I can work on my cell phone if need be."[8]

The ease of telecommuting has added another dimension to the demand for second homes. Specifically, it has increased the demand in two areas. First, second homes located within easy commuting distance of employment centers have become more popular and will only increase in popularity as telecommuting increases. These locations allow for contact with the office and clients and customers as well as provide for those occasions when unexpected or emergency trips to the office are necessary.

The second area affected by the capacity for telecommuting is the demand for "wired" homes. Even if it is within commuting distance of the office, the cabin in the woods won't be attractive to consumers if it doesn't come with broadband communications capacity. The ability to use wireless phones and laptops (not to mention cable or satellite TV) is a major drawback for second homes that might otherwise attract the young boomer looking for a second office.

Safety. In the wake of the terrorist attacks on September 11, 2001, finding a haven from the danger of large metropolitan areas entered the minds of second-home seekers as a major consideration. Stories immediately after the attacks featured families that were leaving New York City for the relative safety of Long Island and Westchester. Their motivation was simple: If it happens again, I'm not going to be here.[9]

No one can deny that we live in a very dangerous world. The dangers, both internal and external, seem to be concentrated on areas of large population. Relative safety appears to be associated with more rural areas. The more time spent away from people, it seems, the lower the chances of being caught up in the violence that stalks the environment in which we live.

The desire to find safety has spurred the demand for second homes, particularly in more rural areas. But city dwellers are not the only source

[8] John Carroll, *op. cit.*, p. 43.
[9] The numbers were significant even before 9/11. According to the Census Bureau, in 2000 nearly 2 million Americans (about 4 percent of all movers) moved for the purpose of finding better and safer neighborhoods.

of demand for homes in safer areas. Retirees, or those seeking to retire in the near future, are also looking for a quieter environment where the hassles of congested areas are absent. In more popular areas, like Florida and Arizona, gated communities are growing in great number. These afford the advantages of community while screening out the dangers that are always present in city life. In the next section we take this up in more detail, as there are significant disadvantages to rural areas or gated communities designed for retirees, but there is definitely a flight-to-safety motive attached to second-home demand, and that motive has increased dramatically since 9/11.

Patterns of Mobility

Having looked at why people are motivated to buy second homes, the next question is: Where are they moving? In this section we look first at the general patterns of mobility of over 55s as revealed in the 2000 Census[10] and then look at some more specifics of the type of places people seek out. The habits of older Americans are a proxy for the behavior of the baby boom and ensuing generations. The basic results are unsurprising. There has been a general population movement from the Northeast to the South, both among older Americans and among the general population. And Americans, with the exception of 1998–99 and 1999–2000, have been moving out of metropolitan areas into nonmetropolitan areas.

We first look at the mobility patterns of senior citizens in the last year of the 1990s (Table 14-2).

The numbers here are not surprising. Even though they depict only a single year, they seem to conform to conventional wisdom.

- In percentage terms, the lowest mobility rate for older Americans is in the South.[11] This is consistent with perception that the South is where one finds a second home. Recall that Florida leads the nation in second homes; 13.5 percent of all second homes are in Florida.
- Conversely, the highest mobility rates are in the Northeast. Again, the conventional wisdom says that "snowbirds" migrate

[10] We concentrate here on older Americans for two reasons. First, they represent the most likely consumers of second homes. Second, as the baby boomers age, these are the population cohorts that will be competing in the market for second homes. The patterns we see now will prefigure the march of the boomers into the second-home market.

[11] Partly, these statistics are skewed by the fact that the South is the largest of the Census regions, stretching form Delaware to New Mexico. In a later section, we look at the more finely divided nine Census regions.

TABLE 14-2. U.S. Population Migration, 55 and Over, 1999–2000 (Population in Thousands)

Census Region	Northeast	Midwest	South	West
Total Population	51,364	62,618	94,646	61,592
55 and over	11,541	12,454	21,591	11,420
Percent of Total	22.5	19.9	22.1	18.7
Movers	2,534	2,560	2,190	776
Within Same County	246	234	401	328

Source: *Census Bureau*

south in the winter to their second homes. When they are ready to retire, they stay.[12]

- A large number of movers move within the same county. Even retirement will not cause American households to move far from their roots. Interregional migration is considerable (see below) but the number staying near home is also significant.
- The West shows a relatively low rate of mobility. Part of this is a function of high house prices in many parts of the region. Part of it also deals with the regional climate, which in many cases makes change irrelevant.

To determine where people are moving, we need to look at the migration patterns among regions. These are best summarized by looking at the difference between total numbers of people moving into a region and those moving out. To avoid the impact of immigration—considerable during the 1990s—from abroad, we only look at internal migration. Unlike the previous section, we look here at total internal migration, not just older Americans. (See Table 14-3.)

The analysis of internal migration patterns also squares with expectations.

- The Northeast has shown a consistent loss of population to other areas. In no year during the decade was there positive net migration

---

[12] The figures do in part include snowbirds that split their time between houses. If a household has two homes, the one in which it spends the majority of its time is the first house and the other the second. Thus, if you spend five months in the Northeast instead of seven, the Sun Belt home is the first house and you have officially migrated.

**TABLE 14-3. Net Internal Migration by Region, 1990–2000
(Population in Thousands)**

Year	Northeast	Midwest	South	West
1999–2000	−252	82	227	−57
1998–1999	−163	−171	271	63
1997–1998	−203	120	230	−146
1996–1997	−119	−154	391	−118
1995–1996	−234	68	150	16
1993–1994	−328	−31	376	−17
1992–1993	−334	233	101	−1
1991–1992	−292	−62	224	129
1990–1991	−585	−15	433	167

Source: Census Bureau

from the rest of the United States.[13] This population movement was ratified by the results of the Decennial Census for 2000 and the resulting reshuffling of representation in the Congress.

- The main beneficiary of migratory patterns during the decade was the South, reflecting retirement demand but also the migration of jobs from the more manufacturing-oriented sections of the country.
- The Midwest and the West were minor players in this people movement, with the Midwest losing a bit and the West gaining.

Yet another demographic phenomenon of the past decade has been the movement between city and suburb and metropolitan area and nonmetropolitan area. For the most part, metropolitan areas have seen a decline in population over the decade. The numbers shown in Table 14-4 show this but actually understate the shift. During the decade, the geographic boundaries of metro areas have expanded, so if nothing changed, they should have *gained* population. Yet they did not. Second, there has been a decided shift from central cities to suburbs. Because both are included in the metropolitan figure, they mask a much greater shift out of urban areas into (presumably) less populated areas.

[13] To some extent this was offset by foreign immigration, but the decade shows a net loss when all population movements are considered.

**TABLE 14-4. Net Migration in
Metropolitan Areas, 1990–2000
(Population in Thousands)**

Year	Net Migration
1999–2000	137
1998–1999	71
1997–1998	−182
1996–1997	−216
1995–1996	−275
1993–1994	−86
1992–1993	−317
1991–1992	73
1990–1991	117
1989–1990	128

Source: *Census Bureau*

Some of this is a function of the availability of space and housing at affordable prices. But part of it represents the desire for safety and lower levels of stress offered in less urbanized areas.

The statistics described above were created by the generation that has preceded the baby boomers. Is it likely that they will continue as the boomers age and move heavily into the second-home market? In a word, yes. As the boomers age, these trends are more and more likely to continue.

The movement to the sun from the northern side of the country will continue, but it will exist side by side with the choice of second homes close to the primary residence for reasons of safety and convenience. We expect that the most common choice of a second home will be either in an obvious resort/retirement community or close to home. In addition, we expect the movement from the city to the country (or more accurately from metropolitan to nonmetropolitan areas) to be intensified by the actions of baby boomers that will be seeking places where recreational facilities are cheap and accessible, and where their active lifestyles can be best accommodated.

But there is a second dimension suggested by these statistics. Right now, a large portion of these numbers represent primary home moves, younger households seeking to acquire housing that is affordable and reasonably close to their jobs. This is the case in the Washington, D.C. area with towns like Leesburg, Centerville, and even Harpers Ferry, West Virginia. Similarly, the numbers reflect the need to follow jobs. As the economy has changed and as the technology boom has erupted, burst, and started to flower again, jobs increasingly are located in the Southern and Southwestern parts of the country where costs are lower and unions weaker. These areas also have abundant land and thus low housing costs. Las Vegas, Phoenix, and Dallas can tell this story.

When the boomers hit the retirement and vacation home markets in great numbers, the concept of job location will fade. Either the boomers will be well employed and look to a true second house, or they will be retired and not even entertaining the notion of a job. Potential relocation areas will be looked at for their facilities and environment. The luxury of never again having to shovel, rake, or mow will dwarf either the presence of jobs or the cost of housing. In short, today's numbers tell a story about relocation for economic reasons; the same numbers in the future will tell a story about lifestyles.

Boomerangs

The statistics generated in the decennial census and compiled by the government tell many stories, but some, important for our purposes, can only be told anecdotally. Right now, stories are appearing about retirees settling in traditional areas like Florida and Arizona and then leaving. Either they will sell the house in the Sun Belt and move a bit farther north (say to the middle South or Colorado) or buy a condo back near home to avoid the extremes of weather that afflict traditional retirement areas.[14]

The issue, however, is more than weather. In many cases, retirees are seeking active lifestyles for both their bodies and their minds. You can't play golf or lounge in the sun all day, and never at night. The presence of a full range of recreational and cultural activities is already important to the current generation of retirees and will be even more important to the boomers when they retire.

This means that smaller university communities are an attractive location. This means the obvious, like the research triangle area of North Carolina, but also less obvious places like Hattiesburg, Mississippi, and

[14] See Al Heavens, "'Boomerang'" Retirees Sticking Close to Home," *Realty Times*, December 20, 2001.

Boone, North Carolina. They are situated north of the very torrid weather in much of Florida and south of where home was and family and friends probably still are.

These places scattered through the middle South combine a mild climate, abundant recreation opportunities and cultural activities. They provide a unique mix of ideals for the retiree or even the vacation home seeker. This option will be even more attractive to the baby boomers. The boomers will have spent their lives for the most part in urban environments. They will have becomes used to the easy availability of restaurants, movies, and theaters. Wherever they retire or vacation for long periods of time will have to afford similar amenities.

A Last Word

The numbers indicating migration and second-home demand are right now very strong. But this is only the tip of the iceberg. The real crunch in these markets will not come until we see the boomers leave the labor market in big numbers, after 2010. This suggests that anyone wishing to buy a second home now, for vacation or investment purposes or even to "audition" as a retirement spot, is in a perfect position to act now.

Appendix

Helpful Forms and Web Resources for Second-Home Buyers and Real Estate Investors

2nd Home Living Magazine

http://www.2ndhomeliving.com/

866-484-9141

816.753.6287 x13

e-mail wmaus@mausmedia.net

Online magazine dedicated to second-home living.

AARP Web site

http://www.aarp.org/universalhome

The Home of the Future

Examples of a "universal design home."

ActiveAdultLiving.com

http://www.activeadultliving.com/

S & L LaCount, L.L.C.

3655 W. Anthem Way, Ste A-109/325

Anthem, Arizona 85086

623.551.3479

Fax 240.525.1378

info@activeadultliving.com

Magazine featuring master planned retirement communities for active seniors.

Comparetopcondos.com

http://www.comparetopcondos.com

Bear Technologies, Inc.

2740 E. Oakland Park Blvd, Suite 300

Fort Lauderdale, FL 33306

Phone: 954-630-3737

Fax: 954-567-2659

Feedback@CompareTopRealty.com

Specializes in new and preconstruction high-rise condominiums and luxury ocean front properties.

Ebay Real Estate

http://pages.ebay.com/realestate/

eBay Inc.

2145 Hamilton Avenue

San Jose, California 95125

Bidding auctions for real estate.

Helpful Forms and Web Resources for Second-Home Buyers

EscapeHomes.com

http://www.escapehomes.com/

EscapeHomes

61 Moraga Way Suite 5

Orinda, CA 94563

800-937-9090

info@escapehomes.com

A guide to vacation homes, second homes, timeshares, recreational properties.

Fairway Properties

http://fairwayproperties.com

owned by KLC Properties

381 Wakelee Ave

Stratford, CT 06614

203-459-2995

A directory of homes for sale in golf course communities.

goCountry.net

http://www.gocountry.net/

1-800-685-1025

info@gocountry.net

Offering links to ranches and real estate listings in Montana, Idaho, Wyoming, South Dakota, and Minnesota.

Golfcoursehome.net

http://www.golfcoursehome.net/

71 Head of Meadow

Newtown, CT 06470

Tel: 203-270-9357

Fax: 203-364-0559

Search from the database of golf communities across the United States.

iVacation.com

http://www.ivacation.com
2003 International Vacation Homes, Inc.
9920 S. La Cienega Blvd., Suite 900
Inglewood, CA 90301-4466
Toll Free 800-282-1594
Local Phone 310-568-8510
Fax 310-568-8289

Properties for rent and for sale.

Lakefront.com

http://www.lakefront.com
info@lakefront

Searchable national database of lakefront real estate for sale.
Also:
www.OceanView.com
www.OceanFront.com
www.RiverFront.com
www.Acreage.com

Lots USA

http://www.lotsusa.com/
73091 Country Club DR
Palm Desert, CA., 92260
Fax: 760-328-2339
E-mail:*info@lotsusa.com*

Nationwide listings of lots for sale.

MSN HomeAdvisor

http://homeadvisor.msn.com
Offers real estate information, listings, and advice on every step of the
home buying process.

Oceanhomes USA

http://www.oceanhomes-usa.com

800-450-0646

info@lakehomes.com

Guide to waterfront areas across the United States and regional Realtors.

Private Islands Online

http://www.privateislandsonline.com/

28 -2451 Queen Street East

Toronto, Ontario

Canada M4E 1H7

Email: *info@privateislandsonline.com*

Offers listings of islands for sale or rent in the United States, Caribbean, Canada, Oceania, and Europe.

Real Estate Golf Property

http://www.realestategolfproperty.com
Golf communities by state.

Realtor.com

http://www.realtor.com/

30700 Russell Ranch Road

Westlake Village, CA 91362

Phone: 805-557-2300

Fax: 805-557-2680

Search for a new home or find mortgage rates, agents, and relocation services throughout the United States, Canada, and Puerto Rico. Provided by the National Association of Realtors.

Remote Realty Inc.

http://www.remoterealty.com/

4349 E. Bannock St.

Phoenix, AZ 85044

A worldwide database of rural and remote properties for sale.

Resort Homes Exclusive.com

http://www.resorthomesexclusive.com/newlist.htm

P. O. Box 1087

Branford, Connecticut 06405-8087

Phone 203/488-1507

Fax 203/488-4262

Thomas Gillis: *hthomasgillis@attbi.com*

Advertising forum for agents, brokers, architects, developers. Also: *http://www.premierpropertiesonly.com*

SeniorOutlook.com

http://www.senioroutlook.com/

A division of *ForRent.com Harmon Homes-*

SeniorOutlook.com

5th Floor North

295 Bendix Roa

Virginia Beach, Virginia 23452

Customer Service: 888-539-1150

customerservice@senioroutlook.com

National database of senior living options, information on choosing a community, financial, and estate planning.

SeniorResidences.com

http://senioresidences.com/

4077 Decarie Blvd

Montreal, Qc H4A 3J8

514-484-5033

editor@theseniortimes.com

Online retirement residence guide featuring communities in Canada and the United States.

Ski Resort Homes

http://www.skihomesandcondos.com/

Ski Homes and Condos

PO Box 1087

Branford, Ct., 06405-8087 USA

Telephone: 203-488-4262

Showcases houses and condos in the United States and Canada.

Online Vacations.com

http://www.onlinevacation.com

Phone 843-450-6371

Fax 781-273-7393

http://www.info-asyst.net/plans.shtml

Vacation homes, vacation rentals, and condo rental property, also allows you to trade

VRBO.COM

http://www.vrbo.com/global/links.htm

VRBO.COM LLC

PMB#308 4255 S. Buckley Road

Aurora, Colorado, 80013-2900

Links to vacation, rental, and travel resources.

EXCHANGE AGREEMENT

THIS AGREEMENT is entered into by and between **John & Elizabeth Smith, husband and wife,** hereafter referred to as "Exchangor", and Friendly Exchange Services, Inc., a Washington corporation, hereinafter referred to an "Intermediary".

RECITALS

WHEREAS, Exchangor owns that real property, hereinafter referred to as "Property A", described in Exhibit "A" attached hereto and hereby incorporated by reference herein; and

WHEREAS, Exchangor has entered into Escrow # 231968-ML with Happy Title Co., hereafter referred to as "Escrow"; and

WHEREAS, Exchangor desired only to exchange Property A for like-kind property, hereinafter referred to as "Replacement Property", in such a way as to qualify for tax-deferred treatment under I.R.C. Section 1031 and similar state statutes; and

WHEREAS, Exchangor has been unable to find suitable Replacement Property for accomplishing said tax-deferred exchange; and

WHEREAS, Exchangor with a continued intent to complete a tax-deferred exchange pursuant to I.R.C. Section 1031, is willing to allow the amendment of Escrow to substitute Intermediary as the seller of Property A therein in order to allow for the closing of Escrow and pending the location of suitable Replacement Property as specified herein; and

WHEREAS, Intermediary is willing to accept and to hold the proceeds of Property A, as set forth in and received from the Escrow, and to utilize the same in securing, acquiring, and transferring to Exchangor suitable Replacement Property to complete the tax-deferred exchange according to the terms and conditions as set forth herein;

THEREFORE, the parties hereto agree as follows:

1.   Subject to and conditioned upon the close of Escrow and otherwise subject to and upon the terms and conditions set forth in this Agreement, including the optional authority of direct deeding contained in paragraph 13 hereof, Exchangor hereby agrees to convey Property A to Intermediary, and Intermediary hereby agrees to convey to Exchangor, in exchange for Property A, Replacement Property having an aggregate Exchange Value equal to the Exchange Value of Property A as determined under Paragraph 4 below.

2.   Exchangor shall convey all of Exchangor's right, title, and interest in and to Property A, under the provisions of paragraph 13 hereof authorizing direct deeding, by delivery to Escrow on or before the closing of Escrow, of a grant deed or statutory warranty deed conveying Property A to the Purchaser. Exchangor shall in this event also execute and deliver to Escrow, on or before the closing of Escrow, an Assignment of Real Estate Purchase and Sale Agreement to Purchase for Property A, assigning Exchangor's rights and obligations thereunder to Intermediary.

PROVIDED, HOWEVER, that if Exchangor so requests, and Intermediary agrees, title shall be conveyed by Exchangor to Intermediary who will then convey to the Purchaser (sequential deeding), rather then by direct deeding.

Figure A-1

3.　　　In order to account for and monitor the Exchange Value in respect to Property A, Intermediary agrees to establish an exchange account concerning this transaction in Intermediary's books and records in favor of Exchangor (hereinafter referred to as the "Exchange Account"). The opening entry for the Exchange Account shall be reduced from time to time by (i) Intermediary's fees and costs, (ii) the Exchange Value with respect to each Replacement Property (i.e., all amounts expended by Intermediary in connection with the acquisition of each Replacement Property, as determined under paragraph 5 below), and (iii) any other payments made or costs or expenses incurred by Intermediary for which Exchangor is obligated or responsible under this Agreement. The balance of the Exchange Value remaining in the Exchange Account also shall be increased in accordance with paragraph 16 below. Intermediary shall provide Exchangor with an accounting, hereinafter referred to as "Closing Statement", of the Exchange Value in the Exchange Account as soon after the one hundred eightieth (180th) day (or closing of the final Replacement Property if sooner) as is practical. In preparing the Closing Statement, Intermediary shall be relying upon information and settlements supplied by third party escrow companies, and Exchangor hereby releases Intermediary form any liability whatsoever in connection with such reliance.

4.　　　In respect to Property A, "Exchange Value" shall mean the total consideration received by Intermediary from the closing of the Escrow. All real estate commissions, prorations of income and expenses (including rents, interests on encumbrances, real estate taxes, etc.), closing costs, title insurance premiums, escrow fees, and any other amounts otherwise chargeable to Exchangor in the Escrow as seller of Property A shall be chargeable to Exchangor in the Escrow as seller of property A shall be charged to Intermediary and shall reduce the Exchange Value of Property A.
Cash received by Exchangor from escrow in the amount of $ _____

will be boot subject to tax in the hands of Exchangor and shall not be included in "Exchange Value".
_____**INITAL**

5.　　　In respect to the Replacement Property, "Exchange Value" shall mean the total costs and expenses incurred by Intermediary, in accordance with the provisions of this Agreement in connection with the acquisition and conveyance thereof to Exchangor, including, without limitation, the aggregate amount of all deposits and expenditures by Intermediary in respect to the purchase price, real estate commissions, prorations of income and expenses (including rents, interests on encumbrances, real estate taxes, etc...), closing costs, title insurance premiums, escrow fees, and any other amounts otherwise chargeable to Intermediary in connection with the acquisition and conveyance of the Replacement Property to Exchangor, but excluding any existing mortgage, trust deed or other secured loans which may be assumed or taken subject to by Exchangor.

6.　　　At the close of Escrow, the proceeds, including cash, shall be transferred, assigned, and/or conveyed to Intermediary and be held by Intermediary pursuant to the terms of this Agreement.

7.　　　Intermediary is instructed to deposit all cash funds received into banks, savings and loan accounts, money market deposit accounts, repurchase agreements, in time deposits, or in such other investments as Exchangor may direct.

8.　　　In no event shall Intermediary be required to make a cash payment to Replacement Property, including all costs and expenses of said purchase, in excess of the amount of the Exchange Value then remaining in the Exchange Account.

9.　　　In the event additional cash is necessary to acquire the Replacement Property, said amount (i) shall be advanced by Exchangor to Intermediary; (ii) shall be used by Intermediary to acquire the Replacement Property; (iii) shall be considered an interest-free loan from Exchangor to Intermediary (fully satisfied upon the conveyance of Replacement Property to Exchangor); and (iv) in the event the Replacement Property is not conveyed to Exchangor, shall be repaid by Intermediary to Exchangor, upon the written demand of Exchangor; OR said amount (v) shall be advanced by Exchangor to Escrow Agent of the Replacement Property.

10.　　For purposes of this Agreement:

Figure A-1 (Continued)

(a)   The period between the "conveyance date" and midnight of the 45th day thereafter is defined as the identification period; and

(b)   The period between the "conveyance date" and midnight of the earlier of the 180th day thereafter or the due date (including extensions) of the taxpayer's tax return for the taxable year in which the transfer of the relinquished property occurs is defined as the exchange period.

11.   Within forty-five (45) days after the transfer of Property A from Exchangor to Intermediary, hereinafter referred to as the "Conveyance Date", Exchangor shall by written notice to Intermediary identify Replacement Property anywhere in the United States. Such notice from Exchangor shall unambiguously identify the Replacement Property by street address or legal description. Thereafter Intermediary shall undertake to acquire the Replacement Property upon such terms or pursuant to such agreement as Exchangor has negotiated with the seller of such Replacement Property. Provided, however, that Intermediary shall incur no liability to Exchangor hereunder if efforts to purchase Replacement Property shall be unsuccessful. All agreements to purchase Replacement Property shall be recorded, executed by or assigned to Intermediary and title to the Replacement Property shall be recorded in Intermediary's name. Intermediary shall immediately thereafter convey the Replacement Property to Exchangor subject to only such title defects or exceptions as Exchangor has approved, in writing, prior to the acquisition; provided, however, that Intermediary's conveyance to Exchangor shall constitute full compliance with any express or implied warranties to which Intermediary would otherwise be subject. In the alternative, title to the Replacement property may be conveyed by direct deed from the seller to Exchangor, in accordance with paragraph 13 hereof.

12.   The Intermediary shall not be required to make any warranties or representations regarding Property A which are not guaranteed by Exchangor. Furthermore, the Intermediary shall not be required to make any warranties or representations regarding the Replacement Property, which would survive as to the Intermediary following conveyance of the Replacement Property.

13.   To the extent permitted by I.R.C. Section 1031 and the Regulations promulgated thereunder, legal title to Property A and/or the Replacement Property may be transferred directly from the Exchangor to Purchaser, or from the Replacement Property Seller to Exchangor. The means for accomplishing such direct deeding may require the execution of an Assignment of Real Estate Purchase & Sale Agreement between the Exchangor and the Intermediary for Property A, and a separate such agreement between the Exchangor and the Intermediary for the Replacement Property.

14.   Exchangor acknowledges and agrees that:

(a)   The Intermediary shall not be required to assume any secured loan on any Replacement Property or to execute any promissory notes or other evidence of indebtedness in connection with such acquisitions which would impose any personal liability on officers and/or directors of the Intermediary for the payment thereof.

(b)   In no event shall the Intermediary be required to pay a cash amount for the Replacement Property, including all costs and expenses incurred in connection with such purchase, in excess of the Exchange Value then held in the Exchange Account.

(c)   The Intermediary shall act only in accordance with the written instructions of Exchangor and on the terms of this Agreement in making said acquisition, and may refuse to proceed with said acquisition, in the event said instructions exceed the scope of this Agreement.

15.   Except for payments made from the Exchange Account to reimburse Exchangor for expenses paid by Exchangor for the sale of Property A or the acquisition of Replacement Property, such as appraisal or title reports, earnest money, etc., which reimbursement shall be permitted upon written request from Exchangor and which payments are authorized under Treas.Reg. 1.1031(k)-1 (g) (7) (ii), the Exchangor shall not be entitled to receive any portion of the exchange account or any growth factor thereof nor to

Figure A-1 (Continued)

receive, pledge, borrow or otherwise obtain the benefits of money or other property prior to the termination of this agreement.

16.   If interest is earned on the Exchange Account, it shall be for the benefit of Exchangor, and shall be reported as interest income on Exchangor's tax return, regardless of whether said interest is applied to the purchase of Replacement Property or is received by Exchangor in cash as part of the distribution of the Exchange Account to Exchangor upon termination of this agreement.

17.   This Agreement shall terminate and the Intermediary under the following conditions shall pay the Exchange Account to Exchangor:

(a)   If the Exchangor fails to identify Replacement Property, within 45 days after the Conveyance Date, the exchange has failed and this Agreement shall terminate and the Intermediary shall pay the Exchange Account to Exchangor after the 45th day.

(b)   If Exchangor has timely identified Replacement Property, after Exchangor has received all of the identified Replacement Property to which Exchangor is entitled, this Agreement shall terminate and the Intermediary shall pay the Exchange Account to Exchangor.

(c)   If Exchangor identifies Replacement Property, following the occurrence after the end of the identification period of a material and substantial contingency that (i) relates to the deferred exchange, (ii) is provided for in writing, and (iii) is beyond the control of Exchangor and of any disqualified person as defined in Treas.Reg. 1.1031 (k)-1 (k), other than the person obligated to transfer the replacement property to the Exchangor, this Agreement shall terminate and the Intermediary shall pay the Exchange Account to Exchangor.

(d)   Otherwise, at the end of the Exchange Period.

18.   Any dispute as to the interpretation of the content, extent, or applicability of this Agreement or Exchangor's instructions to Intermediary shall be immediately arbitrated.

(a)   Exchangor shall select any arbitrator on the then existing arbitration panel of the King County Superior Court, who primarily deals in real property matters.

(b)   Within three (3) working days after the arbitrator's selection and acceptance of appointment and written notification to Intermediary, Exchangor and Intermediary shall each furnish to the other and to said selected arbitrator a written statement of their respective positions regarding said dispute and shall furnish, as reasonably requested by arbitrator, any further answering or explanatory statements that the arbitrator may require.

(c)   The parties agree to be bound by the decision of said arbitrator and agree that said arbitration is in lieu of and instead of any rights to judicial proceedings and determinations that the parties may have.

(d)   Except as provided in subparagraphs (e) and (f) below, the costs of arbitration are to be borne equally between Exchangor and Intermediary and each party shall be responsible for its own attorney fees.

(e)   In any controversy, claim, or dispute between the parties hereto arising out of or relating to this Agreement or the breach thereof the prevailing party shall be entitled to receive from the other party reasonable expenses, attorney fees, and costs.

(f)   The prevailing party shall be entitled to enforce the decision of the arbitrator by recording a judgment, in the Happy County Superior Court.

19.   All notices provided or required to be given under this agreement shall be deemed to have been duly given, served, and delivered if mailed by United States registered or certified mail addressed to the

Figure A-1 (Continued)

party entitled to receive the same at the address specified in this Agreement; provided, however, that any party may change its mailing address by giving to the other parties written notice of its new mailing address, and any notice so given shall be deemed to have been given, served, and delivered on the date following the date on which said notice was mailed in the manner herein provided.

20.   Time is of the essence of this Agreement.

21.   This Agreement may not be amended or modified in any respect whatsoever except by an instrument in writing signed by the parties hereto. This Agreement constitutes the entire agreement between the parties with respect to the subject matter hereof. If any provisions of this Agreement shall be held invalid, such invalidity shall not affect any other provisions hereof.

22.   This Agreement shall be construed in accordance with the laws of the State of Washington. This Agreement may be executed in duplicate counterparts, each of which so executed shall, irrespective of the date of its execution and delivery, be deemed an original, and said counterparts together shall constitute one and the same agreement.

23.   This Agreement inures to the benefit of and binds all parties hereto, their heirs, legatees, devisees, administrators, executors, successors and assigns.

IN WITNESS WHEREOF, the parties have caused this Agreement to be executed this 26th day of June, 2005.

ADDRESSES FOR NOTICES TO BE MAILED:

EXCHANGOR

_____

_____
(Signature)

Tax ID # _____

_____
(Signature)

Tax ID # _____

INTERMEDIARY:

Friendly Exchange Services, Inc.,
a Washington corporation

By: _____
    Howard I.S. Friendly
    Attorney at Law / President

Figure A-1 (Continued)

ASSIGNMENT OF REAL ESTATE PURCHASE & SALE AGREEMENT

FOR REPLACEMENT PROPERTY

This Agreement is entered into by and between **J. Hopalong Cassidy & Brenda Fairway, husband and wife** (hereinafter called Assignor), and Friendly Exchange Services, Inc. (hereinafter called Assignee).

WITNESSETH:

Whereas Assignor as Buyer entered into that certain Real Estate Purchase and Sale Agreement and any and all addenda thereto, if any, a copy of which together with addenda, if any, is attached hereto as Exhibit A (Legal Description) and is incorporated herein by this reference: and

Whereas Assignor and Assignee have executed an Exchange Agreement in which Assignee has promised to acquire suitable replacement property and to transfer the same to Assignor, in consideration of Assignor's transfer of exchange property to Assignee: and

Whereas Assignor has identified as a replacement property the property which is the subject of Exhibit A;

Whereas Assignee agrees to assume and perform Assignor's obligations under the Exhibit A Purchase and Sale Agreement;

NOW, THEREFORE, the Parties agree:

1.   Assignor hereby assigns to Assignee the Buyer's right, title and interest in, and the Buyer's obligations under the Purchase and Sale Agreement attached as Exhibit A, to acquire the subject replacement property.

2.   Assignee hereby assumes the Buyer's rights, title and interest in, and the Buyer's obligations under the Purchase and Sale Agreement to acquire the same as Replacement Property.

3.   Assignee hereby requests the seller to deed directly to Assignor the subject property to the Exhibit A Real Estate Purchase and Sale Agreement.

IN WITNESS WHEREOF, the parties have executed this agreement as their free and voluntary act and deed, on the date indicated by each signature.

ASSIGNOR: **ASSIGNEE:**

_____   Friendly Exchange Services, Inc.

_____   Howard I.S. Friendly
Attorney at Law / President
Date signed 3/26/05

Figure A-2

NOTICE OF IDENTIFIED
REPLACEMENT PROPERTY

Friendly Exchange Services, Inc.　　　　　　Telephone　(888) BE-HAPPY
919 – So Friendly Road　　　　　　　　　　Fax　　　　(877) BE-HAPPY
Just Friendly, USA 98005

RE: Mr. Kelly 200607104

In accordance with the requirements of I.R.C. Section 1031, I/we hereby identify the following
real property as Replacement Property pertaining to the above referenced tax deferred exchange.

Street Address: _____

_____

Legal Description: _____

_____

Dated this ____ day of _____, 2003.

_____　　　_____
Taxpayer Name (print)　　　　　　　　　　Taxpayer Name (signature)

_____　　　_____
Taxpayer Name (print)　　　　　　　　　　Taxpayer Name (signature)

ATTACH ADDITIONAL SIGNATURE PAGES IF NEEDED

On this ____ day of _____, 2003, Friendly Exchange Services, Inc. the Qualified
Intermediary herein, acknowledges receipt of Taxpayer(s) Notice of Identified/ Designated
Replacement Property.

Friendly Exchange Services, Inc.

_____
Howard I.S. Friendly
President / Attorney at Law

PLEASE COMPLETE THIS FORM AND FAX IT BACK TO US

Figure A-3

NOTICE OF REVOCATION OF IDENTIFIED
REPLACEMENT PROPERTY

Friendly Exchange Services, Inc.   Telephone   (888) BE-HAPPY
919 –So Friendly Road   Fax   (877) BE-HAPPY
Just Friendly, USA 98005

RE: Mr. Kelly 200607104

In accordance with the requirements of I.R.C. Section 1031, I/ we hereby revoke the following real property that has previously been identified/ designated as Replacement Property pertaining to the above referenced tax deferred exchange.

Street Address:_____
_____

Legal Description:_____
_____

Dated this ____ day of _____, 2003.

_____   _____
Taxpayer Name (print)   Taxpayer Name (signature)

_____   _____
Taxpayer Name (print)   Taxpayer Name (signature)

ATTACH ADDITIONAL SIGNATURE PAGES IF NEEDED

On this ____ day of_____, 2005, Friendly Exchange Services, Inc., the Qualified Intermediary herein, acknowledges receipt of Taxpayer(s) Revocation of Notice of Identified/ Designated Replacement Property.

Friendly Exchange Services, Inc

_____
Howard I.S. Friendly
President / Attorney at Law

PLEASE COMPLETE THIS FORM AND FAX IT BACK TO US

Figure A-4

ASSIGNMENT OF PURCHASE & SALE AGREEMENT
FOR RELINQUISHED PROPERTY

This Agreement is entered into by and between **John & Elizabeth Smith, husband and wife** (Hereinafter called "Assignor"); and Friendly Exchange Services, Inc. (hereinafter called "Assignee".)

WITNESSETH:

WHEREAS Assignor as Seller entered into that certain Purchase and Sale Agreement and any and all addenda thereto, if any, a copy of which together with addenda, if any, is attached hereto as Exhibit A (Legal Description) and is incorporated herein by this reference; and

WHEREAS Assignor and Assignee have executed an Exchange Agreement in which Assignor has agreed to transfer the Exhibit A exchange property to Assignee, in consideration of Assignee's promise to acquire suitable replacement property and transfer same to Assignor; and

WHEREAS Assignee agrees to assume and perform Assignor's obligations under the Exhibit "A", Purchase and Sale Agreement;

NOW, THEREFORE, the parties agree:

1. Assignor here by assigns to Assignee the Seller's right, title and interest in, and the Seller's obligations under the Purchase and Sale Agreement attached as Exhibit A, for the relinquishment of the exchange property.

2. Assignee hereby assumes the Seller's rights, title and interest in, and the Seller's obligations under the Purchase and Sale Agreement to transfer said exchange property to the Purchaser.

3. Assignee hereby requests and directs the Assignor to deed directly to Purchaser the property subject to the Exhibit A, Purchase and Sale Agreement.

IN WITNESS WHEREOF, the parties have executed this agreement as their free and voluntary act and deed, on the date indicated by each signature.

ASSIGNOR: ASSIGNEE:

_____   Friendly Exchange Services, Inc.

_____

                                              _____
Date signed:_____   Howard I.S. Friendly, Attorney at Law / President
                                              Date signed: 6/26/05

Figure A-5

NOTICE OF ASSIGNMENT OF REAL ESTATE PURCHASE & SALE AGREEMENT
FOR REPLACEMENT PROPERTY

TO: **J. Hopalong Cassidy & Brenda Fairway, husband and wife**   DATE 3/26/0
          Seller

Our File Number 200607104
Escrow   1052659

      You are hereby notified that the Buyer under the Real Estate Purchase and Sale Agreement, a copy of which is attached hereto, has assigned to the undersigned all of Buyer's rights, obligations and duties under said agreement, and the undersigned, as Assignee, has accepted said assignment and agrees to be bound by all of Buyer's obligations thereunder.

        Friendly Exchange Services, Inc.

        By _____
        Howard I.S. Friendly, Attorney at Law / President

      I HEREBY CERTIFY that I delivered a copy of this Notice of Assignment to the Seller on _____, 2005. **

      _____
      Escrow Officer/ Limited Practice Officer

** A COPY OF THIS NOTIFICATION MUST BE DELIVERED TO SELLER PRIOR TO RECORDATION OF THE CONVEYANCE DOCUMENT!!!

Figure A-6

Index

Index

Index

Index

Index

About the Authors

Tom Kelly is a nationally syndicated radio host and columnist as well as a former real estate editor for the *Seattle Times*.

John Tuccillo is a former chief economist for the National Association of Realtors. He delivers more than 50 public speeches a year on real estate topics.